RESILIENCE OF THE UNBREAKABLE SPIRIT

NAVIGATING CRISIS AND FINDING STRENGTH

YOGESH SRIVASTAVA

Clever Fox® PUBLISHING
Chennai • Bangalore

CLEVER FOX PUBLISHING
Chennai, India

Published by CLEVER FOX PUBLISHING 2025

ISBN: 978-93-7500-327-4

CONTENTS

Acknowledgements .... *v*

Part 1 .... **1**

1. Grounded Skies........ 2
2. The Battle of Uncertainty........ 18
3. The Echoes of Resolve........ 50
4. Nights of Dread, Days of Solitude 72
5. Test of Theory Against Humanity's Greatest Crisis 98
6. The Heathrow and The Journey Home 105

Part 2 .... **117**

7. The Apex and the Abyss 118
8. The Prison of Proximity 130
9. Loyalty in a Corporate Game........ 141
10. The Fractured Past 154
11. Silent Screams, Unseen Battles 169
12. Every Life Matters 181
13. Hope Beckons 188
14. The Silent Pillar 192
15. The Shattering Echoes........ 206

16. The Acid Test 211

17. The Fractured Façade 226

Part 3 234

18. The Seed of Epiphany 235

19. Ripples of a Radiant Future 245

20. The Radiance of the Unbroken Spirit 249

About the Author...254

ACKNOWLEDGEMENTS

As I reflect on the journey of writing *Resilience of the Unbreakable Spirit*, my heart swells with gratitude for the many remarkable individuals who have supported me along the way. This book, rooted in my own experiences during a time of profound uncertainty, owes its existence to the strength and resilience of those around me. First and foremost, I wish to express my deepest appreciation to my wife, Dr. Ruchira Srivastava. You have faced unimaginable challenges with grace and courage, battling against the odds and making countless sacrifices for our family. Your resilience during your darkest moments inspired the character of Priya in this narrative, embodying the spirit I strive to convey through these pages. You are the heart of this book and my unwavering source of inspiration. To my daughters, Riya and Isha, your sacrifices and unwavering support have been my lifeline during these trying times. Despite navigating your own challenges, you have shown extraordinary strength, reminding me of the power of family in the face of adversity. Riya and Ryan, your contributions to the proofreading and editing process have been invaluable, and your keen insights have enriched this narrative immeasurably.

I extend my heartfelt thanks to my friend, Ms Rosaline Kurien. Your valuable feedback from a reader's perspective has been instrumental in making this story more relatable and engaging. Your guidance has ensured that the narrative resonates deeply with readers while retaining its essence. Additionally, I acknowledge the assistance of the staff at Park Inn by Radisson, Heathrow, especially Ms Somkiat and Mr Niel. I am also grateful to fellow members of the UK diaspora—Mr Madhuresh Mishra, Mr Harendra Jodha, the unknown heroes from Southall Gurudwara and the officials from the High Commission of India in the U.K. Your support during my time in London made a significant difference in navigating the uncertainty I faced.

This book is rooted in my real-life experiences set against the backdrop of the lockdown during the Covid-19 pandemic and the collateral damage it wrought. I wish to convey my deepest gratitude to the extraordinary medical fraternity, several of whom are woven into the fabric of this narrative as cherished characters. Your unwavering commitment and relentless efforts—often extending into the late hours of the night—have left an indelible mark on my journey. Throughout the tumultuous days of the COVID-19 pandemic, you rose to the occasion as beacons of hope, consistently surpassing expectations to deliver exceptional medical care amidst harrowing challenges.

In this book, I have endeavoured to capture the immense demands, pressures, and expectations placed upon you by the loved ones of those fighting for their lives. The real scenes illustrated within portray the dramatic realities and emotional vulnerabilities of doctors as human beings, highlighting the precarious tightrope you walk between hospital protocols and the heartfelt expectations of patients' families. Your boundless compassion and steadfast fortitude not only save lives but also provides solace to countless families grappling with fear and uncertainty, rendering you the unsung heroes whose resilience and selflessness ignite a flame of hope and renewal in us all. This book serves as a tribute to your remarkable strength and an homage to the unbreakable spirit that you embody.

I would be remiss if I did not acknowledge the key contributions from my colleagues and seniors at my workplace, whose interactions and decisions have shaped the events documented within these pages.

In navigating our everyday lives, we all face various pains and psychological lockdowns, whether at work, home, or within society. This book aims to acknowledge those daily struggles and is dedicated to the resilience of mankind, carrying a hopeful message.

Finally, I dedicate this book to my parents, Mr S.S. Sinha and Mrs Uma Sinha, to my beloved wife Ruchira, and my daughters Riya and Isha. Your unwavering love, support, and the values you've instilled in me have provided the foundation for my strength, empowering me to write this book and share my story with the world.

This book is also a testament to the resilience of the human spirit and is dedicated to countless others who have lost their dear ones during the pandemic. Your stories and struggles inspire this work, reminding us all of our shared humanity amidst the crisis. Thank you to everyone who has been part of this journey. Your contributions have made all the difference.

– Yogesh Srivastava

PART 1

CHAPTER 1

GROUNDED SKIES

March 21, 2020. Heathrow Airport. The world had stopped. The digital boards at Terminal 5—the ones I relied on as my compass for global traversal—blinked mindlessly, ushering me toward an illusion of routine. Yet, something was palpably different. The departure lounge, once alive with hurried footsteps, continuous announcements, and laughter, was shrouded in a silence so unnatural it seemed dense enough to choke on. I tightened my grip on the luggage trolley and paused to breathe. The air carried none of its usual charm—no perfume from duty-free, no jet fuel blending into the background. All I could taste was the metallic tang of fear, mingling with the cold London drizzle that seeped through the airport's glass facade. And yet, the flight home—BA 199 to Mumbai—still blinked on the board, steady and unbroken, as though mocking me. I rushed to the check-in desk in the Transfers Section straight from Iceland Air FI454 from Keflavik with a purpose; my heavy down jacket, a relic of the Arctic chill I'd just left, was a useless second skin against the relentless, internal bite of misplaced anxiety. Ms Evans—her name plastered on the clipped badge pinned over her British Airways uniform—worked feverishly behind the counter, her trembling, sanitised fingers battling against the tyranny of her keyboard. She was surrounded by a small crowd of equally desperate faces, some clutching oversized bags, others holding restless children, voices rising like a tide. Masks hid their mouths, but not the growing panic in their tired eyes. Ms Evans stood at the centre of the chaos, her crisp blazer immaculate, her blonde hair tied back with an authority that screamed "no-nonsense." But her face betrayed her—she looked cornered, beaten down by the relentless demands of travellers whose only hope rested on her ability to untangle the impossible. Her polite smile had thinned to a grimace as the group pressed closer, their voices growing louder and sharper. "Why can't they organise a special flight for us?" an elderly man in a grey cardigan demanded, his voice trembling with exhaustion. "Do you expect us to live here in the airport?" "We're not entirely sure when flights will resume," Ms Evans responded, her tone clipped but controlled. "As soon as we have information—" "That's not good enough!" another voice snapped from the back. A woman, perhaps in her thirties, with large dark eyes and an oversized suitcase, pushed her way forward. "Do you have any idea what this means for us? I'm supposed to fly home to take care of my father—he's sick, and no one else can do it. Or do we not matter?" Ms Evans stiffened, trying to maintain her composure, but her eyes flickered for a brief second—an indication she was crumbling under the weight of expectations no human could meet today. I felt a pang of pity for her, though it was quickly overridden by the urgency of my own situation.

I hesitated before approaching. I was never one to join a mob—but this wasn't a regular day, and desperation had a way of stripping away pride. Swallowing my discomfort, I stepped forward, blending into the cluster of would-be passengers. "Excuse me, Ms

Evans," I said, striving to keep my voice steady. Years of corporate leadership had honed my ability to command presence in chaos. "I'm booked on BA 199 to Mumbai. Will it depart as scheduled?" My tone exuded certainty, as though sheer conviction might reconstruct the splintering world around me. She paused and looked at me, her red-rimmed eyes like glass over frayed wires. "One moment, Sir," she replied mechanically. Her fingertips danced across the keyboard as her phone rang urgently beside her. Behind me, whispers buzzed like uncomfortable static—a huddle of stranded passengers swapping morsels of rumour and hope. I glanced around. The normalcy of Heathrow had evaporated, replaced by an almost dystopian tableau of abandoned trolleys. Looking for refuge, I checked my Longines Dolcevita: 8:37 PM, it read . Boarding was supposed to start at 9:15 PM. I'd always found solace in order—in schedules, in systems—but now nothing seemed concrete. My throat tightened as I stared at the display board. Cancellations began to overwhelm it, one line at a time. Ms Evans let out a breath, the kind that warned bad news was coming. "Sir, I've just confirmed..." she began, hesitant. "Your flight has been cancelled. India has closed international borders to prevent the spread of COVID-19 ." The words struck me like an electrical surge, cold and fiery all at once. "Cancelled?" My voice rose, unintentionally shaking. "How is that possible? Surely British Airways—surely someone—can arrange alternate routes? Via Dubai/Nairobi? Somewhere?" She bit her lip, her shoulders slumping as she typed furiously. A small delay. Hope. I clung to those seconds like lifelines. "I can check, sir, but..." Her pause rang louder than her words.

"Passengers boarding from the UK are barred from entering India—even via connecting flights. The restrictions are unprecedented." "Unprecedented?" That word again. It hung in the air between us like a blade. My chest rose and fell in short bursts as rage clawed its way into me—a familiar beast now utterly useless in the face of this situation. For a moment, I couldn't process her quiet apology. "Sir, we advise seeking accommodation nearby." She gestured toward the deserted check-in counters where abandoned luggage stood as silent sentinels to ruined plans. I stood frozen like the frozen Gullfoss captured in my lens—Unprecedented? The word grated against everything I knew of the world.

I, Rohan Srivastava, was the man who made the impossible happen. I closed multi-million-dollar high-ticket sales, managed large teams, navigated the chaos of market share and crises, and ensured numbers were delivered and targets were achieved. I controlled outcomes. I bent reality to my will. And yet, here I was, powerless against a microscopic virus. Imprisoned by circumstances I didn't create. Failure clawed at me, a feeling long buried beneath decades of driven success. "You must understand the severity of what's happening. People here need answers. Waiting indefinitely is not a solution." Ms Evans locked eyes with mine. Her politeness vanished, replaced by something closer to exasperation. "Sir," she said, her tone more pointed now, "we are doing everything we can. But organising flights under the current circumstances isn't as simple as making a phone call." Her sharpness startled me, but I pressed on. "I get that things are chaotic. But people here have families, responsibilities. lives waiting back home." "And we all have people we care about stranded on the other side of the world,".

She shot back, her frustration bubbling to the surface. "Do you think the airline staff are unaffected by this? I haven't been home in three days. We're doing our best, but it's a global health crisis. Not a PR stunt." The air between us thickened, the murmurs around the desk quieting as the crowd waited to see what I'd say next. Instead, I stepped back, the reality of her words crashing over me. She was right. None of this was simple. No one was to blame, and yet everyone was. My chest tightened with frustration, not at her, but at my own impotence. Turning on my heel, I walked away, the knot in my stomach flaring as the chaos around me clawed louder. A woman began sobbing near the seating area, huddled over her phone as she whispered into it in rapid Gujarati. A child clung to his mother's leg, begging her not to fall asleep on the bench, his voice high-pitched with fear. The uneasy calm shattered with a bang. A suitcase toppled to the terminal floor near the check-in counters, its contents spilling everywhere: neatly folded saris, wrinkled shirts, undergarments, a stack of books, a box of medicine. A man—middle-aged, thin, his hair sticking to his forehead in damp clumps—threw his hands up and yelled at the staff. "I've had enough! Enough! You people don't understand what we're going through!" His voice echoed through the cavernous space, drawing every pair of eyes toward him. "My mother—she's dying! Dying! How am I supposed to get to her now? How do I explain to her that her son is stuck here because there's no one willing to help?"

Security guards approached cautiously, their presence only adding to the man's escalating fury. "Don't touch me! I'm not causing trouble—I only want answers!" I stood rigid, watching this eruption. Every word he said felt like a mirror of my own silent cries. I wanted to rush forward, to tell him I understood, to tell him he wasn't alone. But before I could move, Ms Evans appeared again, a mask of authority slipping back over her exhaustion, as if she were armoured in thin steel. Watching her attempt to de-escalate the situation reminded me of a juggler trying to catch knives while blindfolded. And I couldn't bear to watch her fail any more than the rest of us already had. My family too—Priya, Siya—were waiting for me back in Mumbai, and Ananya was desperately watching from the USA, four family members caught in three different continents, thousands of miles apart. Dragging my feet across the polished floor, I moved to the glass window overlooking Heathrow's tarmac. Outside, on the vast, rain-slicked tarmac, the wide-body jets stood like beached whales—a graveyard of grounded, silver giants. Their metallic silence pressed the finality of the disaster into the earth. It wasn't a delay; it was the death rattle of the old world, and I was trapped inside the casket.

That sight—a graveyard of grounded, silver giants—felt like the final, shuddering death rattle of a world whose rules I had mastered. Each colossal jet, silent and impotent on the oil-slicked tarmac, was a monument to the world's paralysis. But the real acid in the wound was the cruel irony: my BA 199 was the first London-to-Mumbai route sacrificed. Two hours ago, an Emirates flight—a ghost of possibility—had been allowed to claw its way free of the Earth, screaming across the boundary I was now forbidden to cross. That small margin of missed time felt like an eternal, unforgivable mistake. As the chaos escalated behind me—the man's howl of primal grief finally muted by the quiet steel of security—I retreated, stepping deeper into the background. The terminal was a dizzying, discordant symphony: the echoes of the recent conflict, the thin, desperate sobs of the huddling mother, and the sterile, soulless announcements of flight resumption that everyone knew were lies. Heathrow was no longer an airport; it was a microcosm of global insanity: chaotic, fractured, and standing on the brittle edge of total collapse.

I was left alone with the metallic silence of the grounded fleet. They weren't going anywhere. And neither was I. The crushing, irrefutable finality of that truth forced my hand. I pulled my phone from my pocket—my hand trembling so violently the screen threatened to slip from my grasp. I forced myself to call Priya, pulling my phone from my trembling hand. It rang. Twice. Then her voice anchored me in cracks, equal parts sharp and fragile. "Rohan?" Priya's voice was strained and taut. Even the six thousand kilometres between us couldn't dilute her fear. I could picture her standing in our living room, one hand gripping the remote, the other clutching the phone with white-knuckled desperation. "The news… Are flights cancelled? The tickers on TV keep saying borders are closed. Is it true? Are you... Are you stuck there?" Behind her words, I could almost hear the sound of the TV blaring—the rapid-fire commentary of anchors, the flashing headlines in black and white against the aggressive glow of red and blue graphics—the noise of panic that had seeped into every corner of the world. “Yes, Priya,” I swallowed hard, feeling the words tighten my throat. “India’s borders are closed.” I paused, bracing myself for what came next, but there was no easy way to deliver it. “I’m stuck here. Indefinitely.” Her gasp was not just breath; it was a slice of raw sound that cleaved through the distance. “Indefinitely? What does that even mean?” The panic in her voice felt sharp, urgent—a storm crashing on the other side of the line. “How long? When will you come home?” The questions came quickly, tumbling over each other, as if she hoped that asking them fast enough would somehow force answers into existence. She wasn’t asking me; she was asking the universe for mercy. I couldn’t answer her. Not really. The world itself offered no clarity anymore—just chaos, projections, and numbers that changed each day like the shifting sands of an unstoppable tide. “I don’t know,” I said finally. The truth slipped out, naked and cold, and I felt its weight shove hard against me. “I don’t know, Priya. I wish I did.” Her breathing became uneven, the receiver amplifying each quiver in her voice. “What will Siya do?” Her voice broke then, spilling into desperation so raw I could feel her pain through the static. “She’s under tremendous mental stress since all this talk of lockdown, Rohan. She’s… She’s been watching all this horrific news all day—death counts, infection graphs, terrifying predictions about the pandemic wiping out millions.

Every time a news anchor starts talking about uncertainty about how long the lockdown will last, she goes quiet—too quiet. I—I think she’s… shutting down? She barely talks to me anymore, avoids looking me in the eye, and I don’t know what to do.”

The panic in Priya's tone twisted something deep within me—a knot I'd grown adept at ignoring over the years. She tried to stay composed, but the words were spilling out faster now, like floodwaters overtaking a dam. "She needs you, Rohan! She needs her father. Do you even understand the severity of what's happening here?" Her voice didn't just rise; it soared, cracking like breaking ice under the impossible weight she'd tried so hard to carry alone. "You've seen how she's been struggling—how fragile she's been since... since everything. And now this? Now you're... gone? I... I can't manage this by myself. I'm not enough." Siya's depression. *Our Siya.* The words struck me with the force of a physical blow. I hadn't let myself fully acknowledge the extent of it, lazily brushing it aside as the natural turbulence of adolescence. She was a teenager, I'd told myself. It couldn't be that bad. But even from thousands of kilometres away, separated by an ocean and the closing sky, Priya's anguish cut through my denial like jagged glass tearing through skin, exposing the raw, ugly truth I'd worked so hard not to see.

The memories came unbidden, a rapid, agonising slideshow of my neglect: the way Siya's presence had started to feel smaller over the years, shrinking like a shadow at sunset. Her quiet, almost monastic withdrawal at family dinners, the way she'd stare at her untouched plate as the rest of us—Priya, Ananya, and I—laughed or bickered or shared our hollow triumphs. The fragile tremor in her voice when I'd ask about her day, her hesitant, often monochrome replies that never seemed to match the innocent sparkle she once had. I'd dismissed it all as teenage mood swings and paid her no mind—the colossal, glittering distractions of my career towering over the fragile, essential pieces of her world.

Now, Priya's words painted the full, agonising picture of my absence. It was a portrait of a crumbling foundation. I wasn't there when she needed me. I hadn't been present when she started to fade, and now, in the middle of a global crisis that demanded absolute proximity, I was trapped on the other side of the planet, a useless, impotent figurehead. My stomach curled into knots as guilt, hot and caustic, clawed its way up my throat, tasting of ash and failure. I'd failed her. My relentless career ambitions had overshadowed everything—my wife's mounting exhaustion, my daughter's silent, desperate pain—and now I was exile personified, stuck in London while Priya bore the terrifying brunt of it all alone.

"Rohan, say something..." Priya's voice broke through again, uneven now, ragged from the weight of her pleading. I swallowed, forcing out the lie before it could sour on my tongue. "It'll be okay, Priya," I said, willing the words to sound stronger than I felt. "I'll find a way home." The promise, hollow as it was, rolled out automatically—the smoke and mirrors of reassurances I'd mastered over years of corporate decision-making. "I promise. I will fix this." But her silence on the other end told me she didn't believe me. Neither did I. As much as I wanted to have Priya's trust, as much as I wanted Siya to feel safe again, the truth was that I had no control. India's borders remained shut, Heathrow stood eerily silent, and I might as well have been on the moon for all the good I could do. I wished I could say more, anything to convince her, but my throat closed up, too tight to let anything meaningful slip through. "Rohan…" Priya whispered after a long pause. Her voice had softened, though the ache in it remained. "Just… just figure this out. Please. For Siya's sake. She needs her father." And with that, the line went dead.

The phone slipped from my hand as I leaned against the cold airport wall, my usual confidence flickering out like a light bulb on its last breath. Priya's voice—the desperation in it, the sadness— lingered in the stillness, reverberating louder than the faint murmur of announcements on the intercom. Siya's pain. Priya's exhaustion. My absence. Even across oceans, it pierced straight to my core, a grief sharper than any I'd felt before. And yet, all I could do was stand here, frozen in place—watching the grounded aeroplanes on the tarmac, their silver bodies reflecting a sun that seemed cruelly indifferent to it all. What kind of father had I become?

Resigned to fate, I booked Park Inn by Radisson, just across the Airport, so that once flights resume, I can reach the Airport without facing the anxiety of long-distance travel. I redeemed membership points accrued due to frequent corporate stay requirements at Radisson Group of hotels, for a ten-day stay, hoping to get clarity by then as the world reconciles and finds a response to the unprecedented situation. Around me, the airport dimmed under flickering fluorescent lights as passengers disappeared into a labyrinth of cancelled flights . The cold, sterile air smelled faintly of jet fuel, but now it reminded me of something else entirely—Solitude—Priya's final words echoing in my mind: "What about Siya? What will we do?"

It was 10:30 PM on the night of March 17, 2020, and Reykjavik's crisp chill wrapped itself around the MAR Seafood Restaurant, where my dream of savouring Icelandic delicacies had been fulfilled under the evening's dim, golden glow. The restaurant is a tapestry of Scandinavian minimalism—matte grey walls accented with delicate wooden trims, flickering candles sitting atop tables dressed in immaculate white linen, and large windows that framed the snow-dusted streets outside. My meal had been ceremonial—a taste of Iceland's heritage carefully plated. First came **Hakarl,** the fermented shark with its distinct tang and briny boldness— a taste not for everyone, but for me, it was a thrill. Then the dessert, **Bragdarefur**, creamy and cool with the sharp sweetness of fruits, a fitting crescendo to the culinary exploration. I had basked in the satisfaction of the meal, snapping selfies with the plates and sharing them on the family group chat, followed by a video call with Priya, Siya, and Ananya. Their laughter and teasing brought a comforting familiarity to this faraway land. Beneath their smiles and jokes about the shark, I could feel the melancholy of their separation.

As I returned to my room at The Radisson Blu, its minimalist decor and panoramic view of the snowy Reykjavik skyline reminded me that I had just three days left in this Arctic wonderland. Northern Iceland awaited—the dream photography tour to Akureyri and Dalvik—a chance to frame the midnight sun kissing frozen fjords and the dancing auroras painting the skies. But then, my phone rang, shattering the night's soft tranquillity. The sharp trill of the ringtone jarred me, almost unwelcome after the serenity of my evening. I glanced at the screen, uncertain whether to answer.

After all, I had just spoken to my family, shared photos, and felt connected—even if just for a fleeting moment. But curiosity got the better of me. "Good evening, Sir," said the voice, smooth yet laced with unease. It was Ramesh, my junior and go-to man of my team back in India. "How's your trip going?" "It's fine, Ramesh. How are you holding up? How's the situation with COVID back home?" I asked, my tone casual but inquisitive. "It's not good, Sir. Cases are surging. Hospitals are overwhelmed. And, Sir," his voice dropped slightly, "I've heard international flights are being suspended—especially from Europe, U.K., China, Singapore, and the U.S. Maybe you should check with your airline." The words hit me like icy water dripping off a glacier.

Flights being suspended en masse? It seemed preposterous. I had flown all my life, relying on the predictability of the airline industry as though it were a divine constant. But doubt bloomed. "Flights cancelled? Surely not mine. I muttered, already dialling British Airways, needing to crush that nascent fear instantly. The helpline greeted me with reassuring, almost synthetic professionalism. "As of now, Sir, all our flights are on schedule. No disruptions have been reported. Please keep checking for the latest updates." I scoured Twitter for announcements, scrolling endlessly through fragmented posts from the Civil Aviation Authority (CAA) of Britain, the Directorate General of Civil Aviation (DGCA) of India, government advisories, and news agencies. No signs of overt chaos—not yet.

The next morning began with unease. I reached out to the Indian Embassy in Reykjavik, asking for clarification. Their answer was noncommittal but ominous: "No decisions yet, sir. But stay vigilant and follow all updates." Despite the uncertainty, I decided not to abandon my itinerary. Northern Iceland's untouched beauty beckoned—a three-day journey to Akureyri and Dalvik as the final leg of my ten-day Iceland photography dream tour. I would navigate fjords, chase auroras, and capture this land's magnificent isolation before starting my journey homeward to Mumbai, with a planned stopover in Heathrow aboard British Airways flight BA 199. It was supposed to be a routine stopover, just another seamless transit across one of the world's busiest airports. But Heathrow, the monolithic gateway to London, had transformed into a ghost of its former self—a strange, foreboding entity that seemed caught between perpetual twilight and looming dread. The scent of disinfectant hung heavily in the air, unwelcoming and oppressive, stripping the place of its usual warmth. Empty corridors stretched like endless veins in an inert body, and the terminals—once teeming with hurried steps, cascading conversations, and the relentless hum of machinery—lay eerily still. Even the chatter of rolling luggage wheels was absent, replaced by a silence so unnatural it gnawed at my nerves. It was a silence that screamed louder than noise.

My taxi ride from Terminal 5 to the Park Inn by Radisson echoed the same eeriness. London itself seemed muted—a city brought to its knees. Billboards advertising exotic destinations were cruel reminders of what had been lost. Streets once alive with urban chaos were barren. The driver didn't speak, his face shielded by a regulation mask as his gloved hands gripped the wheel. His eyes, sunken and tired, reflected the collective anxiety of a world on edge. The hotel loomed large, its modern glass-and-steel facade glinting coldly under the cloudy skies. Inside, the sprawling lobby—marked by its gleaming surfaces and grand chandelier—felt more like a mausoleum than a hub of cosmopolitan energy. The staff moved like shadows behind a high plexiglass barrier, their masked faces almost indistinguishable from one another, their humanity redacted by fear and protocol. This was not a haven; it was a sterile, impersonal box where I would begin my exile.

My room, a standard 23m^2 space, enveloped me with quiet sterility. Beyond the large glass window lay the grounded world of aviation—rows of planes sat dormant on the tarmac, colossal but impotent, their silenced engines echoing a collective defeat. These were the planes that had been lifelines for many like me, symbols of success, wanderlust—now reduced to relics by an invisible adversary. The view was sobering: muted skies stretched infinitely, broken only by faint trails of a few departing flights—a stark reminder that some still fought to escape. Inside, the walls mirrored my mood—neutral and lifeless, adorned with an uninspired print of London Bridge glowing weakly against a dark cityscape. Opposite hung the familiar image of Big Ben, its reflection shimmering lazily on the Thames. It seemed as if these two iconic landmarks, suspended in their frames, might converse with one another—a silent dialogue of history and fleeting moments. London Bridge, stoic in its structure, whispered tales of resilience and change, while Big Ben, the ever-faithful guardian of time, reminded us of life's relentless march forward. The dispassionate prints felt like abstract reflections of my own inner turmoil—a juxtaposition of nostalgia and yearning to leave behind the past. In this moment, I recognised that the walls spoke not only through their decor but also echoed the weight of unfulfilled dreams and muted aspirations. They stood as a canvas, absorbing my introspection while offering nothing in return. Just as the planes ascended into the vastness of the sky, I too longed for a departure—not just from this physical space, but from the emotional stagnation that had settled within me.

I let my backpack slip to the floor and sank onto the edge of the bed, a deep sigh escaping me. The weight of helplessness pressed down against my chest like a physical force. I closed my eyes, but questions roared through my mind. "What is happening back home? Is Priya okay? Are the girls safe? What if I can't make it back?" By nightfall, exhaustion fought with panic, and the monotony of uncertainty set in—a heavy blanket draped across my restless soul. The isolation in that hotel room wasn't just physical—it was a vacuum, a place where time stood still. I was an unwilling witness to a world that had come to a grinding halt. The buzzing halls of Heathrow, the lively streets of London, the crowded terminals—all reduced to shadows of their former selves. I knew then: this was more than a hiccup in travel plans. This was the start of something bigger, something darker. I was no longer just an observer—I was caught in the eye of the storm, fighting against the uncertainty that rippled across continents. With my family thousands of miles away, my fate hung in the balance as the edges of normalcy began to crumble around me. The reflections on the Thames seemed to amplify my thoughts, merging the past with the present, the desires of my heart with the harsh realities of my life.

CHAPTER 2

THE BATTLE OF UNCERTAINTY

Day 2: A World on Pause: The night had been merciless—waves of uncertainty crashing endlessly, robbing me of sleep and leaving me emotionally wrung out by dawn. By the time my eyes fluttered open, the sun was already high, streaks of muted light filtering through the curtained window of my Heathrow hotel room. A dull ache weighed down on me. Breakfast? I didn't have the energy to bother. My body felt heavy, sluggish, as though chained to the remnants of yesterday's disquiet. By lunchtime, hunger gnawed at me, its call insistent enough to overcome my apathy. I trudged across the deserted street from the hotel to a nearby restaurant run by a Pakistani—its glowing neon sign offering the only hint of life in the eerily quiet landscape. The aroma of spices drifting into the air was nostalgic, comforting even, a geographical bridge to distant memories of Hyderabad. I ordered a pack of Hyderabadi Biryani, the smell of saffron and marinated meat wafting out of the bag by the time I returned to my room. Sitting alone in the suffocating stillness, I dug into the biryani, savouring each mouthful like it owed me solace. The flavours were bold and rich, but they couldn't chase away the suffocating blanket of dread clotting the air. And then, my phone buzzed, shattering the fragile rhythm of my meal. The screen lit up, Priya's smiling photo staring back at me. Her name flashed beneath it, offering a brief illusion of normalcy, like a tether to a life that suddenly seemed so far away. The phone vibrated relentlessly, the buzzes growing louder in my ears, more persistent. I'll just finish my lunch and call her back… I thought, yearning for a moment of peace before facing whatever worries lay on the other side. But the calls didn't stop. One after another, the screen kept lighting up, her face appearing like a silent, pleading scream. I paused mid-bite, a sense of urgency clawing its way into my chest. Seven missed calls. My heartbeat quickened, dread pooling in my stomach. Something was wrong. I grabbed the phone with trembling fingers, swiping to answer on the next ring. "Priya? Sweetheart, all okay?" My voice wavered; the calm I attempted was already cracking under the strain of fear. "What, okay, Rohan? There's nothing okay about this!" Her voice seared through the line, sharp, raw, and shivering with restrained panic. My heart sank instantly. Her words were punctuated by jagged breaths, the tremor in her voice betraying how close she was to the edge. "Priya, talk to me—what's happened?" I asked, fighting to hold myself together. She took in a shaky breath, her anguish spilling over in broken fragments. "The news… they're saying it'll take six months for normal flights to resume… Six months, Rohan! How—how are we supposed to get through six months like this? How are we supposed to survive without you? The girls need you… I need you! You need to come home. Now!" Her words slammed into me like a gut punch, each syllable steeped in despair. I gripped the phone tighter, feeling the helpless chasm that separated us growing wider with every second. "Priya, listen," I began, my voice cracking under the weight of my own helplessness. "I'll get home the moment flights resume. I swear it. We'll get through this. We always do." But my reassurances felt paper-thin, even to me. The hollow promises hung uselessly in the air between us. Priya's sobs on the other end of the line were raw, unchecked, the sound of a woman unravelling under the force of her fears. Hearing her cry like that—unrestrained, like a child abandoned in a cold, unfamiliar room—was unbearable. It clawed at my soul, rendering me mute, impotent. Her sobs weren't just cries; they were wounds, piercing deep into my chest, and I hated myself in that moment. I hated the distance. I hated the invisible barrier that this cursed virus had placed between us. But most of all, I hated myself for not having an answer to her pain. I should have been there to hold her, to tell her everything would be alright, and to give her the comfort she so desperately needed. But instead, I was stranded in a stagnant room thousands of miles away, reduced to whispers over a faltering phone line. Priya's sobs eventually quieted, exhaustion overtaking her as she fell into a troubled sleep, the faint static of the call lingering in my ear long after her cries had ceased. I stayed on the line for a moment, listening to the faint rhythm of her breathing, as if holding onto even this fragile connection would lessen the vastness of the distance between us. The room felt impossibly silent after I hung up. The weight of her despair clung to me like a shroud, suffocating and all-encompassing. My mind raced with questions, each darker than the last. *How would I get home? How would I protect them when I could barely manage my own isolation? What if this dragged on far longer than anyone expected?* Forcing those thoughts aside, I turned my focus to more immediate concerns. Today marked the end of my official leave period—I was supposed to resume my duties. I picked up the phone and dialled Mrs. Madhavi, the head of HR, alerting her to my predicament. "Madhavi, I'm stranded at Heathrow. Flights have been suspended indefinitely—I won't be able to return to Mumbai just yet. I'll send an official email." My voice was steady, but a world of frustration simmered beneath my calm tone. Madhavi was understanding, her voice soft but professional. "Don't worry, Rohan. I'll update the CEO and inform the Crisis Management Committee. Things are… chaotic on the business front, too. The CEO is entirely preoccupied with creating a plan for continuity amidst all this uncertainty. But I'll make sure they're aware of your situation." I thanked her before hanging up, but her words did little to dispel the storm roiling inside me. As I composed the email, each keystroke felt heavier than the last. The reality of this limbo began to sink deeper. Even as I typed, the grander picture began to crystallize: the world as we knew it wasn't just on pause—it was unravelling. And I was caught in the middle of its tangled threads, unable to find a way home. It's 6 pm UK time. The confinement of my room pressed down on me, so I stepped outside to the sprawling lawns of the property. Against the grey backdrop of uncertainty, spring colours painted an ironic picture of life's resilience. Cherry blossoms stood in hues of pink and ivory, daffodils and magnolias danced in Spring's breeze. A pair of grey squirrels—oblivious to pandemics and plummeting stock markets—chased each other across the branches. On another cherry blossom tree, a pair of Common rosefinches' whistling tone was competing with the melancholic calls of a lone bullfinch. The sight felt almost rebellious. If nature could carry on, perhaps I could too. Slinging my Canon 90D camera, my all-time companion in solitude, I sought to capture the spirit of life unfolding around me. Through the lens, the world seemed simpler—each click of the shutter freezing a fleeting moment of normalcy. As I zoomed in on a lone Common Rosefinch amidst the cherry blossoms, its melodic whistle swept over me like a balm. I stood there, camera poised, longing to hold onto this fleeting beauty a little longer. But as night fell, so did reality. Planes from Africa Airlines and Kenya Airways occasionally pierced the horizon, taunting me with the illusion of movement. The hotel lobby was alive in dissonance: the murmurs of stranded passengers folding over the crackling news broadcast from a mounted television. Rohan was restless, pacing near the concierge desk, phone gripped tightly in his hand as he scrolled for updates on flights back to India. "Anything yet?" a soft voice asked, pulling him out of his haze. He turned to find a woman in a faded maroon sweater and worn jeans. She looked older than she was, stress carved into the bags under her eyes. Her accent hinted at a life split between hemispheres, British fluidity tinged with a trace of Bengali cadence. "No," Rohan admitted curtly, gesturing toward his phone. "Website's crashed. Customer care isn't responding." He shifted, adding reluctantly, "Same for you?" She exhaled, exhausted. "I called my father in Kolkata just now. He's diabetic and has tested positive for Covid-19 after traveling on the Metro from Diamond Harbour to Maidan. And here I am, marooned in bloody London." Rohan saw it then—the sheer vulnerability of her situation etched right there in her face. For the first time since the shutdown began, he was forced out of his bubble of personal inconvenience. Over the next quarter of an hour, they stood near the coffee stand, exchanging fragmented stories between sips of scalding espresso. Her name was Tanisha, a journalist stationed in London. She spoke of her guilt, of leaving her father to fend for himself in Kolkata, and how the lack of clear communication was hollowing her out. "And you?" she prodded, tilting her head. "You seem… glued to your phone. Wife at home?" Rohan hesitated, his throat tightening at the question. Images of Priya flashed through his mind—her sitting at the edge of their bed in Mumbai, fingers kneading her temples as she dealt with the encroaching anxieties of parenting during this surreal world shutdown. "Yeah," he finally answered, his voice softer now. "Two daughters. My wife… she's probably holding everything together while I'm here, fumbling for answers." Tanisha studied him for a beat. "It's strange, isn't it? Being away from loved ones when something like this happens. It makes you realize how little control we have. In fact, moved by this crisis facing all of humanity, I have sent a proposal to management for conducting interviews of those who are stuck away from their families. Will it be OK with you to share your experiences and feelings?" Their eyes lingered on each other, a mutual understanding forming. "Sure, if sharing helps, I am for it." The crisis wasn't limited to individual predicaments; it was a tangled web of shared fragility. As they parted ways hours later after exchanging their business cards, her words still lingered in his head. He watched the hotel staff navigating their own chaos: the concierge, smiling tightly while explaining, for the hundredth time, that they didn't know when guests could go home; the janitor, humming an odd melody under his breath as he disinfected surfaces no one dared touch. Everyone bore the invisible weight of the unknown. It wasn't just his hotel, he realized—it was humanity clinging on, pocket by pocket, across the globe. But has mankind found a way to handle this crisis? There are talks of a vaccine, but it is still not there. Will it be as bad as the Spanish Flu of 1918-20?

Day 3: The Elasticity of Desperation

The faint light of dawn crept through the gaps in the hotel's blackout curtains, bathing the sterile room in hues of pale grey. As he finished his morning stretching, muscles warming and awakening in the stillness of the room, he felt a gentle anticipation flutter within—a silent promise of the day ahead. He pushed open the door, the hinges creaking softly like the first notes of a morning symphony, a flicker of colour caught his eye—on the floor, a food packet lay like an unexpected treasure waiting to be unearthed. A handwritten post-it note adorned the package, its ocean blue ink vibrant against the monotony of the mundane: "With Compliments." Curiosity piqued, he hastily opened the packet, peering inside to unveil its delightful contents. My breath hitched—a muffin, glistening with a sugary sheen; a chocolate croissant, its flaky layers beckoning like a siren's call; two golden butter cookies, rich and inviting; and a cheese sandwich, neatly wrapped and bursting with promise. "Wow! This is enough," he muttered with a sense of wonder threading through his words like a golden ribbon of delight before placing the bounty on the main table. In a moment of distraction, he caught sight of his reflection in the mirror, his hair tousled and rebellious, mirroring the thrill of the unexpected treat. With a quick, careless flick of his fingers through his hair, he exuded a casual charm—a mere mortal preparing for a divine feast. As he stepped out of the sanctuary of his room, he found the corridor stretching before him like a pathway of adventure waiting to unfold, the air cool and crisp, carrying the scent of distant promises. The gym remained locked, its doors steadfastly closed, but he brushed the thought aside.

Today, he would break his fast not with sweat but with the rich, aromatic allure of coffee brewing in the lounge. The lounge lay just two hundred meters away, a straightforward journey lined with the allure of nostalgia. As he walked, he passed a gallery showcasing haunting images of old aircraft, their elegant frames whispering tales of distant skies and lost times, each photograph a window into a world where dreams took flight. The Icons bar and the enticing Flini Italian Cuisine restaurant lay on his right, their tasteful elegance a comforting presence as he ventured onward, pulse quickening in anticipation of the coffee that awaited him—and the unwritten stories cradled within that unexpected feast. Rohan set his resolve with quiet determination, making his way to the reception counter, where the hum of travel buzzed in muted tones around him. The lobby, with its polished marble floors and shimmering chandeliers, felt like a world caught in limbo—a sanctuary for those yearning to journey home. A lingering glance at the airline crew member who stepped away after checking in—the only other trace of life from his homeland standing amidst a sea of foreign uniforms—only reinforced Rohan's solitude. "Good morning, Ms. Somkiat," he initiated with a hopeful lilt, glancing at the nameplate embedded on her crisp uniform. "Do you have any updates on flight resumption to India?" "Good morning, Mr. Srivastava," came her response, a hint of empathy lacing her words. "I'm sorry, but we don't have any further updates just yet. We'll let you know as soon as we do." Rohan furrowed his brow, the mystery of her familiarity nagging at him. How does she know my name? In this fog of uncertainty, he found himself feeling like a solitary island in an ocean of transience, surrounded by airline crews donned in crisp uniforms from Emirates, Kenya, and South Africa—each a fleeting silhouette against the backdrop of a world he yearned to reconnect with. "Thanks, Ms. Somkiat, I really appreciate it," he said hastily, retreating from the counter, his heart beating a little faster. The rich aroma of coffee called to him, a siren song promising warmth and solace in the chilly morning. He poured himself a steaming cappuccino from the machine nestled next to the hotel's makeshift office in the lounge, each swirl of foam a fragile moment of temporary joy. Pouring his cappuccino, he sought refuge on the porch, where the cold air wrapped around him like a velvet cloak, reminding him of his favourite Arabica Coffee in White & Red Alluring Fields Noritake cup lovingly served by Priya. His mind began to drift, thoughts entwining in a labyrinth of yearning and nostalgia, images of home flickering like distant stars. Once back in the cocoon of his room, he dialled Priya, Ananya, and Siya, the familiar voices on the line becoming lifelines in an ocean of uncertainty. But as he listened, his heart sank; Priya's tears fell like a relentless rain, each sob echoing the weight of longing that pressed against his chest. After finishing the complimentary breakfast, he picked up "Man's Search for Meaning" by Viktor Frankl—a book he had fondly purchased at Viking Book Store in Reykjavik, its pages promising refuge from his scattered thoughts. He nestled into a corner chair, diving into the profound depths of Frankl's narrative, yet the day hung heavy around him. Time, often an invisible fabric woven into the hustle of his corporate life, seemed to unravel without purpose. Rohan stirred as the soft buzz of his phone vibrated insistently on the nightstand, breaking the fragile stillness of the early hour. He groaned, reluctant to face the day, but the name glaring on the screen brought a flicker of recognition—and with it, the obligation to answer. Mrs. Madhavi. Her name carried more than just the weight of formality. Rohan had come to trust her, respect her, and even, in their professional spheres, rely on her judgment. The Head of Human Resources might not have been a frequent caller, but when she did call, she always had her reasons. And today, her voice barely masked the tension brewing behind the words. "Good morning, Rohan," she began, skipping pleasantries, her tone deliberate yet tinged with concern. "I wanted to reach you first thing. The top management is quite worried about your situation. The CEO asked for an update yesterday, and I'll be forwarding a detailed report to the Crisis Management Committee shortly." Rohan rubbed the sleep from his eyes, his mind sluggish from the cumulative exhaustion of sleepless nights and unresolved anxieties. "I appreciate the concern, Mrs. Madhavi. It's… frustrating. To say the least. Heathrow feels like a prison at this point." "You're not alone in this, Rohan. Everyone's hoping for a resolution soon," she replied softly, a rare warmth slipping into her otherwise formal cadence. There was comfort in her words, but it was her voice—the familiarity of it—that carried an unspoken solace. Rohan smiled faintly, a flash of nostalgia breaking through his foggy mind. He might have been stranded thousands of miles away, cut off from his family and grappling with uncertainty, but in an odd way, this call grounded him. Mrs. Madhavi wasn't just a colleague; she was part of the web of professional relationships Rohan had spent years cultivating—not out of some ambition to climb corporate ladders, but because he understood the power of human connections in the rigid constructs of business. Rohan leaned back, his memory drawing him back to a different chapter of his career. Years ago, when he was Regional Director for Bihar and Jharkhand, operating out of Patna, Mrs. Madhavi was steering insurance sales for one of their partner banks. She wasn't the Head of HR then—she was a relentless force on the ground. His career had intersected with hers in the heat of high stakes and ambitious targets, where numbers weren't just metrics; they were lifelines, whispers of success or survival in the competitive business environment. Rohan remembered the dim-lit cubicles lined with papers, reports, and the hum of conversation. Despite the persistent challenges of that region, low awareness about insurance, and the fierce demand for adaptability, he had thrived. And Mrs Madhavi had been unwavering alongside him, navigating her own hurdles with a sharpness he admired. Their camaraderie had grown slowly but surely, rooted not in office gossip or political manoeuvring but forged through joint efforts and results—tangible proof of their shared focus on performance rather than drama. Together, they had steered their teams through countless campaigns, celebrated shared victories, and tackled seemingly impossible challenges until their success became inevitable. When she joined the corporate headquarters last year as Head of HR, it hadn't surprised him. Her diligence, thoughtful leadership, and instincts made her a natural fit for the role. And yet, the warmth of their professional rapport hadn't been lost in the shift to formal hierarchy. Rohan prided himself on relationships like this—not the shallow kind sustained by rumour mills or the toxic politicking that plagued corporate corridors, but connections built on mutual respect and shared values. He had no patience for gossip vines, whispered intrigues, or the sly manoeuvres that seemed to occupy far too much bandwidth in workplaces. To him, all of that was noise—an unnecessary distraction from what truly mattered: performance, delivery, and the brilliance of raw numbers. Numbers, in Rohan's eyes, held an unparalleled beauty. Their shine was undeniable, untainted by subjective opinion. Performance was binary—it either existed or it didn't. Excellence, for him, was a pattern achieved through repetition, creating a rhythm that became muscle memory in his life and career. It was why he didn't need to play games to get noticed; the shine of his results spoke louder than any loud hallway whispers ever could. His approach didn't just earn him accolades—it earned him trust, unwavering and rock-solid. Whether it was past CEOs, juniors, peers, or partners, people respected Rohan not just for his work ethic but for how he navigated human relationships without the bitterness of office politics. Pulling himself back to the present, Rohan let out a breath, gripping the phone tighter as the stillness of his room loomed over him. "I'll hang tight here for now," he said to Mrs. Madhavi. "Not much else I can do, but thank you for updating me on the management's sentiments. It means a lot to know they're invested in resolving this." "We're all here to support you," Mrs. Madhavi reassured him before adding, "Stay strong. This situation won't last forever." The call ended with a lingering sense of connection—a thread that pulled Rohan back into the fabric of his professional network even as the world around him seemed frayed and disjointed. And as he set the phone down and stared out the window at the barren tarmac beyond, Rohan couldn't help but reflect on the gratitude that relationships like these inspired during times of crisis. In a world fuelled by chaos, uncertainty, and isolated hotel rooms, the quiet resilience of bonds forged in the fire of performance offered him a glimmer of steadiness. Food became a desperate quest. His survival depended on a small department store at the gas station opposite the hotel and the next-door restaurant run by a Pakistani, which was only serving take-away biryani. Muffins, artificial sweetness of chocolate bars, and the salty crunch of crisps—poor substitutes for real nourishment—were another source of fuelling. "Is this my new reality? Scrounging for stale cookies? I used to dine in fine restaurants, close deals over exquisite meals. Now I'm a refugee in a five-star prison, counting calories from cookies and chocolates." The indignity of it all was suffocating, he wondered. The evening, particularly, stretched like shadows across his solitude, devoid of the busyness he had long considered a comfort. In a bid to reclaim a sense of purpose, Rohan picked up his camera gear—his faithful companion in capturing the fleeting beauty of moments. Outside, he wandered into the garden, where nature unfolded its story in vibrant hues. There, he spotted a pair of Common Starlings foraging amidst the branches, their glossy black feathers shimmering in the dappled sunlight. It was a delightful irony—their name suggesting banality, while they possessed an elegance that ignited his spirit. He watched, entranced, as they flitted from perch to bush, then gracefully landed on the ground—a performance in perfect synchrony with an aircraft gliding towards the distant horizon of Heathrow. Each delicate movement—the starlings pecking at the earth, snatching up worms—mirrored the ritualistic dance of travel as planes taxied, refuelled, and boarded passengers like enigmatic shadows preparing to take flight. Amidst the backdrop of soaring metal birds, Rohan lost himself in the starlings' repetitive ballet, pondering when his own plane would arrive, when he, too, would refuel with the solace of home, board the waiting escape, and once again take to the sky, leaving this tapestry of uncertainty behind. Rohan stared at his phone for what felt like an eternity, willing the screen to show something other than the "No Flights Available" notification he'd been refreshing every alternate hour. The overall mood was quieter today at the hotel—most of the stranded passengers had checked out, as many airlines from various countries were still operational, ferrying their stranded citizens. He sighed as he dialled Priya's number, rehearsing his words in his head. Despite his mounting sense of helplessness, he couldn't allow her to sense it. She needed strength, not burden. The ringtone echoed in his ear until her voice broke through, soft but measured. "Hi, Rohan," she said, and for the first time in days, he detected a steadiness in her tone. "Priya, how are you holding up?" he asked, his voice calmer than he felt. "I'm better," she replied immediately, her words practiced yet convincing. "I think Siya slept better last night. The new routine seems to help. We did some breathing exercises and meditation together, and she didn't wake up crying as much. I think we're turning a corner. By the way, did you meditate today?" There was a pause—a beat too long—and Rohan could hear the sound of her labouring exhale, the kind that betrayed her struggle before she masked it again. For anyone else, Priya might have been flawless at hiding cracks in her Armor. But Rohan knew better. "That's good," he said cautiously, adding, "Hmmm.... Kind of.... no, not really, in fact, I just forgot." "I'm glad she's responding to the routine. And you... you're okay?" The question was weighted, designed to break through her wall. A faint chuckle escaped her, but it was fleeting—almost forced. "Me? You don't have to worry about me,

Rohan. I'm fine. I promise." "You say that like I don't have reason to worry." He softened his voice, his concern pushing against her defences. "Priya, you're holding everything together back there, and I'm just… stuck here doing nothing." "You're *not* doing nothing," Priya interjected firmly, her tone almost scolding. The sudden change in energy startled him. "You're trying your best to get back to us, and that's the most anyone could do right now. Don't beat yourself up for things you can't control." "But Priya—" "No buts, Rohan." She cut him off, a rare show of steel in her voice. "Siya doesn't need you guilt-ridden when you return. She needs you whole. And right now, what you can do is stay calm and remain strong. That's it. Do you understand?" Her words pierced through him, equal parts comforting and commanding. She had always had this ability—to ground him even when everything felt like it was spiralling. He imagined her now, sitting on the edge of Siya's bed, a hand brushing away her errant curls while she whispered reassurances in the quiet hours of the night. Priya had taken on the mantle of caretaker, but he hated the thought of her drowning under its weight. "I don't deserve you, Priya," Rohan muttered quietly, the admission slipping out before he could stop it. "Don't say that," her voice softened again, the steel slipping away to reveal warmth. It was her way of holding his hand, even from miles and oceans away. "We're a family, Rohan. We take care of each other, even when it hurts. You'd do the same for me." Rohan hesitated, unsure whether to press further or let her words rest where they fell. But the gnawing worry in the back of his mind wouldn't let him stop. He took a breath. "Priya," he said carefully, "is everything okay? You'd tell me, wouldn't you? If something was wrong?" Another pause. This time, it felt heavier.

He could almost hear the gears turning in her head as she decided how much to reveal. "I won't lie to you," she began, her voice quieter but steady. "Things are… hard. Siya is struggling, and I won't pretend otherwise. She's anxious, restless—she still asks for you every morning when she wakes up, even though she's trying to be brave. And I—" She stopped suddenly, her voice catching. Rohan sat up straighter, his grip tightening on the phone. "Priya," he said gently, "talk to me." "I—I'm okay," she continued quickly, brushing off the slip. "It's just been… a lot. But I'm handling it. We're managing. And once you're home, it'll get better. It has to." Her words carried optimism, but Rohan could hear the cracks forming between them now. She had perfected the art of reassurance, but there was something raw and unsteady beneath her calm facade—something she didn't want him to see. Forcing the issue wasn't a solution, but neither was pretending he didn't notice. "I hate this, Priya," Rohan murmured, leaning forward as though it would close the distance between them. "I hate that you're dealing with this alone. I hate that Siya thinks I've abandoned her. And I hate that you're trying to protect me, even when I should be the one doing that for you." "You're not abandoning anyone," Priya replied sternly. "And I'm not alone—I have Siya, and she has me, and we both have you, even if you're far away right now. You'll come back to us, Rohan. I know you will. So don't let this guilt eat you alive, okay?" Her words were a balm, soothing him in a way only Priya could. Rohan closed his eyes, his grip on the phone loosening slightly. "I'll keep trying to get back home," he said finally, his voice heavy with promise. "No matter what it takes, I'll find a way." "And we'll be here waiting," Priya said, her tone gentler now. "Your family will be here waiting." As the call ended, Rohan sat back in his chair, staring out at the empty tarmac. He could still hear Priya's voice echoing in his mind—strong, unwavering, even as she carried more than anyone should. If she could face the storm at home, then he would face the storm here. Because she was right: they were family, and family didn't break even under the worst of circumstances. "No matter what, I will find a way…" Rohan whispered to himself as he paced the cramped hotel room, the polished marble floor slick beneath his slippered feet. His voice trembled with determination, though it was barely audible over the relentless hum of the air conditioner—a mechanical rhythm that felt all too similar to the suffocating redundancy of his stranded routine. The haunting strains of Priya's tear-soaked words—"We will be here, waiting"—wrapped around him like a noose, pulling him deeper into the weight of expectation. Her voice wasn't just a memory; it was an anthem of hope, a vulnerable plea that he couldn't shake. It buoyed and burdened him in equal measure. Priya and his daughters were waiting for his return, for answers, for a reprieve from this chaos. And Rohan vowed not to let them down. He stared out the window, his gaze caught by the desolate view of Heathrow's tarmac—a scene eerily devoid of motion, cluttered with rows of grounded planes, their once-proud fuselages now spectral reminders of a world paralysed. The sky above was a pale grey, streaked with clouds that hung low as if even nature had surrendered to the weight of uncertainty. "Leverage your contacts, Rohan," he muttered with renewed conviction, his voice louder now, sharper, fuelled by the echo of Priya's words. "Something will work out… it has to."

Rising to the challenge, Rohan shed the helpless daze that had gripped him for days. This was no time for aimless waiting. If the skies were blocked, he would carve out a path—on the ground, through influence, using every ounce of his charm and network to bend the gridlock to his will. He reached for his phone, scrolling through the names in his contact list, lips pressed into a thin line as his mind sifted through possibilities. He dialled his first number—a contact in South Block, the power epicentre of Delhi's bureaucracy, where decisions were carved and livelihoods pivoted. South Block was a fortress of influence, where the corridors whispered of power plays and policies that shaped the nation's course. Rohan had long understood the value of forging connections in places like these, with many of his friends and relatives being the key decision-makers, not for his own career but for moments like this—moments of desperation when every phone call could morph into a lifeline. But his optimism took an immediate blow. Even his contacts, individuals entrenched in the power dynamics of Lutyens' Delhi, were grappling with their own crises. Each call was a mirror of helplessness—bureaucrats caught in webs of overwhelmed hospitals, trying to secure beds for family members who had tested positive for COVID-19. The rising infection numbers had stretched India's health infrastructure to breaking point, leaving even the mighty vulnerable. Everyone was fighting their own fight, whether for survival or desperately attempting to rescue stranded loved ones scattered across shutdown cities. The air felt heavy with unspoken anguish, the world crumbling under waves that brought both isolation and sickness.

Refusing to take defeat at face value, Rohan dialled another number, his hand tightening around his phone as nerves mounted. This wasn't an ordinary connection; it was a man who carried the weight of legacy and influence—Mr. Bhagat, a Padma Shri awardee and a figure who belonged to Delhi's fabled list of "Who's Who." Bhagat wasn't simply well-connected; he held sway at the highest levels, a man with strings to pull and corridors to unlock. Rohan had met Mr. Bhagat years ago through philanthropic projects as part of his company's CSR initiatives. Their relationship hadn't merely been transactional; it was genuine, built through honest collaboration and mutual respect. Rohan had gone above and beyond to support Bhagat's vision, lending his time and resources to initiatives that addressed tribal and rural health, education, and employment opportunities generation. He'd seen Bhagat, a highly revered person of eminence and fondly called Baba Ji by people, work tirelessly, his aura magnetic, his charm intoxicating—and his influence unmistakable. Surely Bhagat could help. Rohan's heartbeat accelerated as the call connected, and the familiar rasp of Bhagat's voice came alive on the other end. "Rohan! I heard about your predicament. You're stranded at Heathrow, yes?" Bhagat's tone was steady, but there was a hint of weariness beneath his words, as if the weight of the pandemic had dulled even the brightest of minds. "Yes, Baba Ji, I'm desperate to find a way home. Flights are suspended indefinitely. Priya and the girls are back in Mumbai… they need me there. I need to be there." Rohan's words spilled out, the urgency in his tone unmistakable. Bhagat sighed deeply, the sound crackling over the thin tether of the phone line. "I wish I could say I have a solution for you, Rohan. Trust me, if it were within my power, I'd move the skies to get you home. But even at the topmost echelons, people are scrambling. This virus hasn't spared anyone—bureaucrats, ministers, industrialists—it's chaos everywhere. I've tried pulling strings for others in similar situations, but there's little anyone can do right now." For the first time in years, Bhagat's voice carried the unmistakable note of helplessness, like a general confessing defeat before the battlefield. And hearing it struck Rohan deeply, a stark reminder that even the mighty weren't immune to the storm engulfing the world. Rohan leaned back in his chair, staring at the phone now silent in his hand. The call had been his trump card, his ace in the deck, and yet it folded under the harsh reality of a virus that had reduced even the most powerful connections to whispers against the tide. If Bhagat—the man with power coursing through his veins—was overwhelmed, what hope was there for someone like him? As the minutes ticked by, Rohan's thoughts wandered to the state of his homeland. India, a country brimming with resilience and vibrancy, was now grappling with hospitals stretched beyond their breaking point, testing the elasticity of its health infrastructure with each passing day. COVID-19 numbers had surged to unthinkable levels; news reports painted a grim tableau of survival. Cities choked with ambulances, families begging for oxygen cylinders, crematoriums overwhelmed by an unrelenting stream of the departed. It was chaos not measured in mere statistics but in lives upended, futures dismantled. And here he sat, stranded, powerless to shield his family from its feral advances. Despite the blow, Rohan refused to sink into despair. I have to keep going. There's no alternative. Priya and the girls are counting on me. He clenched his fists, his jaw tightening as he willed himself to keep searching, to dig deeper into his reservoir of contacts and creativity. There had to be a solution. The echoes of Priya's words—"We will be here, waiting"—returned with renewed vigour, ringing in his ears like a clarion call. Rohan closed his eyes, letting them guide him forward. *I will find a way,* he promised himself, *even if it means fighting every battle until there's nothing left to fight.* The world may have conspired against him, but Rohan wasn't a man who accepted defeat easily. If the foundation of his success had always been relentless perseverance, then this, too, would be another opportunity to rise against despair, against inertia, and against the odds.

Day 4: A Flicker of Light

Rohan woke to the sound of raindrops tapping against the glass like insistent visitors demanding entry. The dim haze of dawn seeped through the hotel curtains, casting a greyish glow over the room. Another day. Another packet of breakfast left outside his door. Another attempt to wrest some semblance of normalcy from the chaos of his stranded existence. He peeled open the packet mechanically, almost resentfully, and found himself staring at the usual contents—flatbread, a portion of scrambled eggs. Familiar, routine, lifeless. He pushed the tray aside, grabbed his phone, and started refreshing Twitter, the digital lifeline to a world where answers still seemed scarce. But first, he needed strength. He trudged downstairs to the small café next to the hotel lobby and completed his morning ritual: a cappuccino. It wasn't just caffeine anymore—it had bloomed into a universe unto itself, a tiny act of rebellion against helplessness. He watched as the barista carefully tilted the pitcher, pouring steam-kissed milk onto the coffee's dark surface, sculpting a delicate foam that stretched taut like a moonlit canopy. It was art, fleeting and fragile. As the cup warmed his hand, Rohan inhaled deeply, absorbing its promise—a brief oasis among shifting sands. He took the first sip, letting the bitterness coat his tongue before it melted into a sweetness he wouldn't find anywhere else. The faint floral notes reminded him of warm evenings in India and the cheerful hum of local bazaars. He closed his eyes and leaned into the sensation, savouring the ephemeral beauty of it all. But the moment was not meant to last. "In the dim light of my hotel room later that morning, isolation pressed in on me like a thick fog," Rohan muttered, his voice breaking into the silence. He didn't realize he was articulating his thoughts—monologuing out loud felt less suffocating than internalizing everything. "Each passing moment more suffocating than the last. Every unanswered tweet, every airline cancellation, every pressed redial button... they all pull me further into this void. How long before the void swallows me whole?" Suddenly, the intercom buzzed, startling him out of his reverie. He stretched his hands to pick up the receiver. "Sir, one Mr. Harjeet Singh Jodha wants to meet you," the voice crackled. His heart skipped a beat. A stranger? Why? But even as his mind raced with questions, he felt something stir—a flicker of hope. Rohan bolted toward the reception desk, his feet moving faster than his thoughts. But halfway there, a comical realization struck: he hadn't flushed the toilet in his bathroom before leaving. A small, mundane oversight. He laughed in spite of himself, the absurdity of it breaking the monotony of his despair. If nothing else, this moment reminded him that life—however chaotic—still had room for silliness. At the reception, a warm presence greeted him. "Mr. Srivastava, I'm Harjeet Singh Jodha," the man introduced himself with a kind smile, his eyes alight with purpose. He looked nothing like the strangers Rohan encountered every day—those polite yet detached faces that passed without notice. Jodha leaned forward slightly, as if bending to shield him from the loneliness of lockdown. "I'm a volunteer," Jodha said, his voice resonant with conviction. "I've been working with the Indian diaspora here in London. The tweets you sent to the High Commission—they reached us. You're not alone in this fight. Let us know if you need anything, truly. We're here to help." The simplicity of the words hit Rohan like waves. *You're not alone.* The words rippled through his heart, knocking down walls built out of days and nights of isolation. "I… I don't know what to say," Rohan stammered, feeling his throat tighten. "I've been so—so lost. Just waiting for someone to—" Jodha reached into his bag and handed him a heavy packet. Its weight pressed into Rohan's palm, tangible evidence of human kindness. "Food. Enough for two days," Jodha said briskly. "Biryani, kheer, snacks, a little cake." He smiled again—this one softer, tinged with the warmth of quiet understanding. "Enjoy it. Consider it a small celebration. These times don't mean we stop celebrating." Rohan blinked. "Celebration?" "Yes." Jodha rubbed his hands together, the tips slightly red from the late-March chill creeping into London. "It's my birthday today," he said matter-of-factly, as though dropping this detail was the most natural thing in the world. "And what's a birthday without sharing? We have enough fear to go around; at least we can try to part with a little joy." A lump formed in Rohan's throat. This man, a stranger, had chosen to spend his special day reaching out to him—a lonely, stranded soul—without hesitation, without expectations of reciprocation. Jodha swiftly handed over his phone number before adding, "Call me anytime you need something. Anything. We're in this together." And just like that, he turned and walked away, his purposeful stride leaving behind a warmth that lingered in the cold, indifferent lobby. Rohan stood rooted to the spot for a moment, staring at the packet in his hands as its significance sank in. He walked back to his room, his steps slower now, the weight of gratitude mingling with the ache of longing for home. Back in his dimly lit sanctuary, Rohan opened the packet. The rich aroma of the Veg Biryani instantly filled the small, sterile space, transforming it into something homely and inviting. The kheer glistened like liquid silver in a humble container, and the slice of cake—its edges slightly smudged but no less enticing—sat nestled beside the sweets. He let out a small laugh, surprising even himself. "A birthday feast from a stranger," he whispered to the empty room. "Somehow, that feels more meaningful than half the birthdays I've spent surrounded by people who never saw me." Taking his first bite of the biryani, Rohan closed his eyes, letting the spices tell nostalgic stories of home. His thoughts wandered to Jodha, this extraordinary stranger who had dropped out of the ether. What compels someone to reach across the chasm of fear and isolation? Rohan did what he did best to find answers—he searched. A quick scan on Facebook revealed the layers of Jodha's life: a physics teacher, a farmer's son from Rajsamand, Rajasthan, who'd carved a path here in London to become a UK citizen. His page brimmed with photos of cultural events, volunteer drives, and gatherings with the Indian diaspora, but every few posts bore testimony to something deeper—a longing. Rohan spotted a caption under a photo of yellowed fields back home: *"You can leave your soil, but your soil never leaves you."* "How?" Rohan muttered aloud, shaking his head. "How does someone do what he does? When everyone around me says stay put, hunker down, survive… How does Harjeet Singh Jodha walk into the uncertain, dragging along hope for those of us who've forgotten what that looks like?" He took another bite, this time pausing to savour the kheer, its creamy sweetness wrapping around a part of him he hadn't realized was starved. His mind spun back to every phone call he'd made recently to friends and relatives in London—a collective chorus of caution had met him at every turn. "Don't risk venturing out. The city's a danger zone." "Stay where you are for now. When this clears up, we'll figure something out." Rohan didn't blame them—fear had wrapped its thorned vines around everyone. But the contrast between their worried voices and Jodha's unflinching confidence gnawed at him. It wasn't that Jodha was immune to fear; it was that he chose kindness despite it. "Some of us hoard safety," Rohan mused to himself, "while others distribute courage." For the first time in days, Rohan felt something stir within him that wasn't dread or exhaustion—it was optimism. The crisis hadn't passed, his tickets back to India hadn't been confirmed, but maybe… just maybe… humanity wasn't breaking as much as he'd feared. Some people, like Jodha, were knotting threads of goodness into this tapestry of chaos. He raised the small slice of cake, angled the fork to cut a corner, and paused. He glanced at the clock. It was late enough in the day for Jodha to have moved on to whatever other kindness awaited him. But even across this strange, distanced connection, Rohan felt the need to acknowledge him. He sent a message: *"Happy Birthday. Thank you for making a stranger's day so much brighter. The food was phenomenal, but the hope you left behind… that's something else entirely."* As Rohan finished his feast, he sat back in his chair, relishing the fullness of his stomach and a soul that now felt a little less empty. Tomorrow's uncertainties hadn't disappeared, but tonight, he had discovered something resilient within himself. He thought back to the floral notes in his morning cappuccino—the fleeting beauty and quiet reward for simply taking the time to savour what remained in front of him. He decided something in that moment: until he could leave this city and fly home, he wouldn't spend his days lamenting what he'd lost. He would hold onto the Harjeet Singh Jodhas of the world, the tiny universes in his ceramic cups, and the quiet wonder of being alive even amid chaos. Because even if the world felt like it was falling apart, there *was* still warmth in it—and Rohan had just been wrapped in its shawl. The sunlight was beginning to fade, London casting its dusky hues into Rohan's hotel room. He sat by the window with the remnants of the biryani, now packed away neatly in a sealed container, and the last piece of cake sitting beside his laptop. Tonight, he planned to call home—not just Priya, but Siya and Ananya too. It hadn't been easy to coordinate everyone's time across school schedules, assignments, and Priya's mounting responsibilities, but somehow, the stars had aligned. He pulled his phone closer to him and opened the family group chat. Rohan: *"Video call time. Let's catch up!"* Priya: "Finally! Siya's ready, Ananya's still finishing her assignment, but she'll join." Siya: "Papa, call now, video call please! I made something for you today!" The message was punctuated with emojis: a splash of hearts, an airplane, and a face beaming with joy. For the first time in days, Rohan smiled as he tapped the call button, a sense of anticipation bubbling up inside him. The screen came alive with tiled faces: Priya's slightly tired but loving expression filled the top left; Siya's excited, bouncing frame filled the middle; and Ananya's annoyed-by-assignment but relieved-to-be-done smirk appeared on the bottom right. "Paaaaaaaapa!" Siya screamed, her voice ringing out louder than the speaker settings could handle. "Siya, you'll give me a heart attack one of these days," Rohan laughed, holding up his hands as if shielding himself from her exuberance. "Papa, guess what?! I made a caricature of you!" Siya squealed, holding up a piece of paper to the camera. Though the image was shaky, Rohan could make out a rudimentary stick figure of him with squiggly hair, a suit resembling the one in his passport photo, and, hilariously, two massive bags under his stick eyes. "If I didn't know better, I'd say you've captured me perfectly," Rohan teased. "The zombie look is spot on, Siya!" "Papa, noooo!" Siya whined. "You're not a zombie! You're my superhero! I drew the bags under your eyes because superheroes work soooo hard to save people!" Rohan's heart contracted. "Well then, I'll treasure this forever," he said softly, his smile gentle. Priya's voice cut through the indulgent banter. "Rohan, you seem… different today." She furrowed her brow slightly as if assessing him through the screen. "Not as stressed. Did something happen?" Rohan leaned back into his chair, letting out a deep sigh before speaking. "You wouldn't believe me if I told you," he began, shaking his head with a small chuckle. "But let me tell you anyway." "Storytime!" Ananya chimed in, her face lighting up. "Finally, Papa has drama to share!" "A LOT of drama," Rohan said, settling into a rhythm. "So today, I received a food package—that's normal enough, right? But let me tell you how it happened…" As he recounted the day, his family listened with rapt attention. He told them about sending tweets into the void—about the hopeless moments scrolling endlessly for flights and the knock on the bathroom intercom announcing Jodha's visit. Siya gasped, Ananya widened her eyes, and Priya frowned in concern at the details, but each held their breath when Rohan described Jodha handing him the food packet and sharing his birthday. "He didn't know me. He had no reason to care. And yet, he celebrated his birthday by helping a stranger," Rohan said, his voice growing quieter as he reflected once again on the encounter. “You know how everyone keeps telling us to stay inside, stay safe, survive—and that’s fine, but Jodha chose something entirely different. He didn’t let fear decide his kindness.” “He sounds like a superhero, too, Papa!” Siya declared with wide eyes and a dramatic fist pump. “I have to make a drawing of him next!” “Please give him a clap ” Ananya said lightly, rolling her eyes but smiling. “But also, can we talk about the biryani? Was it spicy? Did it taste good?” “Ananya,” Priya chastised mildly, shaking her head, “Not everything is about food!” “But food is life,” Ananya retorted, smirking. “The biryani was incredible,” Rohan said, rolling with the jokes. “The kheer—perfect. Sweet, creamy. And there was even cake! This man doesn’t do birthdays halfway.” Priya pressed her lips together, her gaze softening. “Rohan, that… It’s so heartwarming. I just—” She hesitated, glancing at the girls as if weighing whether to continue. She lowered her voice slightly. “We’ve had such a hard time back home, and hearing stories like this reminds me not to give up hope. People like Jodha—they’re proof that there’s still so much good out there, even though things feel impossible right now.” “Exactly,” Rohan said, leaning forward. “It’s easy to get buried under all the bad, under the worry, the uncertainty, the endless news alerts. But Jodha reminded me of something—a simple truth: even small acts of kindness can be monumental. Even a stranger can make you feel seen, respected, cared for.” Siya interrupted the pause that followed, her bubbly voice full of excitement. “Mama, Mama, maybe we can do something like Jodha too! When Papa comes home, we’ll throw a party and invite everyone—even people from outside!” “Maybe,” Priya teased, smiling and shaking her head. “But first, Papa needs to come home before we plan anything." Ananya leaned in conspiratorially, smirking again. "So, Papa. Important question: Did you cry?" Rohan looked mildly affronted. "Now, why would I cry?" "Because nice people make emotions happen," Ananya replied with mock seriousness. "Oi! I didn't cry, Ananya. I just…" He trailed off for a moment but recovered quickly. "Okay, maybe I teared up a little. But that doesn't count!" "It totally counts," Ananya replied, grinning. "Well," Priya said, her tone softening as it carried a weight only Rohan could fully understand. "You do deserve moments like that, Rohan. You've been carrying so much, trying to get back to us. Even if we're apart, don't forget that you're still part of us. Always." Rohan swallowed hard, a lump forming in his throat. "And I won't give up," he said. "You've been holding the fort all this time, Priya. You're the real superhero. I'll keep pushing, keep doing whatever I can to come home. It might take some time, but I'm going to get back to you, to Siya, to Ananya." Siya clapped her hands. "You'll come flying back, Papa! Superhero style!" "Hopefully minus the bags under my eyes," Rohan joked, winking at his daughter. The call wound down gradually, laughter and gratitude intertwining like threads of a tapestry. When each face disappeared from the screen, Rohan felt a warmth that reminded him of Jodha's biryani: rich, comforting, and lingering beyond the moment. He leaned back in his chair, staring at the empty cake wrapper. In the quiet afterward, Rohan murmured to himself, "We're all just searching for connection, aren't we? Sometimes, it comes from strangers. Sometimes, from the ones we love most. But it only takes a flicker of kindness to remind us that the world isn't as dark as it seems." Tomorrow would be another battle. The flights still weren't confirmed, his blood pressure medication still hadn't been sorted, but tonight, in front of his laptop, surrounded by love across continents, Rohan allowed himself to believe that things would be okay. "Maybe, just maybe, kindness was enough to light the way home. Maybe Priya and the girls were cheering him up. Maybe Priya was hiding something much deeper than he could think of." He wondered whether he understood Priya despite 28 years of company.

CHAPTER 3

THE ECHOES OF RESOLVE

Day 5: Bonds Forged Beyond Office Walls

The muffled glow of dawn was still hours away when the sharp, unrelenting shrill of my iPhone tore through the abyss of night. It wasn't just the sound that startled me, but the weight it seemed to carry—the kind reserved for desperation. Priya's name glowed on the screen, trembling as if it held the same restless energy that reverberated through my veins. "Rohan!" Her voice shattered as soon as I answered, brittle yet fierce, laced with panic that clawed its way across oceans to reach me. "I can't do this anymore… I can't. When are you coming home?" Sleep fled, chased away by the escalating pitch of her anxiety. "Priya," I tried, but her words spilled over, relentless in their torrent. "There was a man in the corner of my room tonight. That man was staring at me! He was lurking in the corner of the room, inching closer. I screamed! And then… Siya came rushing in." Her words tumbled out in fragments—fast, irregular, sharp—but each landing felt like another hammer to my chest. "Mom, what happened?" Siya's innocent voice broke through Priya's panic like a sliver of light fighting against shadows. Priya continued, her voice shaking as though trying to steady itself: "I pointed toward the corner, where that monstrosity was lurking. But Siya just tilted her head and said, 'Mom, it's just you and me in this room.'" The silence that followed her confession was heavy—not the silence of absence, but of something immeasurable lingering between the lines. Then came her gasp, a broken exhale that carried the heavy burden of her helplessness: "Rohan, I think I'm losing my mind. Siya is also under stress, and she has become quite distant. The kitchen—it's deserted without the maids; it feels haunted. I cook, but I can't force myself to eat. Last night, I recited the Hanuman Chalisa and Achyutam Keshavam from YouTube over and over until exhaustion finally claimed me. And then the gasp. A broken exhale, wrapping her exhaustion and despair into one unbearable sound. The worst had come true; my hunch that Priya was hiding something last evening came true. She is slipping into the abyss of mental health. "Priya," I whispered, counting my breaths in an attempt to steady her through the phone, though helplessness bit deep. "Listen to me. You're strong; you've always been strong. Remember Shivani's stories? Prem Chand's characters? Their resilience? You need to let your mind wander into the worlds they've built—escape for a few hours. You're not alone. Believe me." Her reply was nearly hollow, like a thread unravelling. "Rohan, how do you stay occupied? Doesn't this isolation crush you?" I opened my mouth to explain the little routines—the meals left by strangers, the impersonal muffled voices through an intercom, the endless waiting for news that wouldn't come—and realized none of it would soothe her. So I answered instead with what she needed to hear: "I think of you, Siya, and Ananya. It helps me hold on. The thought of being home again is enough to keep me moving forward, Priya. This will pass. Trust me." She was silent for a while, then said, "I'll try, Rohan. But please... hurry home." When she finally excused herself to take a shower and disappeared into her bathroom, I collapsed inward, wrestling against the stark realization that despite technology and the illusion of 'connection,' my helplessness remained absolute. The morning carried no reprieve from the haunting stillness of the night before. I went through my own motions of solitude—an unremarkable breakfast thrown together from faded packets—and let the weight of reality settle over me like damp fog. It had been four days since I last tasted freedom. No laundromats operated under the lockdown protocol, leaving me with a mountain of despair staring back at me: the pile of worn, used undergarments from the last 15 days. A flimsy detergent sachet sat on the edge of the sink, bearing the burden of my expectations. Resigned to necessity, I turned the bathtub into a vessel of redemption, scrubbing my clothes as water swirled like muted chaos around me. The act was humiliating, a quiet and relentless reminder of the erosion of the comfort, control, and structure I once took for granted. Each scrub bit into me, as if it was not the fabric being cleaned but the residue of helplessness clawing at my edges. When the task ended, and the water ebbed away, I hung the clothes on my balcony, their damp presence absorbing the hybrid sunlight that filtered unevenly through scattered clouds. It felt like the weather mocked my spirits, playing hide-and-seek with a fragility too battered to rise to the game. The intercom crackling to life interrupted my stillness, sharp and bright like an unfamiliar note in a symphony of muted tones. "Mr. Srivastava," came Mrs. Somkiat's clipped, professional voice—a beacon amidst a world seemingly devoid of human interaction. "There's a gentleman here to see you near the parking in front of the porch." Curiosity fluttered, fragile but insistent, as I peered out of my window to the world beyond. Even as my existence blurred into confinement, the rhythm of life outside flowed on, unaffected. I moved toward the entrance, feet shuffling with restrained urgency, as if this encounter could puncture the bubble of desolation encasing me. And there he stood—near the gleaming white Pajero that dominated the emptiness of the parking lot. His bright, vibrant turban seemed almost defiant against the pale pink cherry blossoms sprinkled overhead, their fragile beauty scattering onto the cement floor below like pieces of hope. The blossoms transformed the cold geometry into a fleeting mosaic of renewal, starkly contrasting with the weight I carried. As I approached, my eyes met his—warm pools visible even through the strict confines of an N95 mask. They carried a silent compassion that extended beyond the physical fabric. He introduced himself simply but profoundly, his voice muffled yet strong: "Sat Sri Akal. I am Jaspreet, a volunteer from the Southall Gurudwara." "Sat Sri Akal." I pressed my palms together instinctively, greeting him, gratitude welling silently as his hands mirrored the gesture. From the trunk of the Pajero, he produced a humble food packet, nestled like a quiet promise within the larger folds of his vehicle's interior. With practiced care, he handed it to me—no words were needed, yet the moment carried more depth than a thousand spoken lines ever could. In that small exchange—the unspoken understanding etched within his gaze—my helplessness momentarily eased. This stranger had seen the struggle in my eyes, read my unvoiced dread, and extended a shard of warmth into the frigid expanse of isolation I inhabited.

His simple explanation that future meals would be left at the reception served not merely as a logistical detail but as a tether connecting me to humanity's shared strength. When Jaspreet left, I lingered there, standing amid the quiet rustle of cherry blossoms dancing around me. Hope, faint and fleeting, stirred within. For a brief heartbeat, I felt part of something larger than solitude—connected not to my fears but to the threads of compassion binding us all in this web of shared existence. In that instant, the echo of kindness made my world, however fractured, feel a little less daunting. Gurudwaras, a place of worship for Sikhs, are known for their benevolence and selfless humanitarian services to all irrespective of caste, creed, and religion. Southall Gurudwara was about 6 miles from Heathrow, and around 200 male and female volunteers were working round the clock to help stranded people due to the lockdown. Gurudwara offered 24/7 langar service and served thousands of people from all nationalities. I pictured a mosaic of faces bound by compassion, and for the first time in days, truly believed: Kindness might still tilt the world back into balance. Why had the volunteers opted to leave food at the reception instead of handing it to me personally? Was it weariness from confronting the desolation carved across my features, or an effort to maintain the invisible boundaries necessitated by these extraordinary times? The question haunted me, its answer elusive and intangible, floating just out of reach. Frustrated, I pressed my palms into my thighs, murmuring a half-hearted monologue in search of clarity. The uncertainty was a gnawing presence, a ghost whispering at the edges of my increasingly repetitive days. The air outside was crisp, with a gentle breeze threading through the imposing iron gates of Park

Inn. Even in isolation, the evening stroll had become my lifeline—a private ritual to stave off madness. The flowers in their orderly beds exhaled faint sweetness, their symmetry in contrast to the chaos of the world. As I returned to my room, the elevator doors grinding shut behind me, my phone buzzed, jolting me back to reality. It was a call, perhaps overdue, but unexpected nonetheless. President Satindra Kumar's booming voice greeted me before I had even fully wrapped my head around his name flashing on the screen. "Rohan! Hi there, how are you managing, my friend?" He spoke with the rapid-fire energy of a man running three meetings simultaneously but somehow still landing attentive. "Listen, I heard from Madhavi about your situation. We've been discussing it in the committee—it came up in our Crisis Management meeting, actually. How are things? Everything okay with the family?" I paused briefly, considering what "okay" meant in times like these. "Thank you for calling, Sir. I'm fine, though home… well, home has been a challenge. Priya and Siya are struggling to hold themselves together. They're under tremendous pressure mentally, especially Priya. It's been tough. I was thinking of arranging a psychiatrist for them." Mr Kumar's response was immediate, direct, and reassuring, like the mentor I remembered. "Don't worry, Rohan. Leave that to me. I'll tap into my team and identify someone suitable. Just give me a little time. If you or your family need anything, just let me know—whether personal, professional, or logistics support. Please, don't hesitate." His tone softened toward the end, carrying an unmistakable sincerity that pierced through the static of the call. "Thank you, Sir. That truly means a lot," I replied, humbled by his concern. My gratitude wasn't formal—it was deeply personal. When Mr

Kumar hung up, I sat for a moment, staring at the pale-blue wallpaper of my hotel room. This man, my mentor from years ago, had once taught me how to navigate the rough seas of corporate life with resilience and practicality. Through his guidance, I had learned the trade's nuances—the calculated risks, the diplomacy of empathy, and the importance of carrying steadfast composure in storms both personal and professional. Yet here he was not as a boss, not as a leader, but as a friend, extending his hand across the miles that separated us. Within moments, my phone buzzed again—a WhatsApp message. It was from Mr Kumar himself. "Dr Khurana," the text read, followed by the contact number for the psychiatrist. His efficiency hadn't waned a bit over the years; I could almost imagine him pacing in his study, firing off instructions into multiple phones simultaneously. I quickly dialled the number. The video call connected, and I found myself face-to-face with Dr Khurana—a man whose calm demeanour and considerate eyes radiated quiet authority. I explained everything, outlining Priya's struggles and the blanket of stress suffocating my family. He nodded attentively, interrupted occasionally by the rustle of papers on his desk. "I've been seeing patients during this pandemic, selectively though, and strictly by appointment," Dr. Khurana explained. "I'll fit Priya in tomorrow. Meanwhile, ask her to try breathing exercises. Trust, Mr. Srivastava, we'll manage this together." The word 'together' clicked into the widening chasm of my disconnect, feeling like scaffolding rather than solace. I told Priya about the appointment later that evening. Her response was hesitant, tired, but tinged with relief—a tiny flicker on the horizon. Not long after, Ramesh, my trusted lieutenant from the office, called me. Ramesh had always been sharp, reliable, and fiercely protective—a right-hand man through thick and thin. "Sir, my wife mentioned knowing a counsellor who's excellent with stress management. I'll pass on your wife's contact details, and we can arrange virtual sessions if that works. We'll make sure Priya has someone to talk to in these times." The conversation felt like a buoy—a life raft extended from hands that I trusted unconditionally. "Thank you, Ramesh," I said, allowing him to hear the gratitude steeped in my voice. "Let's make it happen." Just as I thought the day had offered all its kindness, Nisha called next. Nisha, my loyal secretary, whose presence in my professional life had been a constant, unwavering beam of support. She had managed impossible schedules, handled my travel madness, etc., in her professional capacity, and kept chaos at bay with the grace of a seasoned sailor navigating unrelenting seas. This time, though, her voice held a different texture. "Sir, I've been worrying about Madam and Siya every day. I can visit them whenever you need. Really, don't hesitate—I *want* to help. Just say the word." Her voice cracked slightly, betraying her emotion despite her professional tone. The lump in my throat grew heavier, and warmth spilled through the cold spaces of my isolation. "Nisha, you've always been there for me—from calendars to crises. But… this call? It matters more than you know. Thank you. I'll let Priya know you offered, but even hearing it helped me more than I can express." Her silence spoke volumes before she added, softly, "Anything you need, Sir." When I finally collapsed onto the edge of my bed, my heart was heavier than before—but not because of dread. It weighed with the sheer force of gratitude and connection—threads stretched out by those who refused to let my isolation define me. From mentors to colleagues, from friends to strangers, a web of concern had been spun across continents—a silent acknowledgment that though the world seemed fractured, kindness still stitched its seams. The evening stroll suddenly felt symbolic. Standing amidst buds of fresh flowers in Park Inn was never just about exercise; it was about witnessing resilience—the quiet insistence of petals bursting forth despite howling winds. I thought of Priya and Siya, and for the first time in days, I pictured them not surrounded by dark corners and mental strain, but by new colours blooming unseen. Maybe tomorrow would hold more light than shadows. Maybe kindness would bridge the gaps of our loneliness. Maybe we weren't so alone after all. In that hopeful silence, I closed my eyes, ready for another chance to make it through.

Day 6: Echoes of New Normal

Each day, a hot meal enough for lunch arrived as the city descended further into lockdown—a once-vibrant metropolis reduced to the quiet eeriness of department stores and restaurants shuttered in unison, like iron gates closing against the tide of humanity. I was left stranded in a monotonous existence, alone amidst cchocs of a world paused in an unnatural rhythm. The langar they provided was simple yet profoundly nourishing, and to me, it tasted like manna from heaven—a direct link to the communal spirit I longed for with increasing desperation. The aroma of warm dal and freshly made roti, carried through the air like a gift, enveloped my lifeless hotel room in a cocoon of comfort. It was akin to the embrace of an old friend, a tender reminder of the warmth I'd been missing. That steaming plate of food was an unspoken promise, whispered through its simplicity, of the human capacity for compassion even in the darkest of times. However, for dinner, I had to still manage with some ramen cup noodles, cookies, and chocolates hoarded before the store closed. As twilight draped itself over the skyline in its rich velvet of impending night, breaking my brief reverie, my phone rang suddenly, jolting me from my drifting thoughts. The name of the caller made me pause; it was Mr Niel, the Park Inn's General Manager. Until now, he had been a figure I'd glimpsed only in passing—a man who moved with brisk efficiency, his presence understated but commanding in its controlled aura. I imagined him as all business, a professional who had little time for nuance. Yet this call proved otherwise. His voice carried an unexpected warmth, tinged with subtle concern, blending gruff practicality with something uncharacteristically comforting. "Mr. Srivastava," he began, his tone measured but genuine, "I understand you're having some difficulty with meals. While our kitchen is mostly closed, I've been preparing a few basics for my staff. Would you allow us to send you a light dinner instead? At a discount, naturally." For an eternal second, gratitude swelled in me, lodging itself in my throat. I scrambled for words, suddenly overwhelmed by the enormity of this gesture against the backdrop of my isolation. "Mr. Niel, I… I don't know how to thank you," I stammered, my disbelief evident as emotion surged. "This is beyond anything I could have anticipated. Your kindness… it means more than I can put into words." At my faltering reply, his response was steady, tinged with exhaustion but anchored in human empathy. "We're all in this together, Mr. Srivastava," he said, exhaling with equal parts resignation and hope. "Just doing what we can. We're human beings first, hoteliers second—especially in times like these." The smallness of his offer belied its monumental impact on me. This light dinner was not merely sustenance; it was a crack in the Armor of isolation I wore, a flicker of the humanity I often feared forgotten in the collective despair. It served as an undeniable reminder that the persistence of compassion, even when besieged by fear, remained a force capable of softening the razor edges of crisis. Yet the erosion of normalcy continued unabated, gnawing away at the little semblance of stability that remained. The hotel's housekeeping services were indefinitely halted under the shadow of new COVID protocols, a seeming necessity that brought its own muted chaos. I found myself thrust into a strange procession of room changes every three days—each sterile chamber indistinguishable from the last, all locked in a restless cycle of monotony. Every door I opened ushered me into yet another prison of identical walls, a fresh reminder of my utter lack of control. Each space reverberated with silence, reflecting the empty hum of confinement I could never shake. Days fused into one another like sand in an hourglass, their passage rendered shapeless and unremarkable. But in the cascading void of time, nature offered an unintended reprieve, a lifeline against disquiet's toll. With sunlight pooling over the hotel's exterior, I wandered outside, my thoughts momentarily quieted by the presence of birds. They flitted and perched, wildly indifferent to the weight of human turmoil, their chaotic movements a joyous anarchy beyond our mortal burdens

Their dance was pure freedom—unbound, ego-less, an expression of instinct uninhibited by invisible rules. Dusk's cool breeze carried me toward the hotel's narrow entrance passage, flanked by untrimmed bushes that harboured their own nocturnal mysteries. Two shapes emerged from the shadows into the dim light, small and nimble entities about a foot and a half in height. Cats or jackals—they blurred the line between domesticated charm and untamed curiosity. I stared, marvelling at their fluid outlines before realizing, for them, the distinction didn't matter. They simply were. An effortless coexistence. But even as nature sought to weave its serenity over me, thoughts of my family returned with relentless force—each face a vibrant strand in a tapestry of worry. Priya, Ananya, Siya—they occupied every empty moment of my consciousness, a loop of longing carved deeply into my memories. Before long, I was once again curled upon the sofa of my gilded cage, a cage whose confines tightened with the suffocating weight of another endless evening.

The evening sun draped my room in hues of amber, wrapping everything in a blanket of fragile calm. Priya's voice pierced through my reverie, halting me mid-thought. It wasn't rushed, nor broken, but carried the weight of muted exhaustion—like someone who'd just emerged from battle, weary but still standing. "I visited Dr. Khurana today," she began, her words deliberate, stitched together from threads of vulnerability. "He said I need to sleep, Rohan. To sleep, meditate, eat well, and take my meds on time." A pause followed—a pause filled with hesitations demanding space. "I confessed to him that I haven't really slept for three nights. I just… can't. The quiet gets so loud." My grip on the phone tightened as Priya's voice faltered. I could picture her sitting on the corner of our bed, her face dimmed like the fading daylight outside my window. I imagined Siya in the same room, perhaps gripping her mother's hand, her world shrinking beneath the weight of what no child should carry—the sight of her mother unravelling. "And Siya?" I asked gently, keeping my voice anchored. "He said the same for her," Priya replied, barely audibly, as if Siya's heartache weighed heavier on her than even her own. "She's holding up better than me, but not by much. She's trying to be strong for us. For me." That last word slipped into silence too heavy to fill. How does one comfort a family fractured by distance—a sea of isolation separating hearts desperate to connect? I offered her what little I could: "Priya, you'll get through this. We'll get through this. One step, one breath at a time. Dr. Khurana knows what he's doing. Trust his advice. And… trust me." "Okay," she whispered, her voice almost too small to reach me. But it did. Ramesh called shortly after, his voice brimming with concern. He didn't bother with pleasantries; that wasn't his style. "Sir, how are things on your end? Did Priya Madam manage to see the doctor? Is everything stable now?" "Ramesh, she did see Dr. Khurana," I answered. His sharp exhale told me he'd been holding his breath for updates. "The doctor suggested meditation, sleep, and proper meals. He's given Priya and Siya the same advice. Things are… moving along. Slowly, but moving." "That's good to hear," Ramesh said, his sincerity cutting through the distance like a balm. "Anything else you need, Sir? I'm still trying to reach that counsellor—the one my wife mentioned. If there's anything else, tell me. You know I've got your back." "For now, we're fine, Ramesh. Thank you for following up. It means more than you know." Nisha was next. Her calls had become as regular as clockwork—a lifeline of consistency in my otherwise scattered days. But today's tone felt different, softer, like someone was holding back tears. "Sir, I've been thinking about Madam and Siya all afternoon. I wish I could do more," she murmured, her voice betraying her attempts at professionalism. "At least let me visit them. No one should feel this alone, Sir. You know I'll take care of everything without question." Her offer broke something within me—a dam of gratitude I had no words to express. How does one repay unwavering loyalty infused with kindness? How do you thank someone willing to stretch beyond the limits of duty? "Nisha," I said, forcing my voice to remain steady, "you've been my pillar for years, at work and now through this. Just calling Priya, checking on her, is enough. You've already done more than I can ask for." "Sir, it's not about asking," she insisted, her tone resolute. "You're family to us. And family looks out for each other." Those words lingered long after the call ended. As the night deepened, my phone became a portal to a deluge of well-wishers. Friends, colleagues, relatives—all streaming in with calls or texts, each one echoing concern or lending bits of advice wrapped in hope. Their voices ranged from cheerful attempts to distract me to sombre assurances that I wasn't alone. I stood by the balcony as the last of the callers' warmth dissipated into the cold London air. Below, life ambled on—the occasional car passing, its headlights splitting the streets into shards of black and white. I was lonely, still surrounded. Satindra Kumar's swift actions. Ramesh's unwavering reliability. Nisha's limitless compassion. Priya's fragile resilience. Siya's silent strength. Dr. Khurana's measured advice. Friends and family distant but present. The threads of connection wrapped tighter around me, stitching themselves into my fractured state like a patchwork quilt. Stranded wasn't synonymous with abandoned. My conversations through these five days had proven otherwise. Tomorrow, things might not be perfect, but they would move one step closer. Priya would rest better knowing she had guidance. Siya might smile, even faintly, just by seeing her mother less burdened. Calls from my lifelines—people who refused to forget me—would continue to soften the jagged edges of isolation. Kindness, I realized, wasn't about grand gestures or headline-worthy deeds. It was in the quiet persistence of care—a daily ritual, a heartfelt message, a steady voice at dusk. It was the bridge spanning the gaps of distance and desolation, ripe with optimism for what awaited next.

Days 7 to 9: A Calm before Storm

Thousands of miles away, my elder daughter, Ananya, wrestled with her own lockdown-induced anxieties, trapped by travel restrictions and unable to join her mother and younger sister. Bright and ambitious, she seemed dulled by the trauma of witnessing Priya's illness unfold—distilled into pained pixels on our WhatsApp video calls. Her tear-streaked face, raw with torment, and tremulous voice conveyed everything I feared but could not mend. "Papa, she looks so weak," Ananya whispered one evening, her voice wavering with subdued urgency. "The doctors… they just keep saying these are testing times for all of us, advising to take care of mental health. What if she... what if she doesn't get better? I can't even be there. And Siya—she's forcing herself to be quiet, trying to hide how much she's struggling mentally. She's not herself." Each syllable from her mouth struck me like a thunderclap, igniting fears I had tried and failed to suppress. I fought to find words that would console us both, but, like always, what came out felt hollow—fragile vessels trying to carry the wreckage of my emotions. "She will be okay, Ananya," I assured her—or tried to assure myself—and hoped my voice didn't betray the growing void inside me. "We have to believe in her strength. Focus on your studies. We will get through this together." Yet even as I uttered these words, they felt like flimsy protections against the storm gathering around us. My reassurances were ripe with inadequacy, shaken by the immense uncertainties looming over us all. I was losing them—the laughter of my family, the promise of tomorrow—and every moment apart edged closer to my breaking point, threatening to tear away the threads connecting me to the people I loved most. As I hung up, the image of Ananya's anguished eyes lingered in my mind, joined by haunting visions of Siya's quiet suffering and Priya's pale, fragile form. The guilt was suffocating, a barrier built not just by geography but by the weight of my own helplessness—a prison constructed from the rubble of dashed hopes and unanswered prayers. Somehow, instead of disappearing into despair, I swallowed it whole as my voice echoed in the hollow chamber of my quarantined soul. The days blurred on, punctuated by moments of terror and despair. If redemption existed, I couldn't yet see its light. For now, the storm refused to relent. Same routines across continents, same fears hidden in the corners of bedrooms and dorms, same echoes between calls that pretended to be connection. Yet in these monotonies, hope began to stir. It wasn't loud or bright, but always there—an underlying pulse of quiet care binding Priya, Siya, Ananya, and Rohan in their shared longing for strength, healing, and togetherness. Every call, every hesitant conversation, every moment of reflection looked toward a day where monotony might finally give way to a deeper connection, a chance to confront pain with hope instead of despair. It was the thread they clung to when everything else felt brittle.

Day 10: Search for Shelter

The bland walls of the Park Inn, devoid of character, seemed to shift closer, encasing me like the indifferent embrace of a prison. And as the fibbers of repetition wound tighter, today brought its unique milestone—it was, at last, time to check out. The date loomed heavy: March 31st. No hotel could harbour guests beyond this threshold without exception. A temporary community, hastily constructed by the Indian diaspora, extended its hand to stranded compatriots. Makeshift shelters in banquet halls, communal washrooms, fleeting comforts—each accommodation was a testament to collective endurance. The High Commission offered suggestions for long-term stays, including properties under OYO Rooms that promised affordability but teetered on elusive reliability. I booked one through the app, grasping at hope's flickering light as my time at Park Inn ticked away. Yet, little did I know, this fragile hope would soon disintegrate into an unfamiliar darkness. Still, doubt lingered like an unwelcome shadow as I prepared to leave Park Inn, wrapping my fraying sense of security in fragile optimism. At the front desk, I encountered Ms Georgia—the blonde-haired COO with turquoise-blue eyes, deep and captivating. She was officiating at the front desk in view of the skeletal staff available on duty, her presence anchoring the weary air of uncertainty. Her gaze softened when it settled on me—a kindness subtle yet profound, like a gentle touch on a raw wound. "Mr Srivastava," she said, her voice weighted with compassion and a polite tenderness that seemed all too rare, "I wish you an early flight back home and a comfortable stay at your new place." Her words momentarily eased the tension gripping my chest, but as she spoke, her gaze wavered. There was an unspoken weight behind her eyes, a hesitation that hinted at understanding something deeper than protocol. Carefully, she retrieved a business card from the drawer and extended it to me, her fingers almost trembling. "If you need any assistance," she added quietly, her voice catching ever so slightly, "please feel free to call me." I took the card with a sense of mixed gratitude and trepidation. These threads of shared humanity felt precarious, yet they were all I had as I ventured off to the new place—a patched-together semblance of hope and uncertainty. I was determined to withstand whatever turbulence fate threw my way. But I hadn't anticipated just how turbulent it would be. Upon arrival at the hotel, dread seized me like a vice. The door stood locked, its surface unforgiving and lifeless, reflecting the hollowness of my momentary optimism. It was purportedly a hotel, yet it bore the washed-out appearance of an abandoned bar. The battered sign mocked me, cruel in its irony. I knocked, first timidly, then frantically—five, seven, ten minutes stretched on, each frustrated thud hammering my sense of hope further into oblivion. Through the grimy glass, shadows moved faintly in the darkness. I attempted to communicate through frantic, exaggerated gestures, but my silent pleas were met with rejection. A figure appeared, shaking his head firmly, lips forming but one relentless word: "Closed." The muted echo of the refusal reverberated within me alongside rising disbelief. "The hotel has been closed for renovations for the last three months," he said in a raised voice. My mind raced to reconcile what I'd heard with what I saw, but the gravity of my predicament swiftly pulled me under. Desperation bubbled over as I paced the streets of Hounslow, dragging two oversized suitcases—my stroller camera bag hanging uncomfortably from one shoulder, while a messenger bag, heavy with necessities, swung against my torso like a constant reminder of the weight I carried in every sense of the word. Hotel after hotel rejected me, their closed doors signalling the same dire reality. Every attempt met failure, and I felt the crushing weight settle upon me like the earth itself threatened to swallow me whole. The idea of sleeping on the streets gripped me like icy fingers wrapping around my throat, stealing my breath. Faces blurred past me, indifferent to my plight—a carousel of strangers who seemed to drift by, untouched by my growing despair. Should I turn to charity-run homes for shelter against the unforgiving night? The spectre of contracting COVID in an overcrowded haven whispered threats at the edges of my mind like Chitragupta himself judging my sins. What misdeeds had brought me to this crossroads, stranded and battling the spectre of total abandonment? As I grappled with these apocalyptic spirals of thought, my hand instinctively dug into the folds of my lavender-coloured Massimo Dutti down jacket—purchased during another life in Milan—and within its depths, my fingers brushed against the fragile salvation Ms. Georgia had offered me. Her business card. A lifeline. I dialled the number, praying for it to pierce through the silence. The executive at the central reservation of the Radisson Group answered, his voice draped in polite indifference. All reservations, he said, were on hold. When I insisted on speaking with Ms Georgia, he reluctantly placed me on hold, the line wavering between hope and despair finally got disconnected after a long hold. After three failed attempts with phone lines being busy, I could finally get connected, and there she was—my lifeline in this turbulent sea of uncertainty. "Ms Georgia," I said, desperation clinging to every word, "I checked out just hours ago, and the OYO room I had booked is... closed! No hotel here is accepting check-ins! What am I supposed to do?" "Relax, Mr Srivastava," she replied soothingly. "Let me see what I can do. Can I put you on hold for a moment?" "Of course," I whispered, clinging to the hope she could conjure something amidst all the chaos. What was she seeking? Permission, approval, or merely a moment to gather her thoughts before possibly dismissing me? Trepidation gnawed at my insides, imagining her eventual refusal. What if she can't help me? What if the street becomes my inevitable fate? Visions of the beggars lined outside the department store flashed through my mind like haunting premonitions. My ritual offerings of muffins and cookies to their trembling hands suddenly transformed into ominous imagery of myself joining their ranks. Would I be there, clutching my expensive camera—a relic of some distant, better life—pleading for scraps to survive another day in this indifferent city? "Mr. Srivastava," her voice broke through my tumultuous spiral of despair, carving out a lifeline I hadn't dared hope for. "Please come to the hotel. We have something arranged for you. Don't worry." "Something?" I echoed, bewilderment slipping into relief as her words soothed the sharp edges of my turmoil. A flash of pure gratitude illuminated my heart—raw, aching, yet alive. At that moment, even the humblest room would have been salvation enough. A garage, a storage closet—it didn't matter. I had always believed God appears in myriad forms and names when we are at our most desperate, and this felt like divine intervention in its most stunningly human guise. I clung to the promise she had offered, dragging my weary body, along with my shame and my suitcases, back toward the semblance of safety I'd known just hours before. Arriving at the hotel, I realized Ms. Georgia had already left for the day. The check-in counter was now occupied by Somkiat, whose calm demeanour radiated both comfort and uncertainty. Perhaps she had been briefed, perhaps not—her eyes spoke of neither disdain nor pity, and in them, I found the quiet strength to proceed without sinking deeper into humiliation.

CHAPTER 4

NIGHTS OF DREAD, DAYS OF SOLITUDE

DAY 11 - A Meeting in the Shadows of Chaos

The call came at 11 AM, breaking the monotonous hum of my day. Tanisha had a calm urgency in her voice as she introduced herself—a resident correspondent for a leading English news channel in India, currently stationed in London. She was eager to meet, requesting a 5 PM appointment at my hotel in the Heathrow area. "I'm working on a series about Indian lives affected by the pandemic. Your story… It's important," she said, her words careful but imbued with sincerity. Her intention wasn't casual; it carried the weight of purpose. By the time I met her in the hotel lobby, the dim light filtering through the frosted chandeliers lent the scene a muted urgency that mirrored the day's weary rhythm. Tanisha arrived precisely at 5 PM, punctual to the second—a trait that spoke volumes about her discipline. A slim figure, sharp yet graceful, she carried herself with poise that belied her youth. Just 23 years old, she could have been mistaken for younger were it not for the penetrating gaze in her eyes—eyes that seemed to hold vaults of untold stories. Behind her trailed a cameraman, lugging gear with the practised ease of someone accustomed to shadows rather than limelight. He was an Odiya man, UK-born but tethered to his Indian roots in quiet ways—a second-generation immigrant who'd inherited the rhythms of two lands. His curt nod acknowledged me without ceremony, his professionalism as much a wall as a shield. Tanisha wasted no time. "There will be no retakes," she told me matter-of-factly before we started, her voice crisp but compassionate. "Everything as it is—pauses, emotions, even tears. We want truth, not a polished façade." Her words struck a chord in me, echoing the absurd rawness of the times we were living through. Truth seemed like the only anchor in a world where normalcy had been ripped apart. The interview began in the garden behind the hotel, a desolate patch of green bordered by weathered iron benches and dry, dying hedges. The cold breeze whispered through the leaves, a quiet accompaniment to Tanisha's unyielding questions. The camera lens seemed to bear into my heart, its silent, mechanical gaze peeling back layers I hadn't realized I carried. Tanisha asked everything and spared nothing—the pain of separation from my family, the hollowness that looped through my days stranded in London, and the despair palpable in every video call with Priya and our daughters in Mumbai. She looked directly at me the entire time, her empathetic nods pulling my words into existence even when they threatened to fail me. The air was heavy but electric—weighted with emotions too potent to ignore. Once the shoot was done, we wandered back inside. The vending machine sputtered to life in the corner of the lounge, dispensing cups of coffee that felt almost comically meaningless against the larger backdrop of our conversations. Yet, there was solace in the act—in the simple humanity of sitting together and sharing experiences without preteens. In the lounge, time felt like it was suspended. I recounted the grim loops of my nights spent calling Priya from my room—hours stretching from 3 AM until sunrise, her face framed by the harsh digital light of my phone screen, tears slipping down her cheeks as we struggled to hold onto hope. Tanisha listened intently, rarely interrupting, her expression shifting from curiosity to empathy. In turn, she opened up about her own burdens—her mother battling late-stage cancer back home in India, her father a diabetic struggling to maintain stability amidst the chaos of the City of Joy, Kolkata. For a moment, the journalist's polished walls crumbled, and the vulnerable 23-year-old layered beneath shone through. She spoke quietly, almost as if afraid to let the words exist too loudly. I noticed tears pricking the corners of her almond-shaped eyes when she mentioned that it was her father's second marriage, as her mother had eloped with someone who abandoned her when she was hardly three years old, and that her stepmother took a vow not to bear her own child to ensure uncompromising love, attention, and upbringing of Tanisha. She also talked about her boyfriend back home—her pillar of support, the one tending to her parents as relatives had shown nothing but indifference. Bengalis often introduced themselves as hailing from Kolkata, a city emblematic of culture, poetry, and nostalgia. But Tanisha had peeled back the veneer and revealed herself to be from Asansol—a town that hummed with slower rhythms, burdened by the coal dust of its industrial history and that her father moved to Kolkata with her immediately after his second marriage and never visited Asansol again. It was a poetic unravelling of sorts, much like the narratives she sought as a journalist. Our conversation stretched into forty-five minutes, the lounge bathed in the muted light of evening outside. The cameraman's voice cut through the intimate fog of our shared space: "Madam, shall we go for the next shoot now?" His tone was calm but insistent, a reminder that time was moving even if our stories made it feel suspended. He stood just a few paces away, his stocky build silhouetted against the frosted glass doors, a quiet but persistent presence that seemed to exist on the periphery of everything. Tanisha turned toward him with a nod and stood up gracefully, smoothing the creases on her modest, yet smartly tailored blazer. "Just a moment," she said, before turning back to me. For a second, the busy journalist melted away, leaving behind the young woman burdened with her own battles. "Thank you for sharing... all of it," she said softly, her eyes locking with mine. It wasn't a platitude. It wasn't routine. It was gratitude forged in the fire of raw vulnerability—hers, mine, and the shared humanity of these turbulent times. With a fleeting smile, she gathered her notebook, leaving behind a faint trace of her floral perfume in her wake. It lingered in the air as I watched her disappear through the doors, her cameraman following closely behind, weighed down by equipment and the heaviness of unspoken stories. She was a paradox—soft and unyielding, young but wise beyond her years, a seeker of truths in a world that often preferred comfortable lies. Tanisha wasn't just another journalist chasing soundbites; she was a warrior armed with a camera and a pen, fighting to tell the stories that mattered. Her journey to this place—standing in the garden of a Heathrow hotel, capturing the fractured lives of Indian citizens caught in the unrelenting grip of a global pandemic—was as compelling as the stories she sought to tell. A brilliant scholar and a fiercely independent spirit, she'd earned her place in London on a scholarship—an achievement that spoke volumes of her determination and grit. But beneath her polished exterior lay the burdens she quietly carried: an ailing mother, a fragile father, and the guilt of being thousands of miles away from the people who needed her most. Her voice had only cracked once during our conversation when she admitted her fear of losing her mother to cancer while stuck in a city that felt both alien and familiar, comforting yet distant. Her eyes darted down as she spoke of her boyfriend—the unsung hero holding the fort back in Kolkata, caring for her parents in the absence of anyone else. What struck me most wasn't just her story, but the spark of resilience that refused to dim. In a profession notoriously scorned for its sensationalism, Tanisha had found a niche—covering stories that mattered to the Indian diaspora, from Non-Resident Indians to Persons of Indian Origin, and the occasional tourists who found themselves caught in her human-interest lens. Her authentic approach to journalism had opened doors others couldn't even approach. She'd walked into places where even BBC correspondents met resistance, not because of her badge, but because of her heart. As the evening deepened and Tanisha's absence left a quiet lull in the lounge, I reflected on the sameness of my days.

Day 12 to Day 45 A Ritual in the Shadows :

The world outside was spinning out of control, but my routine in that hotel had ossified into an unchanging cycle of despair and hope. The days slid into each other like rainwater pooling on slick pavement, indistinguishable and unyielding. But then there were the nights. Unlike the days, my nights had purpose—though not solace. From 3 AM to 9 AM, my life condensed into pixelated connections with Priya, my wife, and our daughters. The light of my phone screen bathed their faces in harsh contrast, simultaneously illuminating their pain and emphasising the distance that separated us. Priya's tears lingered in the grainy video feed, spilling over like fragile crystal beads as she clung to hope. I tried to mirror her strength, swallowing my own fears while silently cursing the miles, the virus, and the helplessness that tied my hands. Those calls were rituals—structured and predictable, but far from comforting. We spoke of plans that couldn't be made, of futures that felt like far-off dreams. Between the lines of our conversations, silence breathed and stretched, teetering on the edge of despair. Yet even in the quiet moments, there was something unspoken that bound us—a promise to fight, to endure, to hold on until the tides turned. Tanisha's visit had been an interruption, yes. But it was also a reminder—that in the cacophony of crisis, there were still people fighting to bear witness, to immortalise pain in words and images so it could, perhaps, be transformed into something greater. As I sat in that dim lounge, sipping the now-cooling coffee from the vending machine, her lingering presence felt strangely comforting—a small but enduring ember in my collapsing days. Somewhere out there, she was already chasing her next story. And somewhere back in Kolkata, an old couple—her resilient parents and the boyfriend who stood in for absent family—were waiting for her return with the kind of love that held worlds together through sheer force of will. In that moment, as the hours dissolved into the night, I realized that perhaps survival wasn't just about endurance. It was about connection—about the threads we wove through each other's lives, threads that refused to break even in the face of an unfeeling world. Priya's face appeared on the screen, pale and restless, framed by the muted glow of her bedside lamp. The room she sat in had once been filled with laughter and warmth. Now, it seemed reduced to a hollow shell, the heavy curtains sagging as if the room itself had grown weary of pretending. Behind her, the faint outline of Siya emerged, her small figure perched silently in the corner like a guardian who had no power to fight the demons plaguing her mother. On camera, Priya's eyes trembled with suppressed emotion, her cheeks sunken, as though the very air around her was stealing her strength. "I meditated this morning, Rohan," she whispered, her voice barely strong enough to travel through the connection. "But it doesn't work. My chest still feels tight. My hands… keep shaking. And Siya—she tries to help, but she shouldn't have to. She's too young to carry me like this." I responded with encouraging words—meaning well, yet knowing the limits of shallow comfort. But Priya wasn't just speaking to me; she was speaking to herself, voicing truths she couldn't suppress anymore. When the video call ended, Priya slumped back against the bed, her fingers tracing invisible patterns on the blanket she had wrapped tightly around herself. The room smelled faintly of lavender, from a diffuser that now seemed futile in its attempts at creating peace. Her inner monologue began again—loud and intrusive. *"What happened to me? I could make dinner while Siya played her favourite tunes on guitar in this very room. I would sit there laughing as Rohan told stories of his coworkers and their quirks. Now this room feels suffocating, like the walls are closing in around me. I should be better. If not for me, for her."* Priya's gaze flickered to Siya across the room—her child, now carrying the weight of adult worries at just ten years old. Siya now stared blankly at her tablet screen, reading books on Kindle; she didn't even laugh anymore. "Siya, honey, what do you want for breakfast?" Priya forced herself to ask. But Siya didn't even look up from the tablet. "Anything is fine," she murmured. Priya's wounds deepened. She turned to the mirror in the bedroom, her reflection brutally honest. The ghost of herself stared back at her—a woman capable but faltering. She exhaled deeply, remembering Dr Khurana's words: *"Meditate, Priya. Sleep. Nourish yourself. Find one small thing that makes you feel alive, even for a moment."* Her fingers pressed against her temple as she repeated his advice like a mantra. *Meditate. Sleep. Find life.* The living room, once Siya's kingdom of endless colours and carefree laughter, now felt like a tired portrait robbed of its vibrance. The faded floral curtains draped the windows in reluctance, letting only timid slivers of sunlight sneak through, as if wary of intruding on the grief that had pitched its tent inside. The air was heavy, almost too thick for a child to breathe. Her schoolbag lay discarded on a forgotten stool, the zippers half-open, spilling notes that no one cared to pick up. Siya sat curled up on the family couch—a large, plush relic that had once been the beating heart of the household. Flanked by overstuffed pillows that no longer offered comfort, she stared at a tablet that failed to distract her, its smooth surface mirroring the reflection of a girl she barely recognised. Young, yes, but with a shadowed maturity that clung to her like an ill-fitting winter coat. Beside her, the guitar her father had gifted her for her last birthday stood abandoned, resting against the wall like a mute witness to her growing solitude. Dust hugged its strings, suffocating chords that once sang bright melodies during family evenings. In the stillness, Siya's small hands trembled slightly as she fingered a fraying thread from the couch. Her thoughts felt too big for her small body, swirling like restless clouds threatening a storm. The questions that filled her mind were jagged and painful, questions no child should ever have to ask. Why does Mom cry all the time now? Is it my fault? Why doesn't she laugh the way she used to? Dad says everything will be okay, but how can he fix anything when he's stuck all the way across the ocean? She bit her lip and glanced toward the hallway where the door to her mother's room loomed, half-ajar like a fragile secret. Dusk painted the walls with faint streaks of gold, but no light seeped from under her mother's door. Priya's silhouette shimmered faintly, a restless pacing shadow against the battered wood of the door. Priya—or "Mom," as Siya had known her—the once-invincible centre of the family, now felt like a fragile, fractured lamp that no one knew how to repair. Siya placed the tablet down carefully on the table, mechanically aligning it with the edges as if bringing some structure to its placement might bring structure to her spiralling world. Her slender fingers hesitated before wrapping around the brass doorknob of her mother's room. The knob felt cold in her palm, its coolness a quiet rebuke to the warmth she longed for. She sighed, pressing her forehead briefly against the door, letting the faint wood grain scrape against her skin. “How do I even talk to her anymore?” she wondered. The tears brimmed, but she swallowed them quickly; she had decided long ago that crying only made things worse. She was too young to realize that grief needed expression and too old to believe her own pain didn't matter. “I don't know what to say. If I ask her what's wrong, she might cry again. If I try being good and quiet, it still doesn't help. I miss her old smile. The one that lit up like Christmas when Dad walked through the door.” For a moment, the thought occurred to her that she wasn't supposed to understand these things—that she should only worry about homework and guitar practice and bedtime stories. But that childlike simplicity had been stripped away, leaving behind someone too young for the burdens she carried. With a deep breath, Siya released the doorknob and turned back toward the couch, her shadow long and lonely on the marbled floor.

Ananya: Battles of the Mind in Boston

Thousands of miles away, under a dusky Boston sky, Ananya stared at the hurricane of papers and chaos consuming her dorm room. Commonwealth Avenue hummed with life just outside the window, but the world within her four beige walls felt like it was crumbling. Her desk, a mess of abandoned intentions, brimmed with the evidence of her unravelling: coffee-stained study guides, towering stacks of binders, and an assortment of pens—most of which didn't work, not that she tried anymore. At the edge of the desk, a lone yellow Post-it note fluttered under the fluorescent glow of her desk lamp, mockingly insistent. *"Submit Project X by 12 PM Monday."* She read it again for the hundredth time as though the words would change, her eyes distant and unfocused. The laptop screen in front of her was a maze of deadlines and half-finished assignments, glaring with the cruel efficiency of a machine unfazed by human exhaustion. Ananya sat cross-legged on her squeaky desk chair, her shoulders sagging as her hands gripped the ends of her dishevelled jet-black waves. Her mind spiralled in chaotic bursts, moving far too fast to catch a foothold. How do I finish any of this? Dad's alone in London, still trying to get back home. Mom's falling apart, and Siya—Siya's still so young. Does anyone even notice how she's holding up? Does anyone even care? The guilt hit her like a train. Every time she thought of Siya and Priya, it was like her chest caved inward. She nudged aside the unfinished assignment on her desk and reached for her phone. Her fingers scrolled absently through texts from Priya, rereading the messages with silent longing. They were frustratingly short, clinical even—words exchanged not as a mother and daughter plotting their way through heartache but as distant pen pals ticking off life's boxes.

"I miss when she was strong," Ananya thought, her heart aching. "When she didn't just tell me to solve my problems—she showed me. 'Pace yourself, Ananya,' she used to say. 'One problem at a time.' Well, the problems are here all at once, Mom. I don't know how to pace myself when everything's falling apart." The untouched tray of lasagna she'd ordered hours ago sat on the edge of her desk, its edges curling dry. Hunger gnawed at her stomach, but the sight of food felt almost offensive now—another task she neither had the energy nor the interest to complete. Restless, she pushed herself from the desk and moved toward the window. She stood there with crossed arms as the murmuring city of Boston moved beneath her dorm. People were laughing, shouting, existing—oblivious to the crushing weight pressing against her chest. The evening chilled the window ledge under her palms as she gazed at the far-off flickering lights of a student-run café, its promises of warmth utterly meaningless to her now. The phone buzzed faintly on the desk behind her, its vibration a soft plea against the ambient hum. Her father's name flashed across the screen—his familiar face frozen mid-animation as the video call request lingered. She hesitated, her breath hitching as she hovered between resistance and longing. "Do I answer?" she thought, her throat tight with unshed tears. "If I do, he'll hear it in my voice. The panic, the guilt, the exhaustion. Maybe I should. Maybe he needs to hear it. Mom can't keep carrying this alone. Maybe… I can't either." For a moment, her hand lingered on the edge of the desk, fingertips brushing the cold surface—not yet ready to pick up, but not ready to let the call go unanswered either. In the split-second indecision of her heart, the world outside Boston carried on, but for Ananya, it waited. And in that pause, as dusk stretched its muted light across the room, she felt the invisible ties pulling her across oceans back to a family fractured by distance but bound by the shared weight of endurance. A silent prayer echoed in her heart. For Mom. For Siya. For herself. Dad, pick up. I can't hold this alone.

The emotional weight of Priya's deteriorating mental state fused with the omnipresent dread hanging over our children, Siya and Ananya, whose lives seemed tethered to shadows darker than their fleeting smiles could conceal. Morning blended into evenings marked by futile distractions: sifting through grim headlines, firing off tweets like lifeboats into a sea of indifference, and wrestling with marauding thoughts that left me disoriented. I would attend official online meetings on Microsoft Teams and would try to keep my team motivated and focused even when I was losing my mind. While it was usual in the corporate world to have video conferences, that was confined mostly to senior management meetings. Switching entirely to online meetings, managing teams, and ensuring deliverables was initially challenging. But soon a new normal was accepted by all. It was my duty as a leader to ensure that business continuity was maintained and the show went on. "I am not the hero, I am just a director; my team members are heroes." The mere thought of not being the central character in the movie helped me in moving from a "by me" narrative to a "through me" narrative. Occasionally, evenings gifted me fleeting solace in isolation—a duo of elusive red foxes performed their nightly ballet outside my window. Yet even such brushes with nature's elegance couldn't mask the staleness creeping within the sterile confines of my hotel room. Gradually, the shock of being stranded began to give way to something more insidious—a gnawing haze of solitude, cloaking the walls that seemed to edge closer to me with every passing hour. My internal monologue, once sharp and strategic, devolved into the relentless echo of despair, staging whispered rebellions against my attempts to maintain composure. Pressing my forehead to the cold glass of the hotel window, I sought solace in the grounded planes that stretched before me—a ghostly airport turned cemetery of silenced giants, their stillness a reflection of my confinement. I was utterly irrelevant, stripped bare by this microscopic adversary, and the weight of that irrelevance gnawed at my soul. The indignity of my situation was a shroud I couldn't shed. The sharp sting of degradation clung to me, most notably in the cold, rough surface of the bathtub as I scrubbed my worn underwear—a task so mundane it had become emblematic of my fall from grace. The soap bubbles offered no relief, fading into fragile ghosts amidst the swirling water—reminders of where I once was and what I had become. Food, too, had transformed. Once a source of pleasure and social significance, it now symbolised my predicament—the Gurudwara's langar, a single meal borne of noble generosity, spoke of unending dependence. Mr Niel's complimentary breakfast and discounted dinners—gracious gestures, no doubt—came with a quiet sting. Each morsel reminded me of my dwindling self-reliance, burying the vestiges of corporate opulence I'd once taken for granted. Gone were the crystal glasses chiming in unison, the laughter punctuated by sips of fine wine shared among colleagues. In their place: paper boxes bearing quiet scars of circumstance, and plastic cutlery that mocked the comfort and freedom I once enjoyed. The constant barrage of worry and mental fatigue was unrelenting, hammering the very foundation of my being. I was supposed to protect them, fix everything—and yet here I was, paralyzed and impotent, trapped in this gilded cage that was slowly stripping away the essence of who I was. Dejection wrapped itself around me like an oppressive cloak, suffocating my will and spirit. The bland walls stood silent, mocking the emptiness that echoed within. "What's the point of going on? What's the point of anything if I can't even be there for them? All that ambition, all that … for this? To be stuck in a hotel room, watching my life unravel from a distance? To be so close, yet so utterly useless?" The thought, dark and insidious, flickered at the edges of my consciousness—a cold, tempting whisper of oblivion. Maybe it would be easier if I just… disappeared. No one to disappoint. No one to answer to. No responsibilities. The words emanated from a shadowed corner of my mind, feeding the emptiness that consumed me. The temptation felt vast, endless, as though it could swallow me whole. But then, like a raw nerve struck, I snapped. No. Stop it, Rohan, I admonished myself with silent fury. You can't go there. You won't. Not now. Not ever. Not when Priya and Siya need you. Even if you feel like nothing, you have to fight. I clenched my fists, my nails digging into my palms, the sharp sting anchoring me to reality. Shutting my eyes tightly, I fought against the encroaching darkness, willing it away with every ounce of strength I had. My mind conjured their faces, distorted by the distance and despair—a haunting image burned behind my eyelids. That was all I had left to cling to: the tether to the ones who tied me to survival, even in the abyss. As the London sky transitioned to a bruised purple in the evenings, I discovered an unexpected solace. The relentless suffocation of my room could not hold me; there were moments when I escaped its hold, walking aimlessly to the Hatton Cross Bridge—a concrete path suspended over the road connecting Heathrow to London. The wind whipped around me in sharp gusts, harsh yet strangely comforting—a cold, lonely embrace that masked the ache within. But the open space, vast and infinite under the sky, gifted me a fleeting sense of freedom. I stood there for hours, unmoving, staring at the expanse above—a silent sentinel embracing solitude as a balm for chaos. Occasionally, the sky welcomed the ghostly arcs of distant planes—cargo flights or repatriation charters—cutting across the emptiness with subdued hums. Their lonely journeys reminded me of motion, of survival, of a world that continued slowly, hesitantly, even as mine stood still. In those moments on the bridge, I turned to old habits, rediscovering fragments of who I'd once been through photography. My wildlife photography skills, honed over years of chasing elusive tigers in Ranthambore and identifying vibrant bird species in the hills of Sikkim and Darjeeling, now found a quieter purpose. I captured fleeting snapshots of life braving the edges of the airport's suffused quiet—the kestrel hovering with poise, its wings like whispers against storm clouds; a murmuration of starlings swirling like ink against the twilight; and, on rare evenings, a pair of russet-hued red foxes, their playful scampering a fragile explosion of vitality against the cold, grey concrete. These moments stitched together fragments of beauty in desolation. They became a quiet ritual—a personal meditation to ground myself in a surreal reality that threatened to rip me apart. As solitary as these acts were, they reminded me of two paradoxes at war within me: the stillness I had never known under the endless grind of my corporate climb, and the piercing silence imposed by a global lockdown. One loosened the intangible, invisible chains of my professional life; the other shackled me more tangibly than ever before within this new, unforgiving world—both golden cages, but vastly different in their grip. While one had tethered me to ambition, the other threatened to undermine all that ambition had built. As the days passed, time became molasses—slow, suffocating, indistinguishable. Desperately, I had tried all possibilities off lying through a chartered plane with others; I also tried to leverage all my contacts in bureaucracy, political, and social change makers, but to no avail. Everyone was helpless. The news of wards of IAS officers, IPS officers, ministers, and judges not getting hospital beds or oxygen cylinders was so overwhelming that my crisis seemed to be too small. I had to reconcile and resign to fate. However, somewhere in the back of my mind, I had the confidence that I would fly back by the first available flight. My routine remained more or less intact—meditation, meals, strolls, and Tony Robbins live webinars at night, promising optimism with talk of "priming" and "breakthrough." The Tony Robbins phrase, "Life doesn't happen to you. Life happens for you. Make it a breakthrough opportunity." Forty-five days had crept by like a thief in the night, stealing from me every certainty I had once thought invincible. Suspended in limbo, lost in a torrent of isolation and doubt, I fought daily against the weight pulling me under. This was survival, but only just. I stood on that bridge every evening, resisting the tide of despair. And in those moments of fleeting beauty, amidst kestrels and foxes, I glimpsed threads of resilience—scattered and fragile, but enough to keep me standing still. I had faith in God. I believed in myself. I believed in all that I had known about the virtues of helping others and doing good... This too shall pass.

Day 46: A Glimmer of Promise

The monotony of days—an endless gravy haze that blurred their edges—had tightened its chokehold around me. Locked within the walls of my London hotel room, I had scrolled mindlessly through the morning's news, my fingers going through the motions without expectation. Every headline bled the same grim narrative: rising numbers, grounded planes, collapsed borders. It was suffocating. Hopeless. Until... A tweet. It wasn't just another headline. No, this one blazed with a ferocity that cut through the relentless gloom like a beacon in the dead of night: "Repatriation flights to India. Heathrow inaugural departure scheduled for May 9, 2020. Bookings open soon." I froze, my breath caught somewhere between a gasp and a sob. I read it again, each syllable pounding like a drumbeat in my weary skull. Once. Twice. Three times. I didn't dare blink, terrified that the words would vanish into the digital abyss. My thumb hovered over the screen, untrusting, until reality hit like a thunderclap: This. Was. Real. The joy that erupted within me was almost foreign, a forgotten sensation that surged through every nerve ending like electric fire. My legs found strength as if powered by some latent reservoir of energy, and before I knew it, I was standing, then pacing, my heart racing to catch up. A sound bubbled up from deep inside—half-laugh, half-sob, wholly uncontrollable. My fingers fumbled for my phone before my thoughts could catch up. "Priya," I choked into the line the moment she answered, my voice shaking with raw emotion. "Priya, there's a flight!" The syllables tumbled over one another in their eagerness to escape. "May 9th! I'm coming home!" For a moment, there was silence, a breathless, trembling silence that stretched across the virtual chasm. Then her voice, hushed and tear-soaked, whispered back, "Rohan... really? Are you sure?" "Yes!" My voice broke with the sheer force of my excitement. "It's been announced. I'm booking it as soon as they open. Tell Siya... tell Ananya..." My chest seized as their names escaped—memories of my daughters' laughter flashing cruelly against the reality of their absence. "...Tell them Daddy's coming home. I'm really coming home." And then I heard it—something so pure, so needed, that it brought me to my knees: Priya's sobs, not of grief but of relief. I could almost feel the weight lifting off her chest, hear the cracks forming in the armour of hopelessness she'd been wearing for months. Her tears were loud and unrestrained, blending with my own as we cried together across the unforgiving miles. By evening, the news of my celebration had spread, carried down the sterile halls of the hotel like wildfire. Mr Niel, a kind stranger who had become an unexpected friend in our shared isolation, marked the occasion with a private but thoughtful gesture. A knock at the door revealed a small yet radiant token of solidarity: a bottle of champagne perched alongside a handwritten note. "Here's to the beginning of your journey home. Cheers!!! - With love, Niel." The cork popped with a soft thump, the sound reverberating in my otherwise silent room. Pouring myself a glass, I stepped onto the balcony that overlooked the glittering skyline of London, now shrouded in a reluctant darkness. The glass caught the dim light as bubbles raced upward in endless pursuit, each accompanied by the bittersweet taste of hope. I sipped, eyes drawn to the silhouetted planes grounded on the runway below, their hulking forms mute sentinels of a world still in waiting. The memory of joy felt faintly reminiscent of a better time—a sip from a champagne flute in Room 3618 of the Park Inn, long before this ordeal. But tonight, there was no room for surrender.

Day 47: The First Domino Falls.

The next morning brought certainty to what had previously been hope's flickering flame. An official email appeared in my inbox, its subject line practically glowing: Your Repatriation Flight Details. I opened it slowly, savouring the anticipation that burned at my fingertips. The instructions were meticulous, the timelines rigid but manageable. I devoured every sentence, highlighting critical points and double-checking the process until it was etched into my mind. Payment. Documentation. Deadlines. It all felt manageable—no longer the nebulous swirl of uncertainty that had plagued me for weeks. The moment I hit "Submit" on the transaction, relief swept over me, although not entirely. There was still one more person I needed to share this with. Pulling out my phone, I sent a text to Jaspreet, a volunteer from the local Indian diaspora who had been my rock throughout this ordeal. "Jaspreet, I won't need food after May 8th. Thank you. Thank you for everything." The words looked inadequate on the screen, painfully insufficient for the weeks of meals, calls, and encouragement she had selflessly provided. My gratitude sat heavy in my chest, unable to find form in something as simple as text. But for now, it would have to do. I promised myself, silently and fiercely, that this kindness would not go unacknowledged.

Day 48: A New Beast

The relief of yesterday soured into a new terror: silence. The ticket confirmation—the final piece of this precariously constructed puzzle—had yet to arrive. My inbox was barren, and every refresh became more maddening than the last. The confirmation of payment sat mockingly in my email, a cruel reminder of progress but not completion. My breaths came quicker, shorter, as worry twisted its way into the spaces hope had only just begun to occupy. What if this was a mistake? What if the ticket was lost in some tangled mess of bureaucracy? What if— I shook my head violently, chastising myself: Stop this. You've come too far to spiral now. But the questions didn't stop their unrelenting march. I crafted an urgent tweet, tagging every official channel I could think of—Air India, the High Commission, anyone who might see it. The words were sharp and desperate: Non-receipt of ticket confirmation after successful payment. Can you please help me urgently? As the tweet took flight into the digital ether, I found myself back on the balcony, staring at the towering, grounded planes that now felt almost like adversaries. Their immobility mocked me as I stood, powerless, waiting for the next flicker of hope to spark. Yet even as anxiety threatened to consume me, I knew one thing with absolute clarity: I would get home. I had to.

Day 49: The Chain Must Continue

Salvation arrived—for real this time. The lifeline I had clung to for two days finally materialised: a ticket confirmation email. Seeing it felt surreal. I collapsed into the chair, a breath escaping my chest in a rush as though my body had been holding it for weeks. Relief came in waves, staccato bursts—joyous yet strange, exhausting as much as it was intoxicating. I allowed myself precious minutes to revel in the certainty of progress before the impulse to act urged me forward. I decided this day would not be spent pacing or waiting. Today would be about gratitude, action, and making connections beyond the void of digital notifications and email replies. Today, I resolved to meet Jaspreet—the volunteer whose selflessness had ensured the arrival of meals at my door through all these weeks of uncertainty and isolation. Humanity, I thought, wasn't just the act of giving; it was the act of connecting, of fostering meaning in the moments we're less alone. The labyrinthine parking lot of the hotel spread out before me like a maze, indistinguishable lanes wrapping around the grey drizzle of the morning. Then, cutting through the dullness like a blade, I saw a sleek blue BMW pull into view. It was not Jaspreet. The young woman who stepped out was striking—a calm presence in stark contrast to the weary limitations of this pandemic-riddled world. Her black hair cascaded like liquid midnight. She had yet to speak, yet something about her demeanour disarmed me. "I just… I wanted to thank you in person," I stammered, my voice thick with emotion. "Your work, your kindness… Your team has been my lifeline. Without your help… I don't know how I would've…" My words faltered, stuck, unable to convey the depth behind them. "No, Rohan Ji," she interrupted, her voice firm yet gentle. She raised a hand in a quiet yet profound gesture. "Please don't thank me. It's our duty to help each other in times of need. If you truly want to do something out of gratitude, please help someone in need. This chain has to stay intact. It's the only way we truly get through this world." Her words settled over me like a balm, soothing something deep within—a place that had long been raw and tender. I nodded, unable to articulate the gratitude brimming at the edges of my being. Before I could say anything more, she folded her hands respectfully, stepped into the BMW, and drove away, her exit both swift and profound. I stood rooted to the ground, my eyes tracing the car until it disappeared. She had been like a fleeting star, dropping briefly from the heavens to illuminate one small corner of my life, only to vanish back into the ether. I only realized much later that I hadn't even asked her name.

Day 50:The Weight of Goodbye and the Promise of Tomorrow"

The end of my ordeal felt tantalizing and overwhelming—a bittersweet convergence of relief and unexpected heaviness. When I opened my eyes that morning, two envelopes waited for me on my breakfast tray. One bore Mr. Niel's name, while the other came from Somkiat. With trembling hands, I opened Mr. Niel's note first. It was crisp, professional, and printed but carried an unmistakable warmth: a thoughtful farewell from a man who had watched me fight through days of uncertainty. Then I opened Somkiat's letter. Her handwriting was neat and deliberate, her words striking a hammer against the deepest parts of my soul. *"Dear Mr Srivastava,"* her letter began, *"You have been family to us in these uncertain times…"* By the time I finished reading it, I found the words smudged by tears, rendering the ink like the echoes of an unfinished symphony. My own tears blurred the expressions of gratitude and empathy she had painstakingly penned. At the reception, Somkiat waited, standing behind the desk, her own eyes glassy with unshed emotion as I approached her. "Somkiat," I started, my voice cracking under the weight of my emotions, "I don't know how to…" "You shush now," Somkiat interrupted with gentle authority, stepping around the desk and stopping short of embracing me in a soft hug due to social distancing protocol. "You're just like a brother to me. What else could I do but look out for family?" She pressed a small bag into my hands—fruits, cookies, cakes. A modest but profoundly thoughtful gesture, her parting gift a promise of care that transcended goodbyes. By the time the tall cab driver greeted me at the entrance with a booming "Good morning, Mr Rohan! May I help you with the luggage?" I felt hollowed out yet somehow whole. "Good morning, Mr David," I replied faintly, forcing the semblance of a smile. "Thanks. I'll manage my luggage," I added, though the weight in my chest rivalled that of the suitcase in my grip. The airport was five minutes away, each endless meter trudging toward the culmination of fifty arduous days. For fifty days, I had been stuck in limbo—a prisoner, anchored by circumstances beyond my control. Yet, as we approached the gleaming entrance of Heathrow, I felt a thread within me tighten. It wasn't just hope anymore. It was something stronger, something unshakable. *The chain of humanity continues.*

CHAPTER 5

TEST OF THEORY AGAINST HUMANITY'S GREATEST CRISIS

All those gleaming certificates, the lofty case studies dissected in mahogany-panelled classrooms, and the endless discussions around managing complexity—Rohan had soaked it all up during his years at the premium management institutes. He had breezed through modules on "Navigating VUCA (Volatility, Uncertainty, Complexity, Ambiguity)," armed himself with insights about risk matrices, and mastered the art of strategy under pressure. Back then, it had all seemed so profound, so essential. He had taken pride in his ability to find structure amidst chaos, to chart a clear path when others hesitated in uncertainty. But nothing—*nothing*—in all those years of academic rigor had prepared him for *this*. No case study, no leadership simulation, no management article could have equipped him for the relentless, soul-crushing crisis that now gripped his life, the world, and the very fabric of human existence. This was no corporate challenge with tidy profit margins at stake. It was survival—not just his, but humanity's. An existential crisis that defied equations and trampled over strategies. Rohan sat alone in the near-empty hotel room, one leg bouncing incessantly as his restless energy erupted in small, physical betrayals. Outside the cold, glass-paned window, the planes lay still in their hangars, colossal steel creatures transformed into powerless monuments to a paused world. The sky outside was bruised with layered greys, heavy with the weight of a global silence. Somewhere beyond the clouds, millions were fighting an invisible enemy—a virus—while the rest of them waited, trapped in forced inaction. Rohan exhaled and rubbed his temples, his mind spiralling back to the countless PowerPoint slides on resilience he had once presented to disengaged boardrooms. Phrases like *"crisis management"* and *"adaptive leadership"* had been thrown around so easily then, their weight diluted by the cushions of privilege surrounding him. In those years of professional ascendancy, "uncertainty" had seemed more like a hypothetical exercise than a lived experience. He realized now with bitter irony that he had unconsciously equated "resilience" with a catchy buzzword, not the raw, primal struggle it had become. But here, now, in the midst of the most profound upheaval humanity had seen in generations, resilience wasn't a phrase. It wasn't a neat chart or a clever infographic. It was survival itself—a lesson not learned through glossy textbooks but forged in the crucible of desperation. Rohan leaned back in his chair, allowing his gaze to linger on the walls of the room that had become both his prison and his refuge. The once-modern decor—a minimalist palette of whites and greys enlivened by abstract art—seemed to mock him with its emptiness. A solitary lamp emitted a warm but insufficient glow, its muted light unable to compete with the dark shadows pooling in his thoughts. It was here, in Room 3618 of the Park Inn, that Rohan had taken on the ultimate test of humanity's capacity to endure. Every day blurred into the next as he fought to fend off the crushing weight of doubt. There were no frameworks to guide him now, no case studies to solve this. His toolkit had been stripped to nothing but determination—to wake up, to keep moving, to hope when hope itself often felt like a cruel trick. And yet, within him, something stirred: resilience, not as theory, but as instinctive, unconscious competence. It was not a skill polished in air-conditioned classrooms. It had been forged over years of quiet battles—of parenting late into the night, of handling grief silently, of navigating smaller storms that had prepared him for the tidal wave he faced now. The Trenches of a Global Apocalypse: COVID-19 wasn't just a virus; it was a silent predator, a spectre that forced the wheels of civilisation to grind to a halt. By the time it became clear how catastrophic this global disaster would be, millions of lives were already consumed in its cruel wake. Cities that once pulsed with the melody of human connection had fallen silent, streets deserted, their emptiness carrying the echo of collective fear. The coronavirus wasn't merely biological—it had infected the world's very psyche, a creeping terror burrowing into every mind. The numbers were staggering, almost incomprehensible. By mid-2020, over 7 million people had been infected globally, with the death toll climbing past 400,000—a toll that was as much a statistic as it was countless stories of grief, loss, and shattered families. Hospitals turned into battlegrounds, their corridors overflowing with gasping patients as doctors and nurses fought valiantly like soldiers without armour, often succumbing to the same invisible enemy they risked their lives to fight. Refrigerated trucks became makeshift morgues in cities like New York, gruesome emblems of a reality humanity was unprepared to face. The virus had no bounds—it shredded through borders like paper, sparing no race, no nationality, no gender, no class. Governments issued lockdowns, shuttering economies overnight in desperate attempts to slow its spread—but it was like sealing cracks with water still seeping beneath. The economic impact was grotesque in its scale. Stock markets imploded, shedding trillions in value. Businesses collapsed en masse, leading to surging unemployment that thrust entire nations into economic freefall. Families who once measured a "bad day" by inconvenience were now measuring survival by their ability to scrape together enough to eat. Mass layoffs gutted livelihoods, hunger replaced routine, and millions lived in the gnawing uncertainty of whether they could survive another week. And then there was *the fear*. It was omnipresent, a thick, suffocating fog that settled over every heart and mind. The invisible nature of the enemy made it all the more terrifying. One minute, someone was fine; the next, coughing, feverish, gasping for air, their lungs ravaged, as if drowning without water. Paranoia rippled through society. Masks turned from mere objects into shields of survival; the six-foot distance became law, human touch forbidden. Every cough, every fever, every casual interaction became a trigger for crippling anxiety, panic branded into the minds of billions as if the virus itself had infected the fabric of trust. Amid the chaos, the origins of COVID-19 became a subject of contentious debate, fuelling conspiracy theories and geopolitical tensions. Was it truly the result of a wet market in Wuhan, China—an accident born of unregulated animal consumption? Or was the virus unleashed from a laboratory, an unspeakable error or perhaps something more sinister? Countries pointed fingers, accusations became headlines, and beneath all of it lay the unanswered question: How could this happen, and why weren't we prepared? Meanwhile, humanity scrambled to fight back. Scientists worked against time to comprehend the virus's twisted calculus—how it spread, what it did, and how it could be stopped. The race for a vaccine was launched at a breathtaking pace. Laboratories from Moscow to Massachusetts, from Paris to Pune, surged to decode COVID's genetic map, bringing together virologists, epidemiologists, biochemists, and logisticians in a feverish push to save what felt irreversibly lost. Funding poured into pharmaceutical giants and small research teams alike, driven by an urgency that turned once-divergent researchers into collaborators. The world prayed for breakthroughs, yet all attempts to develop effective treatments remained in the precarious realm between hope and despair. Months passed. Progress crawled. Humanity hung suspended, waiting for the hammer to fall. Humanity's greatest crisis had not broken their will—it had redefined it. Resilience Born in the Trenches of Reality Through the haze of uncertainty that surrounded him, Rohan began to process lessons he hadn't even realised he'd internalised. Every cancelled flight, every delayed notification, every anxious day waiting for updates seemed to sharpen his focus rather than dull his resolve. With each obstacle came a decision to face it, rather than crumble beneath its weight. He thought of the blurred faces he had encountered over the years in corporate boardrooms—senior executives scanning reports with furrowed brows, whispering about "leapfrogging" chaos but never truly understanding its claws. How would they survive in this void without structure or clarity? How much of what they had learned in their cushioned existence could carry them through a crisis that offered no safety net, no guarantee of a return on investment—just raw survival? Here, there was no whiteboard to organise his thoughts, no consultant jargon to lean on. Instead, Rohan's only tools were the battered edges of his own humanity—empathy for others and a core belief that the storm would break someday, that endurance itself was its own victory. The management schools called this *adaptive intelligence,* but here in Room 3618, it felt more like ripping open wounds to grow stronger scars. The tiny victories became his salvation. An email acknowledged. Another email notification for his flight ticket sent. Even the rhythm of small things—boiling water for tea, straightening the creases of his sheets—became acts of defiance. In the smallest rituals of normalcy, he reclaimed fragments of control stolen by the larger crisis. Rohan's thoughts drifted to Priya and his daughters. It was their absence that left a hollow ache in his chest—one that no distraction could erase. Yet, it was also their presence in his mind that gave him the strength to keep going. Every night, as he sat in the high-backed chair beside the hotel window, watching distant city lights twinkle, he whispered promises into the darkness: "I'm coming back to you. I'm coming." Rohan discovered an unshakable truth. Resilience, he realized, wasn't something you could fully absorb from lectures, spreadsheets, or theories. It was something invisible, hidden deep, and only surfaced when you were pushed beyond what seemed survivable. True strength wasn't about erasing fear but carrying it with you and forging ahead anyway. It was about accepting ambiguity while still fighting for answers to the unanswerable. This crisis—the crisis—had shattered the illusion that VUCA was ever just an academic concept. It was now the oxygen of the world, unavoidable and ever-present. Rohan had no choice but to live through it, moment by moment, choice by choice, carrying his own hope even when it felt unbearably heavy. And through all this, one unshakable truth remained: Resilience was not learned in the comfort of a classroom, but in the trenches—in the moments when the ground beneath you gave way, and you still found the courage to stand.

CHAPTER 6

THE HEATHROW AND THE JOURNEY HOME

The waiting hall of Heathrow Airport stretched before Rohan, its sterile expanse a glass-and-steel mausoleum bathed in fluorescent glow. Once pulsing with life—laughter bouncing off walls, heels clicking purposefully—this sprawling terminal now felt like an abandoned opera house after the curtain's final fall. Long queues of masked souls moved sluggishly toward check-in counters, their collective silence heavy with fatigue. Even the machinery, humming faintly, seemed weary of the absence of voices and vitality. Rohan stood at the end of the serpentine line, its slow progress testing his patience—a recurring test he'd failed too many times before. A flicker of memory surfaced, unbidden but welcome: Siya's cheeky voice from a lifetime ago. "Papa, why are you always the last person to join the queue?" she had teased, her tiny fingers pointing with exaggerated disappointment toward yet another long line. It was a McDonald's evening, punctuated by her insistence on a Happy Meal, the kind of moment that lives forever in a corner of the heart dedicated to laughter and shared joy. *Why indeed?* Rohan mused now, shaking his head at the curious symmetry of his life. It had become his default position—not just in lines but in relationships, obligations, everything. Always lagging behind. Always catching up. He sighed and clung to the memory before pulling out his phone to call Priya. "I'm in the queue now," he said, keeping his voice neutral. Behind the façade, his nerves tickled beneath his skin. Priya's relief was palpable. "Alright, Roh. Just stay safe… until you're home. You're almost there." Her words hung in the air, a delicate thread that felt lighter than he'd anticipated, yet stronger than he'd dared hope—probably new medicines of psychiatrist worked. Disconnecting the call, Rohan hesitated for a moment before dialling again—this time, Ananya. His eldest. His "wise soul." "Hi, Sweetie!" he exclaimed, forcing warmth into his voice, hoping it would echo in theirs. Ananya's response was effervescent—a reminder that life waited for him, however fractured it might be. "Great! How about you? Have you reached the airport?" "Yes, my dear. Heathrow. Somehow still standing after all these days," Rohan joked lightly, though the enormity of finally heading home gnawed at him beneath the playfulness. "How's Michael?" he added slyly, testing the waters. Ananya froze, her silence laden with an innocence attempting, poorly, to mask itself. "Michael? Who's Michael?" "Come on now, friends don't lie!" he teased, his smile widening. Siya's gleeful disclosure about Ananya's boyfriend had been delivered like a triumphant secret, her sister's reputation offered up on tiny hands as though it were treasure. "Ugh, so you know about him!" Ananya replied, her huff dissolving quickly into laughter. "Of course I do," Rohan said softly. "Your sister couldn't keep it to herself." The laughter was a balm, soothing wounds both invisible and undeniable. For a moment, it felt as though distance—geographical, emotional—had evaporated entirely. He wanted to keep her on the phone longer, her voice anchoring him as he drifted in the anxiety of limbo. But Ananya interrupted, almost apologetically: "Dad, I've got an online class starting soon. Can I call you back later?" "Of course, dear. Take care. Love you." "Love you too, Dad." Her words carried an undercurrent he hadn't anticipated. "You've reduced a lot over these months. Eat properly when you're back." Reduced. The word lingered far longer than it had any right to. *Not just weight,* he thought grimly. *But time. Presence. Pieces of myself.* For fifty days, he'd been only a shadow to those he loved—a hazy memory flickering on their screens during brief video calls. He sighed deeply, pulling his jacket tighter around his shoulders as the queue crawled forward. Fifteen minutes passed. The line had barely moved. Rohan clenched his jaw as frustration bubbled within, threatening to spill over. Before he could speak, an airport official approached, his surgical mask dulling the depths of expression. "Sir," the man began in measured tones, "we're processing passengers in groups of four to maintain social distancing. Airlines will ensure the boarding gate remains open until everyone has cleared check-in." Rohan nodded, the explanation only partially soothing him. *Social distancing.* What had once been just behaviour was now doctrine, a term grafted permanently into the world's dictionary of survival. He exhaled heavily, allowing resignation to settle over him like an ill-fitting coat. "Vanakkam Anna!" a cheerful voice interrupted his thoughts, jolting him to attention. Rohan turned to see a smiling man in his mid-thirties, his energy as bright as the terminal was sombre. "Namaste, brother," Rohan replied instinctively, his own warmth tentative but sincere. The man, unperturbed, laughed heartily. "I thought you must be Tamil, Anna!" Rohan chuckled, shaking his head. "Not quite. Srivastava, born and raised in Uttar Pradesh."

The stranger clapped his hands as though Rohan's answer was worthy of applause. "Ah, but still Indian! Just as much, Anna!" The man introduced himself as Erumudi Vijayaraghavan Swaminathan, accompanied by his wife Sreelatha and their spirited five-year-old son, who refused to acknowledge Rohan's presence. Instead of offering an anticipated "Good morning," the child mimed racing Formula 1 cars in his head, oblivious to everything around him. Rohan laughed softly, waving the moment away. "So, Anna," Vijayaraghavan continued, lowering his tone conspiratorially, "have you got confirmed tickets?" "Yes, why, what about you?" Rohan threw a volley of questions, his brow furrowing. "Our tickets are not confirmed; they are issued against last-minute cancellations if people don't show up due to Covid." Rohan felt his chest tighten at the revelation. Even the simple act of boarding a plane had transformed into a gamble—a reminder of how fragile and uncertain the world had become. He bit back the automatic itch to cough, knowing full well how such reflexes could incite the fear-filled gaze of strangers. "Lord Murugan will make us fly," Vijayaraghavan declared, his conviction unshakable. Rohan smiled thinly, recalling how he used to infuse optimism and confidence in his sales teams whenever they found budget achievement challenging. Moments later, the line finally began moving, jerking him out of contemplation. Check-in, security, immigration—all blurred into a string of mundane procedures, until at last, he reached the lounge to recover. The unyielding glass door, marked with "CLOSED," laughed in his face. Disappointment pinched his chest, but he turned away, ready for the next step. One step closer to home. The Scarlet Thread of Memories. The airport was an architectural marvel, but now it resembled a ghost town—a hollowed monument to movement that had abandoned purpose. Heathrow, once teeming with life, had been reduced to an eerie mausoleum of silence. The concourses stretched like endless hallways of a forgotten stage: darkened shops with their shutters drawn, their empty interiors resembling tombs. Rohan glanced at a storefront that once displayed rows of Scotch whiskies and Toblerone chocolates, the perfect gifts he'd planned to bring home. Now, the shelves whispered only vacancy. He sighed, the absence heavy in his chest, and trudged toward his boarding gate, gripping his boarding pass tightly like a talisman—a fragile lifeline tethered to the idea of home. The terminal's cavernous quiet enveloped him, amplifying his solitude. He tried to summon strength, repeating the mantra in his mind. *It's fine. It's fine. Just a few hours, and I'll be home.* Before the thought could linger, a voice broke through, urgent and clipped. "Mr. Srivastava! Mr. Srivastava!" Startled, Rohan looked up to see a white-skinned official with sharp blue eyes stepping toward him. Her polite urgency cut through his exhaustion, snapping him back to reality. "You're the last passenger, sir. We're closing the gate now." Awkwardly, he rubbed his eyes, his boarding pass trembling in his hand like fragile parchment. "Thank you," he murmured, forcing his legs to carry him forward. As he crossed into the jetway, his steps were heavy, his nerves frayed—but his heart soared in defiance. He'd made it. *Home.* The word felt as sacred as a prayer. The cabin pulsed with a subdued energy—a quiet but potent mix of exhaustion, apprehension, and, above all, hope. It wasn't the boisterous excitement of a holiday crowd, nor the quiet determination of seasoned travellers conquering familiar routes.

Instead, this was something rarer: a collective journey homeward in the shadow of a shared crisis, each passenger carrying their own burden, their own story. Outside the window, streaks of twilight melted into the endless expanse of clouds, painting the horizon in muted golds and greys. Rohan stared out, his reflection on the windowpane barely registering. His chest ached—not from the cramped space, but from the sheer weight of the moment. He had made it. Finally. Settling into his aisle seat, he clutched his phone like a lifeline. His fingers trembled as he dialled Priya's number. A knot in his chest loosened when she answered on the first ring. "I've boarded the flight," he whispered, his voice betraying an uncharacteristic vulnerability. "Thank God," Priya breathed on the other end. Relief carried across the invisible tether between them, covering continents like a protective shield. "Thank God, Rohan." It was an ordinary phrase, but the raw gratitude in her voice reverberated with an intensity that made his throat tighten. Months of separation, of uncertainty, of longing, condensed into those three words. He tried to respond, but the words stuck, caught somewhere between pride and emotion. Instead, he quickly dialled Ananya next. "Papa!" she exclaimed, her voice bursting with the exuberance of a child who'd been counting down days. "Are you on the plane now?" "Yes, I'm on the plane," Rohan replied, his heart lifting with her unfiltered joy. Her laughter bubbled through the call, wrapping him in the kind of warmth he hadn't realized he was so hungry for. That laughter stayed with him even after he switched the phone off, tucking it into the seat pocket. As the plane taxied toward the runway, he leaned back, his head resting against the cold, curved edge of the window. His legs cramped beneath the narrow confines of the seat, but it didn't matter, not tonight. The thought of home—of smelling the monsoon-soaked earth, of Priya's cooking, Ananya's chatter—was enough to blur the discomfort, if only for a while. Just as he closed his eyes, a jubilant voice cut through his semi-consciousness. "Srivastava Anna! What a journey, no?" He smiled faintly. It was Erumudi, the spirited Tamilian gentleman he'd met back in the Heathrow queue. Erumudi, who managed his humble South Indian restaurant in Hounslow, somehow radiated relentless optimism, as if his spirit had been tempered in the heat of a thousand kitchen stoves. "Lord Murugan has blessed us all." "Indeed," Rohan replied, half-turning in his seat but aiming for brevity. He appreciated Erumudi's effusiveness, but he wasn't in the mood for banter now. "Indeed, God is great." Still, Erumudi's joy was infectious, stirring something deep within Rohan. Their ordeal at Heathrow—the endless queues, the masks fogging up glasses, the tension written on everyone's brow—seemed like another lifetime now. Home was close, tantalizingly within reach. A crackle above interrupted his thoughts, followed by the pilot's voice ringing through the intercom, firm and proud. "Dear passengers, welcome onboard this Air India flight, operating as part of the Vande Bharat Mission. It is an honour to bring stranded citizens home during these challenging times. Jai Hind!" The cabin erupted into applause, a shared expression of gratitude and relief. A man further down the aisle—a turbaned Sardarji with a chest full of pride—rose to his feet. "Bharat Mata Ki Jai!" he exclaimed, his voice filled with unshakable conviction. "Bharat Mata Ki Jai!" the passengers echoed, their weary voices rising in unison, an emotional crescendo that broke through the emotional isolation they had all felt in their scattered lives. For once, they were not alone. Even Rohan, who often chose quiet introspection over public displays, found himself smiling. It wasn't just his family he was returning to—it was his country. Flawed, chaotic, exasperating at times, but unquestionably his. The applause died slowly, replaced once again by the hum of engines and the muted murmur of conversation. A sense of calm settled over the cabin. Behind him, a baby cried—a raw, unfiltered wail of distress. Rohan turned briefly, catching sight of the infant squirming in her young mother's arms, her mask slipping slightly as she fought to console the bundle of innocence. The cry was piercing, primal, and it captured something far larger than one small life's frustration—it was the sound of an entire world turned upside down, of displaced humans longing for a return to stability. The hum of the plane engines was steady, rhythmic, but his mind wandered far beyond the confines of the cabin. Sitting by the window, he rested his forehead against the cool glass, gazing at the sprawling expanse of clouds below but seeing nothing of the present. Instead, his memories unfurled, vivid and relentless, like reels of a film he could never pause. It began with the mosaic flooring of their apartment in Mumbai—little cracks near the edges where faded colours bled into one another, battling for dominance. He could still picture Ananya sitting cross-legged on the tiles, dressed in her bluebell flower frock and mismatched magenta stockings, her tiny fingers poking at invisible patterns in the floor. "Bhaiya, bhaiya! Tamatar lelo, free hai!" she had chirped, her voice a jumbled melody of mischief and innocence. Her laughter was contagious, harmonizing with the clinking of pots in their small kitchen. Rohan acted the part of an amused customer, squatting down with a mock shopping bag, his lips curling into a private smile. She wasn't interested in dolls or tea sets like other children; Ananya built worlds from the moments she absorbed—the ordinary rhythms of life reimagined in her pale hands. Catching her off guard, he had swept her into his arms, her delighted giggles ringing out like wind chimes in the embrace of a summer breeze. He spun her around, their laughter weaving a cocoon of weightless joy, before setting her down gently. "What kind of merchant are you, Anu?" he teased, mock-scolding with feigned outrage. "Selling tomatoes for free? You'll go bankrupt!" She had only grinned wider—the kind of grin that carried all the wisdom in the world while dismissing it entirely. Ananya tugged at his shirt then, that small act she repeated whenever she needed his undivided attention. Something in her eyes shimmered with conviction, as though she had uncovered truths too big for her young heart. She wasn't just his daughter—she was his mirror. His anchor. And, at times, his storm. Memories shifted, like pages turning forcefully in a book. He found himself standing in the hazy landscape of past holidays—Ooty, Bangalore—places where they'd once been more than scattered fragments of a family. Ooty, where Ananya learned to roll down grassy hills, her laughter reverberating across sleepless nights. Bangalore, their first flight together, where two-year-old Ananya waved at strangers and tugged at air stewards for juice. He could still see her little hands clutching orange cartons, joy radiating from her like sunlight breaking through rainclouds. But like all dreams, the brightness faded over time. The fractures began within Priya—her mind fraying slowly, small cracks turning into irreparable fissures. "Why, Rohan?" she had yelled one evening during their worst fight. Her voice cracked, raw and trembling.

"Why do you do this alone? You yell at juniors during the day, drink with them at night! Do you even *see* what you're doing to us? You're trying to play a hero, but I'm the one stuck raising them!" He had slammed the dining table, his fists clenched so tightly that his fingernails drew blood. "What?!" he had spat in bitter defiance. "What doubt, Priya? Oh, let me guess—the *affair*. That's what you think, isn't it? God forbid I even drink water when I come home! I do this FOR YOU. FOR THEM. FOR THIS FAMILY!" Hours of silence had followed, shrill against the tension in the air. And then, Ananya had appeared. Twelve years old. Tiny hands holding a cup of tea. "Papa," she had whispered. "Chai garam?" Rohan's rage had melted in an instant, traded for shame at her quiet forgiveness. He drank the tea in silence. Hours later, he had taken Priya and the kids out for ice cream, desperate to seal cracks that refused to be mended. It was their pattern—a broken love stitched together by fleeting reconciliations. Ananya's sharp eyes, always watching, had absorbed every wound, every whispered conflict. She stood somewhere between blame and peace, carrying the burden of truths too heavy for her small shoulders. Years blurred like streaks of rain against a windowpane. He remembered her milestones—the pride of her admission to Mayo College was a triumph that eclipsed their fractured home. And yet, every celebration reminded him how far she was drifting. Boston, years later, swallowed her whole. Her calls became sporadic, fractured at best. "I don't know how I'll make it through seeing them like this," he overheard her tell friends once. "I just want to go back, to start over somewhere else." And then there was Michael—the shadow in her world that he hadn't yet been able to trace. Rohan knew only fragments, whispers carried by

Siya's gleeful revelations. Boston Shawarma—Ananya's safe haven during storms of homesickness—had birthed this stranger who had evidently helped her weather it. "Who's Michael?" Rohan had asked teasingly on their last call, hiding the weight of his curiosity in a playful tone. Her huff carried something warmer, softer. He promised himself he wouldn't push for answers—not yet. Some truths were better left to unravel in their own time. For now, it didn't matter. Home awaited. And home was everything.

Rohan barely noticed when the cabin crew approached with the meal service. "Sir, Hindu veg?" the stewardess asked softly, her eyes tired above her double mask but kind. "Yes, thank you," Rohan replied, offering a polite smile. Suddenly, a boisterous voice called from across the aisle. "Madam, kuch whisky-sisky milegi?" The passengers nearby chuckled softly. It was the Sardarji again, his mischievous smile only slightly obscured by his mask. His eyes, full of life and charm, crinkled like those of a man who knew how to lighten any mood. The stewardess, an elder member of the cabin crew whose neatly draped Air India sari spoke of years of service, shook her head indulgently. "Sir, no alcohol is being served on this flight. Government orders." She paused, then quipped dryly, "Because of COVID protocol." Unfazed, the Sardarji leaned closer, his voice rich with playful mischief. "But, madam, alcohol kills the virus, na? The government itself told us that sanitiser works because of the alcohol. So technically…" He left the sentence hanging, his grin widening as laughter rippled down the aisle. Even the stewardess cracked a genuine smile, chuckling softly before replying, "Nice try, sir," and continuing down the aisle. For the first time in ages, a small bubble of light-hearted relief filled the cabin. Rohan, too, let out an involuntary laugh, followed by a sigh of appreciation. These were the small joys—fragments of humanity that no pandemic could extinguish. His eyes grew heavy soon after, lulled by the rhythmic hum of the engines. He was startled awake only by the pilot's crisp announcement. "Ladies and gentlemen, we've begun our descent into Mumbai. We will touch down in approximately thirty minutes. Cabin crew, please prepare the cabin." Rohan adjusted his posture and gazed out the window. The streaks of twilight had deepened into a darker indigo, flecked with orange streaks near the horizon. Below, the faint glow of Mumbai's city lights began to emerge, hazy but unmistakable. He tightened his grip on the armrest. Home was close now—close enough to touch, yet distant in ways he couldn't entirely explain.

PART 2

CHAPTER 7

THE APEX AND THE ABYSS

Second week of February 2020: The Mumbai skyline stretched before him, a restless ocean of jagged glass and steel shimmering in the molten light of the setting sun. From the edge of his 35th-floor flat—a minimalist sanctuary perched high above Bandra's chaos—Rohan Srivastava looked down at the human tide swirling below. The city roared like a colossal machine: the cacophony of relentless traffic, the faint cries of hawkers, and the distant grind of local trains dragging the weight of millions clinging to their hopes and heartbreaks. From this height, the people appeared as dots—tiny, frantic, anonymous. "Ants on a mission. Ants with dreams too big for their fragile exoskeletons. Aren't we all ants, ants on a mission? Ants in the labyrinth of huge Corporates carrying more weight than scientifically acceptable. How much weight can a human mind carry?" His eyes lingered on the scene below, his lips curling into a faint, sardonic smirk. "Do you hear it?" he muttered, nearly inaudible even to himself. The 1500-square-foot expanse of curated collection, born not just of success but of taste sharpened over years of travel. Each corner told a piece of his story: an antique Burma teak tower clock stood as a stalwart relic against time; paintings of tiger eyes—crafted in the wilds of Ranthambore—beamed with predatory intensity;

S.H. Raza's Bindu won in an auction at Saffron Arts, collection from various Art Galleries of Mumbai & Bengaluru. The mythological Musk Dear by renowned Chandigarh-based Artist Madan Lal, representing desires bought from Saatchi Art and fine Dhokra sculptures whispered of tribes in Jharkhand, Odisha, and West Bengal, spoke of Rohan's interests and life beyond the corporate corridors. Artifacts from continents, chosen not because they were expensive, but because they resonated with his need for permanence, as if each possession screamed, "Look! I made it out alive. I mattered." And yet, standing before the glittering Mumbai skyline, his reflection caught in the glass like an apparition, Rohan couldn't silence the weariness that curled in the edges of his mind. He could see it now: the man who had what he aspired to staring at a city that had given him more than he'd ever believed possible, yet continuing to question—where did he lose himself in the process? The black sedan parked in the basement, the branded clothes tailor-made to perfection, the international school Ananya and Siya attended, the holidays in the Maldives and Santorini—they were undeniable badges of success, hard-fought and hard-earned. But somewhere in the heart, the curated perfection of his life lingered an aftertaste of dissatisfaction. The boy who spent his childhood at Dabha Semar—then little more than a spot on the map, of Faizabad now reborn as Ayodhya—clung to him still, a ghost shadowing each step he took away from that life. In sharp contrast to the polished finery of his present was the memory of his childhood home: a small, clinging two-room structure held up more by hope than mortar. The walls bore the stains of countless monsoons, soft-edged patches of damp that refused to be defeated. The air there carried a permanent scent of struggle:

the damp musk of earth, the acrid burn of wood smoke curling from the *chulha,* and the faint sweetness of stale jaggery. It wasn't just the walls; it was the voices, too. Cracks in the concrete were mirrored by fractures in his parents' strained exchanges. "Shankar, where's the money for the Diwali clothes?" his mother, Uma, would ask, her voice sharp but fragile, like glass under pressure. "What do you expect, Uma? The salary doesn't stretch. I'm doing my best!" his father would snap, quieter than her but equally burdened. Shankar, a Block Development Officer, was an honest government servant. Too honest. "I won't dirty my hands, not for this. Even if it means dinner's missing a few rotis." In those arguments, young Rohan forged a decision: I'm not going to die hungry just so I can feel righteous about it. His resolve burned white-hot. It wasn't about vanity or riches, not then. It was survival, plain and simple. The suffocation of scarcity lit a fire in him that demanded an escape—and escape he did. He remembered the escape route vividly. Books, always books. Their dusty pages held worlds that felt kinder, expansive. Unlike the overcrowded government classrooms, stifling with too many students and too little attention, the books became portals. Science, mathematics, history—they weren't just subjects; they were lifelines. His teachers whispered words like *brilliance,* knowing smiles and gentle encouragement lighting his path. Through it all, his best friend, Ashok, stayed rooted by his side. Every time his family's fights threatened to overwhelm him, there was a moment with Ashok that pulled him back—a cricket match on sunbaked fields, a playful bet on how far they could run before collapsing on the dusty lanes, rows of sugarcane whistling in the wind. Ashok lived in an obscure village near Dhabha Semar. His father operated a

Barber Shop out of a wooden kiosk on the National Highway connecting the then Faizabad to Allahabad. He was a brilliant student and studied with Rohan after classes at his home because there was no electricity connection in his village. Ashok dreamed of the Navy. He retired from the Navy as Commodore last year. The shadowed weight of sacrifice pressed deeply into the fabric of Rohan's memories, surfacing like a spectre every time he allowed himself to revisit the pivotal forks in his life—the dreams deferred, the paths untaken. They weren't just painful echoes of the past; they were the defining chords of his existence, shaping the man he had become. He had been the star pupil, the prodigy of Dabha Semar, his small, nondescript village nestled amidst the fields of Uttar Pradesh. Rohan's academic brilliance had cut through the shroud of poverty like the piercing rays of sunlight through a dense, morning fog. His diligence earned him a merit scholarship to a government-run secondary school, and his name appeared consistently at the top of every class roster—a rare distinction for someone from a village where education was often a luxury, not a necessity. His dreams burned brightly, consuming him with the promise of escape, of transformation. He could envision the immaculate corridors of the university waiting for him, could almost hear the hum of intellectual discourse, could feel the weight of opportunity in his hands. And then the grinding halt, the sudden rupture in his dreams. The phone call still haunted him. It was Ashok, his childhood friend, speaking with urgency, the tremor in his voice like a blow to the gut: "Rohan!... your father... It's his heart... He collapsed. He's very bad." Rohan had rushed home, and what met him stole the air from his lungs. Bills piled high like mountains threatening to avalanche over his family. His father lay weak and fragile on a hospital bed, his heart betraying the strength he had always embodied. His mother, gaunt and hollow-eyed, pleaded without words—her silent desperation cutting him deeper than anything she could have said aloud. His younger siblings clung to each other in quiet fear, their small worlds unravelling. And in that moment, Rohan understood—there was no choice, he needed to have an alternative to the financial security of the family, as human life can be very fragile and can vanish any moment. This was the first major lesson he learned in his life and helped shape his leadership style at a later stage of navigating uncertainties in business. The future he had envisioned was now secondary to the survival of those who relied on him. The prestigious university acceptance letter, the passport to a new life, became a cruel symbol of a dream rendered unreachable. He folded it neatly and tucked it away into a drawer to gather dust—the tangible evidence of what could have been. Duty eclipsed ambition. The mantra he repeated to himself—This is my duty. My dreams can wait—became his shield against the suffocating disappointment, though his soul bore the bruises of that sacrifice. The transition was abrupt and jarring. He walked into an insurance company as a clerk, leaving behind the vibrant potential of university life for the staleness of an office suffused with the smell of old paper and cheap tea. His three-figure salary, a figure that seemed pitiful against his aspirations, but necessary for survival. Rohan found his anchor in Mr S.P. Singh, the branch manager, a man tempered by wisdom and empathy. "Why give up on education entirely?" Singh had asked one day, his voice kind but firm. "Take study leave. Do what you can—it's never too late." And so, with Singh's guidance, Rohan continued to push against the walls of his circumstances. He earned a Bachelor of Science degree from Canning College, Lucknow University. It was a long and gruelling process, but Rohan had always believed in education—not as a mere qualification, but as empowerment, as a force for growth even amid chaos. He graduated with distinction, a quiet triumph that rekindled the embers of his ambition. But his hunger for more persisted. Always, the question lingered: What is the limit of sacrifice? When does duty end, and the pursuit of dreams begin? Determined, Rohan set his sights on a Master's degree, and he applied to the University of Sussex in Brighton, UK—a prestigious institution that felt like destiny calling him once again. Inlaks Foundation approved him for a scholarship, but by the time the funds were secured, the admissions deadline had passed. Again, fate seemed to intercept his trajectory, pulling him back to reality each time he stretched toward escape. He had pictured himself studying, taking up part-time work in Brighton's bustling streets, sending money home—better than the meagre salary he earned as a clerk. Yet, once more, his ambition met the hard wall of timing and circumstance. The fire in his belly refused to extinguish. Rohan threw himself into a series of competitive examinations, each an attempt to carve a better path for himself while balancing the looming weight of familial responsibility. Undeterred by his repeated failures in Civil Services exams, making it to the Mains but never finding his name among the selected candidates, he pivoted to other Officer-grade exams—Probationary Officers, Assistant Administrative Officers—and was finally selected in several different organisations before choosing the Insurance Industry as his future. But even in his success, there lingered remnants of regret. The memory of his

ISRO interview was particularly vexing, a colourful snapshot of a missed opportunity. The panel of senior scientists had asked him sparse questions, their chatter among themselves seemingly meant to unnerve him, to test his patience. Then came that defining query: "So, Mr Srivastava, have you ever worked on a computer?" He had looked the panel square in the eye, his honesty unwavering despite the laughter that followed. "Sir, I've not even seen a computer. But your advertisement clearly stated that people with aptitude could apply, and I believe I have the aptitude. That's why I'm here." The scientists had erupted into laughter—a cacophony of amusement echoing through the room—but something in his steadfast audacity must have resonated. Way back in 1984, computers were privileged assets of research institutions, scientific organisations, and some other big organisations and were hardly seen in schools, colleges, offices, or other common places. Weeks later, ISRO sent him a selection letter, offering him the position. Yet, practicality prevailed over aspiration—the designation of "Scientific Assistant" and its modest salary lost to the allure of the "Assistant Administrative Officer" title and higher pay. Even now, sitting in his Bandra flat, Rohan sometimes mulled over that decision, his chest hollow with a faint regret that the path of science and exploration had been abandoned for a more secure future. Life had been an incessant negotiation—a relentless tug-of-war between ambition and duty, a balancing act where no choice was free of consequence. But somewhere along the way, the fire in his belly lost its spark, replaced with the suffocating monotony of material success. Rohan had climbed higher and higher in pursuit of security and provision, but at what cost? As the hum of metropolis life rumbled beneath him, he thought of shattered dreams and whispered promises—those he had once made to himself, and those he had yet to make to his family. He had sacrificed much for survival, but now, staring at the glass skyline, Rohan wondered whether survival alone had been enough. Perhaps the time had come to reclaim the life he had long deferred—not for himself alone, but for the laughter he longed to hear within his home. For love. For presence. For all the reasons he had climbed this ladder to begin with. When he finally left, the grit and resilience that Dabha Semar had instilled in him fuelled his rise. First, the scholarships, then the exams—it was a staircase he sprinted up, the fires of his past snapping at his heels. He crammed harder than most, worked smarter than all, and eventually graduated into a world where his talents weren't ignored. By 2020, Rohan had wandered far from the exhaust fumes of his father's scooter rides and the arguments over Diwali clothes. Materially, he stood at the apex, surrounded by every comfort a young boy from Dabha Semar could have imagined. And yet, looking at the life he had built, Rohan felt tired—tired in ways materialistic possessions felt irrelevant questioning his own relevance. He had it all, didn't he? The job, the family, the accolades, the wild escapes to Africa's safaris and now the upcoming Iceland Photography trip next month, every marker of achievement. But deep inside, that boy who played cricket with Ashok and hid during his parents' fights wondered if this world of marble and air conditioning could buy back what he once had. There were cracks here, too, faint but growing. Siya's distance, her inexplicable silences. Priya's discontent, barely concealed beneath her composed demeanour as she called out his long absences and inattentiveness. And beneath it all, his own doubts, surfacing in the quiet moments when life wasn't loud enough to drown them out. The city's lights blinked below him, stretching endlessly into the distance. Somewhere under that shimmering chaos was a younger version of himself, still running toward something, never fully knowing what it was. Rohan took a steadying breath. For the first time in years, he wondered: was it really up here that he was meant to climb—or did he simply lose sight of where he truly belonged? "Beautiful, isn't it?" Rohan said softly, his voice a curious mix of pride and vulnerability. He turned toward Priya, who sat perched on the edge of the velvet sofa in their sprawling flat. Her delicate fingers moved rhythmically across her phone, the faint glow illuminating her sharp features, but her expression betrayed her preoccupation. For a fleeting moment, it seemed as though she hadn't heard him. Then, without looking up, she responded, her voice clipped, razor-edged. "What's beauty worth, Rohan, if it feels like it's only for show? Look around you. This place—your precious artifacts—they may tell stories of far-off, colourful lands, but they're silent about *us*." She finally looked up, pinning him with a gaze that burned as hot as the evening sun dipping below the horizon. "You've surrounded yourself with stories from strangers, yet you're blind to the one unfolding right in front of you. Our story." Those Chanderis, Maheshwaris, Banarsis, Sambalpuris, Kanthas and Mekhlas are bribes which you bought to compensate for your guilt of long absence from family on official tours.

Her words landed harder than expected, a sharp spark igniting in the space between them. Rohan pulled back, blinking as though she'd physically struck him. He turned to face her fully, confusion and frustration colliding in his expression. "What does that even mean?" he asked, his voice rising in protest. "Our home—everything in it—this isn't just stuff, Priya. It's the manifestation of our success! It's the proof that we made it!" "Success?" Priya scoffed, the edge in her tone sharpening. She placed her phone slowly on the marble coffee table, as though anchoring herself in the moment. "If this is success, then why does it feel so empty, Rohan? So cold? Minimalism, sleek furniture, priceless art—all these damned tokens of your climb to the top—none of it radiates warmth. It's like living in a museum curated by someone who forgot what love feels like." Her words were a blade sliding between his ribs, deliberate and precise. He opened his mouth to respond, but no words came out. For once, his silver tongue, honed in boardrooms and battles of wit, failed him. All he could muster was a heavy breath. "This... this is ridiculous," he finally stammered, his voice faltering. "You think this is cold? Priya, this home—we built this. It's everything I fought for. Everything I dreamed about when I had nothing." Priya rose slowly, meeting him eye to eye, the composed restraint in her posture more intimidating than any shouting match could ever be. "You dreamed of this, Rohan. Not *we*. You have so much, but you've lost sight of what actually matters. You don't build a life together by hanging clocks on walls or collecting sculptures from foreign lands. You build a home by showing up for the people in it." Her words were weighted with an undeniable truth, each syllable embedding itself into his chest with the force of decades of suppressed grievances. He turned away from her piercing gaze, seeking solace in the familiarity of the skyline. The city was no comfort tonight. Its twinkling lights seemed to mock him, millions of homes filled with lives either more desperate or more content than his own. "I didn't have a choice," he said at last, his voice barely audible. "You… you know where I came from. You know what it was like. Those two suffocating rooms. My parents—constant noise, constant fear—fighting about money, arguing over whether they could afford even my sister's education, let alone mine. There was nothing there but struggle. Nothing." He exhaled shakily, running a hand through his hair. "I promised myself I would escape that. I thought if I could build this—this life—it would mean something. It would mean I'd won." For the first time, Priya's eyes softened, but she didn't relent. "Won what, Rohan? A race against ghosts? A victory against a childhood that doesn't haunt you anymore, except in your head? I know you worked hard to give us this life, but at what cost? You've locked yourself in this gilded cage and forgotten how to live inside it. You're still chasing that boy you used to be. But you're not him anymore." Her words cracked something open within him, the quiet truth he'd been avoiding. His escape from Dabha Semar may have been triumphant, but it had never felt final. No amount of success seemed to silence the ghost of that small, damp house with its thin walls and muffled arguments—or the gnawing fear that he would somehow lose it all and end up back there. "Do you remember Siya's play last week?" Priya's voice was quiet now, but the hurt was unmistakable. "She looked out into the audience three times before realizing you wouldn't show up. Do you know what that does to a child? To see an empty chair where her father should be?" "I had a meeting—" he began, but she cut him off with a sharp wave of her hand. "Don't," she said firmly, her voice trembling slightly. "Don't say the words *'I had an important meeting'* one more time. You always have something more important. Work. Meetings. Meetings, presentations ... But you don't realize, Rohan—you're closing the deal on losing us in the process." Her words landed with devastating clarity. He couldn't look at her now, his once sharp gaze clouded and distant. He turned back to the window, his reflection dimmed by the darkness gathering outside. Priya's words weighed heavier than the skyline itself. The brutal honesty of her remarks brought forth something he hadn't let surface in years—regret. She wasn't wrong. Somewhere along the way, he had turned his ambition into a refuge, a fortress he used to protect himself from the vulnerability of family, of emotions, of being needed. He had armoured himself against every ghost of his past, only to become a phantom in his own home. "I'll change," he whispered, more to himself than to her. The words felt fragile, like a promise he wasn't sure he could keep. "Don't just *say* it, Rohan," she replied softly but resolutely. "Do it. Be here for us. Not just in this house, but really *here*. For me. For the girls. Before it's too late." The room fell silent, her words reverberating in the air between them. He could feel her waiting, silently hoping—but the fear gnawing at him was deafening. Could he really change? Could he truly face the rubble of his childhood instead of running from it? Could he let go of the unrelenting climb? Outside, the city buzzed as always, indifferent to his struggles. But inside, Rohan was at war, standing at the crossroads of his ambition and his family. The Abyss and the Apex. Which way would he go? Which path could still be saved?

CHAPTER 8

THE PRISON OF PROXIMITY

The memory of those fifteen days in quarantine clung to Rohan Srivastava like a damp, suffocating shroud—oppressive and unshakeable, with its sterile monotony. The torment in Mumbai was cruel, mocking him with every breath. The sweltering humidity seeped through the room's flimsy seals, mingling with the distant, bittersweet scent of jasmine from street vendors below—a tantalising whisper of freedom that hung just out of reach. Rohan had spent fifty long days locked away in the cold isolation of London—a forced exile marked by the absence of family, of love, of purpose. When news broke that limited international flights were resuming, his heart had surged with a desperate intensity he hadn't felt in months. Each second on the Airbus AI 130 stretched interminably, a torture all its own. Priya's face would flash in his mind, fleeting yet vivid: her cautious smile, the light in her eyes when she teased him. Ananya, tense and contemplative, diligently pouring over her textbooks. Siya, her laughter as bright and uninhibited as summer sunlight, filling their home with the melodies of the guitar. But that glimmer of hope was accomplice to betrayal. Even after touching down at Chhatrapati Shivaji Maharaj International Airport, Mumbai wrapped him in a deceptive embrace: its colourful chaos a promise of life, only to be dulled by the blunt edge of quarantine protocols. Freedom, once within tantalising reach, receded like the tide, leaving him stranded in isolation once again. "Rohan Srivastava," a voice cut through his reverie—the sharp tone of a health officer dressed head-to-toe in a PPE suit. Shuffling into line, he cast sideways glances at his fellow passengers, their faces pale and masked, reflecting unspoken anxieties. Herding onto the bus felt like penance, the fogged glass windows reflecting fractured images of his inner turmoil. Andheri, Santacruz, and then Bandra overlooking the imposing Bandra-Worli Sea Link—rushed past, passing as apparitions of a city he once belonged to but now couldn't touch. The quarantine hotel was suffused with sterile indifference—a room painted cream, as lifeless as a hospital ward. A bed, wooden desk, chair—each an artifact of monotony. The mechanical hum of the air conditioner was relentless, and though it cooled the room, it magnified the heat within his chest—the rising frustration, the suffocating ache of proximity without connection. Through the small window, no more than a slit in the wall, Rohan could see what he craved most: his family's building illuminated against the night. He could picture it perfectly: Priya brewing chai, chatting with Siya over her latest fascination with fairy tales, while Ananya asked for help on her homework. That was his life. His world. A mere kilometre away but unreachable, separated by an invisible barricade that felt more insurmountable than any physical wall. His forehead pressed against the window's cold glass, Rohan's anger bubbled up. How had he ended up here, reduced to this state of helpless longing? Each day he stood at this spot—a silent sentinel, staring at the reflections of his own inadequacies. The thoughts burrowed deeper, stabbing at him with the unrelenting sharpness of truth. The urge to dial Priya became unbearable. He reached for his phone, his heart heavy with hope and dread. "Priya?" Her voice flowed through the receiver, warm but tinged with a fragility she tried desperately to mask. "Rohan! When will you be home?" Her tone was steady, but he could imagine the effort it took to sound so composed, the tremble just beneath her words. "I'm here, Priya. Just nearby. "His voice cracked with emotion, betraying the calm front he tried to maintain. "I…I can see the building. Can you see me?" He didn't expect an answer, but he needed to ask—to pretend for just a moment that she could, that he wasn't miles away in spirit even if he was mere blocks away physically. "It's good knowing you're coming home soon," Priya said gently, though her breath faltered. He could picture her wiping away silent tears before their daughters could see, pressing on with a brave smile. "Soon," Rohan murmured. "Just…a few more days." The words tasted sour in his mouth. Fifteen days sounded insignificant to anyone else, but for Rohan, each one stretched endlessly, a mockery of movement while he stood frozen. Hanging up, he allowed silence to coat the room like ash in the aftermath of a wildfire. The flicker of connection with Priya was uplifting but fleeting; his despair returned stronger with nothing else to distract from it. Forced introspection was becoming his enemy—a magnifying glass held too close, exposing vulnerabilities he had spent years burying beneath layers of corporate deadlines and boardroom bravado. Rohan walked back to the window, but this time, his thoughts turned darker. He could see Siya laughing as she played, Priya helping Ananya with her assignments. He could imagine life—his life—happening without him. And the thought twisted like a dagger. Mumbai's cacophony—children shouting in joy, auto-rickshaws honking in maddening unison—was missing outside. But for Rohan, the rhythm was deafening in its absence; the symphony played in a pitch he could no longer hear. Thoughts crept in slowly, insidiously, carving through his resolve. Maybe they didn't need him. Maybe the burdens of expectation and responsibility could melt away if he were no longer a tether to disappointment—a father who was present only in absence, a husband whose corporate armour left marks deeper than affection. "What if I just…" The whisper came unbidden within his mind, seductive in its simplicity. What if I vanished? No burden to carry. No one to disappoint. No hollow assurances of being 'strong' while I crumble inside. But as the dangerous allure of darkness tried to rear its head, a sound jolted him back—a ringtone piercing the silence. Priya again. Of course… Priya, Ananya, Siya—they would call after him even if he fell into the abyss. They were his light, distant but unwavering, reminding him that even from the prison of proximity, love endures. In the muted twilight of his confinement, Rohan Srivastava cradled a heavy cup of tea in his hands, the steam curling into the sterile air like a phantom of home. The robust aroma of Red Label Nature Care, infused with cardamom and the sharp bite of ginger, teased his senses—an ephemeral comfort in the midst of his emotional tumult. He stared down at the cup, trying to steady the tremor in his hands as the scattered pieces of his resolve threatened to disintegrate again. Was it possible to miss something so deeply that even the most trivial rituals—like the act of holding tea—felt unbearably heavy? The quiet hiss of the air conditioner hummed in the background, an unrelenting monotony that mirrored his isolation. With a soft click, Rohan drew apart the thin curtains separating him from the world outside, his fingers lingering on the fabric as though it could somehow soften the ache. The sharp contrast of the sprawling metropolis greeted him, a city impossibly alive yet haunting in its indifference. Mumbai stretched before him, glittering like a jewelled tapestry, its glass-and-steel skyscrapers stabbing the darkening sky. Each glowing window held the promise of lives in motion, laughter, families, purpose—all the things that seemed so painfully distant now. His gaze locked onto one building amidst the sprawling urban jungle—his building. The home where his heart beat in rhythm with his family's laughter and quiet comforts. It stood firm and resolute, a shimmering beacon of his previous life, now reduced to mere shadows on the horizon. A pang of longing tightened in his chest, sharp enough to make him catch his breath. The flickering lights of his building felt like the cruel glare of a lighthouse taunting a stranded sailor, both guide and tormentor. He thought of Priya, of Ananya diligently solving math problems at the dining table, of Siya skipping barefoot through the hallway, her carefree laughter echoing through the walls—and the distance between these moments of happiness and his stark solitude felt like miles, not kilometres. Why do the walls of this room feel like a prison? he wondered bitterly. The tea clutched in his hands was scalding, but it was a poor substitute for the warmth of their presence. He closed his eyes, just for a moment, remembering their last video call, when Siya had held up her latest drawing proudly and Priya had smiled, softly, as though masking her exhaustion for the sake of him. I should be there, was the thought that roared in the back of his mind. Not here, trapped like a ghost watching his family from behind glass. With a sudden burst of determination, Rohan reached for his camera bag, a desperate need for connection pushing him past his despair. His fingers grazed over the sleek body of his Canon 90D and landed gently on the lens he considered his lifeline—his 100-400mm telephoto. It had been some time since he had last felt the thrill of capturing fleeting moments in motion: the quick flicker of a bird's wings, the glint of sunlight on rippling water. But this wasn't about photography. This was about bridging an impossible gap between him and the life just beyond the cruel confines of this quarantine. He mounted the lens with careful precision, the sound of the click reverberating through the silence—a moment of control in a world that was slipping from his grasp. "Just a glimpse," he muttered under his breath, steadying the camera against his palm, anxiety pressing sharply against his ribs. "If I can just… see them." Through the viewfinder, a distorted slice of his life unfolded. He zoomed in, his hands steady despite the desperate beating of his heart. The building he called home came into focus, its windows glowing softly in the deepening dusk. He could just make out shadows moving behind the glass—hazy figures, indistinct and fleeting, yet brimming with motion. Was that Priya, sitting in the living room? He imagined her curled up with her favourite novel, *Kainza* by Shivani, the corners of her mouth lifting in quiet enjoyment of words that had the power to pull her away from the storm. Was that Siya, perhaps, skipping across the hallway, her nimble fingers gently strumming her guitar strings? Through the viewfinder, the tableau played out like an intimate yet distant dream, just beyond grasp. The heavy clouds swirling above loomed ominously, a sombre reflection of his aching heart. He knew it was futile—he knew the shadows were too far away, mere illusions conjured by his longing. And yet, he continued snapping the shutter. Each click rang out like an act of rebellion, a fight against the suffocating weight of his estrangement. He turned the lens outward, capturing the melancholic beauty of the city in monochrome: clouds darkening as night descended, buildings standing tall with their lights flickering bravely against the encroaching storm. When he loaded the photos onto his laptop, the grayscale images stared back at him like reflections of his inner chaos—darkened clouds balanced against illuminated cityscapes, an unsettling dance of hope and despair. He titled the photograph "Mumbai in Solidarity with Kolkata," a tribute to both the tempest ravaging the City of Joy and the storm brewing within his own soul. As he hovered over the "post" button on Facebook, Rohan hesitated. The post felt like an offering—a vulnerable cry for connection in the void that surrounded him. Would anyone understand the ache captured in those images? Could anyone comprehend the loneliness of standing so close to love yet being unable to touch it? He hit "post" and leaned back, the weight in his chest momentarily giving way to a fragile hope that someone, somewhere, might see the flicker of his desperation and respond. The tea on his desk had grown cold, the steam dissipating like the remnants of his courage. He wrapped his arms around himself as the weight of the night deepened. The storm outside mirrored the turbulence within, both threatening to consume him entirely. But just as the darkness reached its peak, a flicker of defiance sparked within Rohan like a dying ember refusing to fade. "No," he whispered fiercely. "I will not let this defeat me. I may be distant, but I am theirs. And they are mine." Sitting up straighter, he felt the pulse of the city beneath him—a rhythm that, for all its chaos, reminded him of resilience. Because love, even trapped behind walls and windows, had an uncanny power to endure. Tomorrow, he thought, I will call Priya again. Tomorrow, I will remind her—and myself—of all that connects us, even in separation. I will close this distance, one step at a time. Rohan's gaze shifted from the mocking skyline to the rhythm in his own chest, steady and resilient. He let the love for Priya, Ananya, and Siya rise within him, undeniable and fierce—his anchor in the shifting storm of uncertainty. Fifteen days may stretch like an eternity, but they were still his. And he, no matter the barriers between them, would always be theirs. Days slipped by like heavy raindrops in a monsoon—slow, suffocating, and relentless. Rohan felt the passage of time constrict around him, each moment amplified by solitude's crushing weight. Quarantine had become a cage, starkly contrasting the cacophony of his bustling city life. Worse still, his absence from home left him grappling with guilt and helplessness as Priya—the vibrant core of their family—slipped further into the shadows of schizophrenia. The illness had stolen her laughter, replacing it with silent cries that echoed in their once lively home, now a muted shell of communal joy. The kitchen, which had once resonated with the sizzle of oil and the dance of spices, now sat eerily silent. Priya's fragrant dishes had been glorious celebrations—her *pani puri*, *momos*, or *kebabs* a cherished centrepiece of their home, a beacon of her love for Rohan and Siya. But now, those memories felt cruel. The clang of pots and pans seemed like distant mirages obscured by the haunting whispers of her mind. Rohan could picture her now—subdued, huddled on their bed, the soft sheets wrapped around her like a shroud. Medication prescribed by the psychiatrist dulled her energy; her movements became awkward, faltering like those of a newborn deer. Siya had already rushed her off to a specialty orthopaedic clinic after finding her crumpled on the bathroom floor. The very space which should have offered refuge had transformed into a hazard of falls and stumbles—a bitter metaphor for the fragility of their lives. Quarantined in a room far away from comforting embraces, Rohan had been reduced to consulting doctors online, their advice offering little solace. Conversations felt spectral, echoes of his helplessness bouncing back to him from blank Zoom screens. His family's focus was consumed by pandemic fears: the grim spectre of Covid had swallowed both the outside world and their home, morphing familiar hospital corridors into sombre war zones. Rohan felt like a spectator trapped in a disaster film, unable to break from a role he detested but couldn't escape.

Priya, once the pulsating heart of their community, had thrived amidst the vibrancy of her connections. Festivals like Ganesh Chaturthi spun magic under her care; her food stalls during festivals teemed with eager faces, her warmth bridging strangers and neighbours alike. As young boys n girls would gravitate toward her stall, wide-eyed with hope and hunger for her culinary masterpieces. "Aunty! Can we have more *pani puri*, please?" they'd plead, their eyes alight with enthusiasm. Those golden days now felt like distant mirages. Schizophrenia had stolen her spark, but perhaps even crueller was how life had unspooled the threads of camaraderie she had painstakingly woven. The friends who once adored her turned away when the burden grew too heavy for them. Loneliness replaced their hollow promises of support. When Priya sought solace in Mrs Singh's company, she was met with the slam of a door—the sound ricocheted through the hollow of Rohan's chest, a painful reminder of the frailty of human compassion. The storm brewing within him felt relentless, swirling with a cocktail of helplessness and indignation. A polite phone call he made to Mr Singh was met with cold practicality, the suggestion to send Priya for treatment at a mental asylum igniting firestorms in his mind. Siya, fierce and unyielding, had marched Priya home. The young girl's voice trembled with fury as she confronted her mother's so-called friends. "Enough is enough, Mom!" Siya had cried. Her face reflected a tempest of anger and sorrow. "You see everyone celebrating with you during good times, but where are those so-called best friends now? Where are they when you need them?" Her words lingered in the air like heavy storm clouds, amplifying Rohan's own helpless rage. This mental pressure was taking toll on Siya's mental health also. What had become of humanity? What had become of them? He pleaded with municipal authorities to let allow him home quarantine as was for pregnant women, senior citizens and children, in view of his circumstances requiring his presence at home. All the pleas fell on deaf ears for the sake of guidelines and circulars.

With just three days left before Rohan's quarantine ended, his thoughts swirled endlessly. What awaited him back home? Would Priya still be lost in the same desolate state, her laughter reduced to hollow echoes? Would his home—a sanctuary for love and laughter—still be recognizable beneath veils of illness and isolation? Finally, the day arrived: May 24, 2020. Rohan glanced at the Longines strapped to his wrist; it's cool metal grounding him amidst his turmoil. The watch ticked silently at 7:38 PM as he slid into the backseat of an Ola cab. The city outside blurred into a mosaic of red taillights and flickering storefronts, each flash distorting the boundaries between past and present. Rohan felt like a bird released from its cage, yet bound by invisible chains. The very essence of home—the place he longed to return to—felt foreign now. Would he find the strength to leap into the warmth of their embrace? Or would fear anchor him to the ground, robbing him of the courage to confront the unknown? The cab rattled over the asphalt as the familiar contours of their street emerged on the horizon. Each bump sent ripples of anxiety through Rohan's chest. He pictured Priya's face as she had appeared in his dreams—the vibrant joy that had once radiated from her now cloaked by layers of depression and isolation. Could he untether her from the darkness? Could he still recognise the woman he loved beneath the scars left by trauma? The answers lay beyond a threshold he hadn't crossed in far too long. He would enter his home to find the promise of reunion—but would it offer healing or only more heartbreak? As the cab slowed, Rohan inhaled deeply, steadying his racing thoughts. Every moment, every fear, every flicker of hope had shaped the man he had become—a man who had to make the leap. Beyond the door lay flickering stars of possibility; perhaps they would illuminate his way. But first, he had to gather his strength. For the family he cherished, for the love waiting like embers of a dying fire, Rohan had to step inside. The weight of absence was crushing—but perhaps it could be lifted.

CHAPTER 9

LOYALTY IN A CORPORATE GAME

The Capital Building in BKC pierced the bruised Mumbai skyline like an arrow of ambition, its steel-clad towers shimmering under the dim blanket of dusk. The soft hum of the city, the distant honk of hurried cabs, and the muted murmur of life outside barely reached Rohan Srivastava as he stood motionless by the floor-to-ceiling window of his apartment. His gaze rested not on the chaotic vibrancy of the metropolis but on the distant silhouette of the towers. The gleaming skyscrapers always seemed alive to him, their stoic brilliance a testament to triumphs he had once tasted—a life where polished floors shone like accolades, intelligent elevators whispered promises of upward mobility, and the powerful mingled with the ambitious. But tonight, they seemed less alive and more accusatory, looming over him like sentinels of a world he no longer trusted. He inhaled deeply, trying to anchor himself, but the metallic tang of the city air mingled with the bitter taste of betrayal—mocking reminders of the success he had endured, and the battle scars left behind. How far away that world feels now, he thought, his chest tightening as memories surged like a tide unwilling to be held back. It wasn't just a career he had built—it was an identity. Rohan Srivastava, the boy who morphed from a modest clerk at a public sector insurance company into an Executive Vice President in a multinational conglomerate. He told himself it was worth it, that the quiet murmurs branding him as "lucky" or the "CEO's fav" would fade away if he stayed the course. But ambition, he was learning, could cut as deeply as it pushed upward. "Rohan, your team's numbers are consistently excellent. You've done extremely well," Ms Kapoor—the cold and calculating President (Marketing) — had said in their last appraisal meeting. Her voice, deliberate and sharp, lingered in his memory the way paper cuts linger in one's flesh—small but incessantly stinging. "But I hear you're spending too much time on 'team building.' Don't let soft skills dilute hard results." It wasn't the words that had cut him, but the quiet flicker of condescension in her hawk-like gaze. She didn't believe in his methods; to her, leadership wasn't about connecting, mentoring, or inspiring—it was transactional, measured only in bottom lines. He had spoken back with unshaken resolve that day. "Ms Kapoor," he'd said, meeting her gaze without flinching, "Strong teams are led by transformational leaders. People management and performance metrics are symbiotic. If we want sustainable growth, we must build the foundation, not chase quick fixes.". It was not a quote from an Ivy League Institution; he was sponsored by his company to hone his leadership skills. It was a conviction he demonstrated and lived by. Her grudging nod of approval had felt like a hollow victory, a moral triumph in a place where emotions were liabilities. But if that memory was a burn, what followed pierced him like ice.

He vividly remembered the upheaval he had been part of 15 years ago when he had not even completed a year in the company.

The day the promotion list was released, humiliation had struck like a thunderclap. His name wasn't there. The luminescent office screen, glowing with the names of those who had leapt ahead of him on the corporate ladder, made his cheeks burn with disbelief. Rohan prided himself on calm, calculated responses, but the omission felt personal, deliberate—a slap delivered under the cover of policy. He recalled the weight of his phone in his hand, how unnatural its smooth surface felt against his palm stained by anxious sweat. Calling Ms Kapoor had felt like walking into a lion's den, but he needed answers. His voice betrayed him when he spoke, trembling slightly. "Ms Kapoor. I… I needed clarity on the promotion list. I was informed—no, assured—that I was in line for the Regional Sales Manager position." For a moment, the pause on the other end of the line felt heavier than the silence left in a room after bad news. "Rohan," she said at last, each syllable rolling out like a pristine judgment. "As far as promotions go, I was not privy to the process. It might be best to speak to Mr Sinha directly." Her tone was neutral—practised, polished—but the indifference was unmistakable. The corporate ritual had played out: plausible deniability. Had she already known? He wondered. Feigned ignorance was the currency of management here, passed from hand to hand as power shifted and stories changed. The first brick in his carefully laid fortress of resolve began to tremble. His mind flashed back to endless months shaping the UP market, to weekends lost to 14-hour workdays, to cold coffee in conference rooms where he promised soaring metrics to executives who barely looked up from their spreadsheets. All for what?

Despite his better instincts, he called Mr Sinha, the then Executive Director of Marketing. The man's genial tone grated against the storm churning inside Rohan's chest. "Rohan!" Sinha greeted him as though they were old friends rather than a chessboard king and one of his pawns. "Congratulations on a solid quarter. You've truly performed miracles in a tough market." "Sir," Rohan interrupted, the desperation spilling out like an open wound, "With all due respect, my performance isn't why I'm calling. I was assured..." He regretted the falter in his words but pressed on, "I was assured a promotion, based on Mr. Sahu's—our former CEO's—assurance. But today..." He could visualise Sinha exhaling, preparing to deliver a half-hearted handoff of blame. "Rohan, your efforts are acknowledged, even celebrated. But you see, the HR policy has changed. Eligibility for promotion now requires twelve months of performance instead of six months earlier ." The words hit him not as information but as betrayal. "You never told me this," Rohan shot back, the anger in his tone barely veiled. "Last week, you said we needed to hit 115% of budget and my team delivered. You said that UP had to over-deliver." His words gained a momentum of their own, each one sharpened by fatigue and indignation. "I've worked beyond capacity. Didn't that policy 'change' exist before my targets were set?" "Rohan..." Sinha's voice took on that familiar patronising tone, at once calming and invalidating. "I understand your frustration. But every organisation has its systems. This isn't personal—it's process." "Process". That word. Its sterility enveloped Rohan, suffocating every last ounce of conviction. Process erases humanity, he thought bitterly. Process ensures no one is truly accountable.

He stood there, staring blankly into his reflection in the skyscrapers outside. All his achievements, his sleepless nights, his strained family dinners, his delayed vacations—they all clicked neatly into a game of corporate chess where pawns worked themselves to the bone for faceless queens and kings. And promotion? It was just another move, dictated not by effort but by whim masked in policies. There was frustration, yes. But buried beneath the surface of anger was something darker. Exhaustion. A profound weariness, not of the work but of the game itself. Rohan clenched his fist, willing himself to calm down. Somewhere, an alternative life beckoned—a life where nobody judged him, where his evenings weren't measured in deliverables, and where recognition wasn't another dangling carrot in an endless maze. The question lingered long after he let out a slow breath: What does success cost when you've lost sight of why you wanted it in the first place?

The truth hit him like a piercing blade, undeniable and unrelenting. Another financial institution had cast its net—a shiny lure with promises of a bigger pay check, greener pastures, and a 'significant market ripe for development.' The offer buzzed in his mind like static on an untuned radio, demanding his attention even as his heart craved peace. Should he stay, bound by loyalty to the soil he had tilled so relentlessly? Or should he leap into the unknown, leaving behind the world he had worked tirelessly to build—a gamble where the stakes went beyond numbers or job titles and seeped into the fibres of his identity? Rohan Srivastava was no stranger to hard decisions, but this one felt different. Leaving wouldn't just mean breaking ties; it would mean abandoning years of sweat, sacrifice, and ambition entwined in a mosaic of branches spread across Uttar Pradesh—a network of 28 thriving locations that had once been mere dots on a barren map. He remembered the long nights, the missed family dinners, the relentless hours spent nurturing his vision of growth. And yet, a small voice inside him whispered of escape, of a fresh start that promised to lift him out of the shadows closing in on him. The question gnawed at him: Was loyalty worth it in a world ruled by betrayal?

What use was allegiance to a machine that rewarded manipulation over merit? Could Mr. Sinha truly be unaware of the lengths he had gone to, or was it all an orchestrated deceit—another sleight of hand wrapped in the cold veneer of corporate policy? The cool glass of the windowsill pressed beneath his fingers felt like an anchor, grounding him against the storm raging inside. His brow furrowed, his mind swimming through tangled thoughts. What was the price of loyalty? Would they ever truly recognize his worth, or would he remain the invisible cog in a faceless machine, turning endlessly in service of those who thrived on empty promises?

As the city of Nawabs pulsed vibrantly below, alive with dreams interwoven into its ancient rhythms, Rohan closed his eyes and made a silent vow—a promise to himself alone. No more waiting. No more drowning in the uncertainty of "what if." It was time to reclaim the wheel, to steer his life toward a path that valued him not just as a worker but as a person. If another opportunity would recognize his worth, reward his passion, and respect his sacrifices, he would take it—even if it meant leaving behind what he had built. A flicker of hope ignited within his chest, fragile but determined. He would rise again, whether within these walls or in a new arena. This chapter of disappointment would become the fuel propelling him forward. "I've worked so hard," he whispered aloud, his voice trembling with exhaustion and longing. "Patience is a virtue. The storm will pass. Maybe it's time to unwind. To spend time with family."

The evening sky surrendered its fiery throne to the indigo embrace of night as Rohan found himself drawn to Hazrat Ganj, the bustling heart of Lucknow. The iconic shopping district was alive with electric energy, a kaleidoscope of sights and scents—an oasis offering reprieve from storms of corporate disillusionment. His daughter, Ananya, twirled around the living room with uncontainable excitement, clutching her crumpled list of culinary adventures, her zeal infectious. "Papa! Are we ready for Gunjing?" she chirped, her eyes shining like constellations. Rohan smiled, temporarily letting down the walls guarding his tired heart. "Absolutely! Are you ready for the best **TokriChaat** (Basket Chaat) in the city?" Her giggle rang out like a bell of pure joy, pulling him into her world—a world where concerns evaporated and life was measured not in deliverables but in simple, fleeting delights.

Hazrat Ganj bloomed around them, a living tableau painted with vibrant storefronts, buzzing cafes, and a sea of people weaving through its colourful streets. Strings of fairy lights hung overhead, shimmering with festive brilliance while the air sang with aromas that tugged at one's senses—the sweet allure of freshly fried snacks mingling with intoxicating spices perfumed the evening, wrapping Rohan in warmth. First stop: Royal Café, home to the famed *Tokri Chaat*. The polished façade of the café hummed with old-world charm, a relic of leisurely meals once savoured without hurry or distraction. Ananya dragged Rohan toward the counter—her energy irresistible. "Four *Tokri Chaat*, please, two spicy ones and two mild spicy !" her voice sparkled, buoyant with anticipation. The wait felt eternal, but when the crisp golden bowl filled with tangy chutneys, creamy yogurt, and a sprinkling of pomegranate seeds finally arrived, it was a masterpiece of flavours—a symphony on the tongue. Rohan and Ananya shared bites amid laughter, her giggles breaking through the silence he had carried in his heart. For a moment, he let himself forget everything—the promotion, the humiliation, the lingering bitterness—and savoured the burst of flavours reminding him that happiness could bloom, even amid chaos.

Now it was turn of **Tunde Kabab**, home to the legendary Galauti Kebabs—tender morsels that disappeared on tongue , rich with spices that told stories of heritage and artistry. Ananya's excitement bubbled over as they sat down, savouring each bite of the indulgent feast- the Kebabs with Roomali Roti . For Priya Paneer Kofta with Pulao was picked up as take away from Vyanjan .

Next, they visited **Prakash Kulfi**, a legendary establishment in Aminabad , where creamy scoops of frozen bliss awaited. The line snaked long into the night, but even the anticipation felt delicious—a prelude to the velvety delight that awaited them. "Can I have pistachio-flavoured kulfi, Papa?" Ananya asked, her voice laced with childlike wonder. "Of course, sweetheart," Rohan replied, a rare smile flickering across his lips. The first bite was magical—a cool, nutty richness melting on the tongue, transporting them to moments untouched by worry or regret. With each spoonful, Rohan found himself surrendering further to the magic of simplicity.

The world outside blurred into insignificance as flavours and laughter enveloped them, a sanctuary from life's storms. And as tradition dictated, their adventure concluded with *Meetha Paan*—a sweet, fragrant indulgence that tied the meal together with a bow of nostalgic charm. Ananya clutched her small, syrupy treasure triumphantly, the world reflected in her sparkling eyes.

As Rohan watched Ananya twirl around the pavement, her hair dancing in the flickering lights, something shifted inside him. The icy despair he had carried began to thaw, replaced by a warmth that whispered of hope and resilience. These moments—shared smiles, tiny celebrations, unspoken connections—were far greater than any list of job titles or accolades. He held Ananya's hand more tightly, her laughter tugging him back from the brink once again. Perhaps the corporate world was unforgiving, a merciless chessboard where he was expected to play without reward. But here, amid the swirling air of joy and the love of family, he remembered the truth: true victories are measured not in numbers or promotions but in moments where the heart beats freely, untethered by the weight of disappointment. Perhaps the clouds would part. Perhaps they wouldn't. But for now, Rohan had one certainty—he was not alone. Amidst storms of ambition and betrayal, this truth was enough to keep him standing.

A New Chapter Beckons The next morning, Rohan woke with a spark of restless energy and a plan that promised to stitch together the frayed edges of his spirit. A family trip to Nainital and Jim

Corbett National Park—just the thought of it was enough to spark life within him. The allure of the mountains, the crisp air of the hills, and the untamed thrill of watching wildlife in their natural habitat felt like a balm for his weary heart. Photography had always been his solace, a lens through which he could temporarily frame out life's complexities. "Daddy, do you think there are tigers in Nainital?" Siya asked, her wide eyes brimming with innocent curiosity as she craned her neck to meet his gaze. Rohan chuckled, a genuine smile spreading across his face for the first time in what felt like weeks. "Not in Nainital, sweetheart. The tigers live in Jim Corbett National Park, near Ramnagar—a little drive from Nainital. We'll try our luck and see if we can spot one. And elephants too." Siya clapped her tiny hands in delight, but Priya wasn't one to let her husband off easily. Her lips curved into a teasing smirk. "You mean like that *tiger* you *thought* you photographed the last time? The legendary 'moving bush'?" "Alright, alright," Rohan laughed, his face breaking into a boyish grin as he threw his hands up in mock surrender. Their playful banter was a welcome reprieve, wrapping around him like a comforting blanket, pushing the shadows of recent doubts into the periphery. He knew those shadows would flicker back, as persistent as they were unwelcome, but for now, he allowed himself to bask in the warmth of his family's joy. The drive back from Bareilly after the three-day safari trip unfurled in rhythmic monotony as the car ambled past fields stretching into the horizon. Rohan's mind wandered, the low hum of the engine lulling him into quiet introspection. Thoughts swirled—some as fleeting as ribbons of smoke, others lingering like ghosts. Rohan was hugely respected by his team as he always empowered them, coached them, and added value. He was very tough from the outside; people would think ten times to approach him for frivolous issues, but he was highly accessible to his people for important issues. He was equated with a coconut shell—hard from the outside and soft from the inside. His nickname was "Tiger" not only because of his penchant for tiger photography but also his courage, energy, and spirit. Priya and the kids, seated in the back, bubbled with chatter, their laughter peppered with rounds of a word association game. It was their own little world, and though Rohan found solace in it, his own realm of worries remained stubbornly in the foreground. The moment cracked open like a dropped plate as his phone vibrated against the dashboard. A missed call glowed on the screen: Ms. Kapoor. Rohan's throat tightened, his mind immediately racing. Why now? What could this mean? He hesitated for a beat before muttering something about needing a quick bio-break. Pulling over on the side of the highway near a roadside dhaba, his fingers dialled her number back with a mixture of unease and anticipation. "Congratulations, Rohan," Ms. Kapoor's voice greeted him—a tone that was inexplicably warmer than usual, almost unrecognizable from her typical curt demeanour. "You've been given charge as the Regional Sales Manager for UP, Bihar, and Jharkhand. I may not be an official promotion, but consider this your recognition—a testament to your hard work over the years." For a brief moment, time suspended itself. Rohan felt the weight of her words strike him like a stone cast in still water, sending shockwaves through his very being. Years of struggle, unrelenting effort, and unspoken sacrifices crystallized into this fleeting moment of validation. He closed his eyes, allowing himself to savour the moment before words spilled out like a tide breaking through a dam. "Thank you so much, Ma'am. Truly. This wouldn't have been possible without your trust and belief in me. I promise you—I won't let this opportunity go to waste." Warmth surged through him—a surge he hadn't felt in months. For the first time, the icy grip of corporate disillusionment melted just enough to let gratitude and hope seep in. The storm clouds that had cloaked him began to lift, a crack of sunlight piercing through. He turned back toward the car where Priya and the kids were still lost in their game, unassuming and blissfully unaware of what had just occurred. He fixed his gaze on them, a sudden urge tightening in his chest. Without a word, he opened the door and reached for Priya, pulling her into an impulsive, heartfelt hug that caught her entirely off guard. "What's gotten into you now?" she asked, laughter dancing in her eyes, her arms wrapping around his waist in response. "Celebrate!" Rohan's voice was electric with elation, the edges of his grin threatening to eclipse the sun itself. "We've just received the best news!" The ordinary roadside dhaba, with its plastic chairs and grease-smudged tables, suddenly transformed into a venue fit for a celebration. Within seconds, the family descended on the small counter, arms laden with an odd assortment of candies, chips, packet cakes, and fizzy drinks. They clinked glass bottles of Thums Up as if they were champagne flutes, their laughter and joy echoing louder than the trucks rumbling past in the background. For once, Rohan savoured the moment wholly, unburdened by pretence. As the kids peeled open their Cadbury bars and Priya raised a toast with her Frooti, the mundane suddenly felt magical, imbued with the weight of triumph and unity. As the car resumed its journey toward home, it seemed as though even the road itself had softened, stretching ahead like an invitation. Rohan's gaze shifted to the horizon, where the sun was painting its departure in swirls of burnt orange and gold, leaving behind a warm glow that clung to the landscape like hope made visible. The euphoria lingering in his chest slowly gave way to contemplation. Would this recognition truly stick? Would it be sustained, genuinely honoured? Or was it merely another token gesture to keep him from straying? The questions twisted in his mind like uninvited guests, refusing to be ignored. But something had shifted inside him. He always believed that no organization can afford to ignore merit in this fiercely competitive world. Maybe Mr. Sinha was right. This time, he wouldn't allow complacency to lull him back into stasis. He had clawed his way out of despair once, and now, more than ever, he was determined to keep rising. The vibrant laughter of his family harmonized with the low hum of possibility that had taken root in his heart. The road stretched on, unspooling like an unwritten story waiting to unfold. This, he realized, was just the beginning—not an end, but an intersection where hope, determination, and resilience converged. Rohan leaned back, inhaling deeply, the faint mix of sweet and salty air coursing through his senses. The journey ahead might still be fraught with challenges, but for now, he embraced the moment—the rare, intoxicating taste of triumph—and prepared himself to write the next chapter of his story. Whether it was for the people who mattered most by his side and the promise of a brighter dawn ahead or just because they did not have better options and Ms. Kapoor's performance depended on Rohan's performance who had proved his mettle in such a short time? He mused and felt ready to face whatever lay waiting beyond the bend.

CHAPTER 10

THE FRACTURED PAST

Five years had passed, yet the memories clawed at Rohan's conscience, vivid and raw, refusing to fade. They were more than recollections—they were spectres. The days following his quarantine in Mumbai remained etched in his mind with cruel precision, like standing on the precipice of despair and staring into an abyss so deep that light itself seemed terrified to venture in. The descent had been swift—cataclysmic—a life carefully stitched together unravelling, thread by thread, under the weight of chaos. Fear tasted metallic in his mouth, its bitter tang coiling around his tongue like iron chains, while silence suffocated the air around him, an oppressive presence far heavier than any storm. When he crossed the threshold of his home—a sanctuary once filled with jasmine-scented evenings and laughter so warm it could hug the walls—a fragment of normalcy greeted him in the faint floral aroma hanging in the air. But comfort was fleeting. Dread followed like a shadow, settling over his chest with the merciless grip of panic. Where was Priya? The question erupted in his mind, relentless as a wildfire. The silence wasn't just an absence of sound; it was an oppressor that stifled every breath, every heartbeat. The door opened to reveal Siya—his younger daughter—now a ghost of the bright, spirited girl he had left behind. Her small frame trembled, eyes rimmed red, her face pallid like the ash of a burned-out flame. "Where's Mom?" The words escaped Rohan's throat, fragile and cracked, as if speaking them aloud would splinter him irreparably. Siya hesitated, her lips quivering as she tried to shape words around her anguish. "Papa…" Her voice broke. "She's… in bed." Sardonic emptiness underlined her reply, and Rohan could feel the weight of truths unspoken. Without another word, he brushed past her—bags abandoned at the entrance as though they were burdens his arms refused to carry anymore. The hallway stretched in his vision, each step feeling heavier as he waded through a mire of dread. Wade. Keep going. Don't stop—because stopping is sinking. The bedroom door swung open, and the sight froze his world. Priya lay on the bed, her eyes fixed vacantly on the ceiling as though it concealed answers she'd searched for in vain. Her once vibrant presence—her sharp laugh, her boundless warmth, the woman who had effortlessly brought life into any room—was gone. Rohan inhaled sharply, his resolve wavering under the sight of what had become of her. "I'm home, Priya," he whispered, words trembling as though hoping they could dismantle the barrier between them. Her eyes met his fleetingly, but the flicker of recognition vanished just as quickly. "Hmm," came her response, flat and distant—no joy, no warmth, no acknowledgment of the man she had once been tethered to. "Kaise ho? Aa gaye? Achha?" (How are you? You are back. Good?) she whispered in mother tongue, Hindi. He tried again, pitching his words into the void between them, hoping for connection. But it only deepened the chasm—an ache expanding like a silent scream as he watched the vibrant woman he adored dissolve, turning into a shell he barely recognized. This was the same woman who had filled their home with the richness of saffron-painted kitchens, the spicy fragrance of cardamom, and laughter that bubbled out effortlessly, bright as sunlight. Now, the once-lively kitchen sat in eerie stillness, abandoned pots and pans gathering dust like memories quietly decaying. Rohan felt the walls closing in, the suffocating bubble of despair constricting his chest. I can't fix this. I can't save her. With trembling hands, desperate to contain the surge of emotion threatening to drown him whole, he fled to the bathroom. There, the sound of rushing water became a sanctuary—a shield between his grief and the reality clawing at him. The faucet roared as he washed his face over and over, but the icy water did nothing to numb the paralysis gripping his soul. "Rise, Rohan," he muttered under his breath—a mantra he had lived by as a corporate executive—but this time, the command felt hollow, a desperate charade against the crushing truth of his failure. It was past 8:45 PM when he stumbled into the kitchen. Cooking—an act that once felt trivial, even mundane—became his lifeline amid the chaos. He didn't want to cook; he didn't need to cook. But he had to—because to give Siya and Ananya comfort, even momentarily, was the only way to soothe the guilt eating at him from the inside. He thought of their favourite meal: Mutton Rogan Josh, a recipe passed down from his father, vivid in its fiery red sauce and burned into his fondest childhood memories. But the pantry mocked him—the shelves scarce, the options dwindling. Only soya nuggets and potatoes surfaced from corners of neglect. Still, he assembled what he could, infusing every ounce of energy left in his weary frame into making a meal from fragments—for them, for himself, for a semblance of normalcy. As Priya lay bound to her bed, her body recovering agonizingly slowly, her enemy shifted from the physical to the mental. The manifestation was subtle at first—forgotten conversations, vacant stares, hours spent gazing at the ceiling. But soon, her fragility fractured deeper. Her once-sharp mind unravelled like a tapestry fraying at the edges, slipping further into delusion's grasp. Shadows danced on walls invisible to anyone but her, voices whispered conspiracies in rooms that left others silent. Psychosis. The word clawed at Rohan, foreign yet terrifyingly real. The accusations began small—mistrusting the nurses' words, rejecting the taste of her food. Then, they escalated. "You're poisoning me!" she screamed at him one evening, a fire of paranoia flashing in her once-kind eyes. Later, Ananya sobbed as Priya accused her of plotting against her—accusations that shattered the young girl's fragile resilience. Rohan tried to console them both, but his corporate expertise was useless here—to navigate Priya's shattering reality was to venture blindly into quicksand. "This isn't her. This isn't my Priya. What is happening? Where did she go?" The questions tormented him. He felt a canyon opening between his former and present selves, his identity crumbling under the weight of irrelevance. The motivational speeches, performance review meetings, and executive strategies he wielded so confidently at work—all of them were ineffectual now. He wasn't a leader anymore; he was just a powerless man watching his family dissolve while the world outside spiralled into pandemic-induced chaos. But fragments of hope glimmered faintly. Siya's face brightened when the scent of their makeshift meal wafted through the air—a fleeting moment of shared comfort, even if imperfect. And though Priya's psychosis lured her into darker corners of the mind, occasionally she blinked, dazed, but looking at him with faint recognition. Don't give up, Rohan. Not yet. Hope flickered weakly, but it burned.

The chapter wasn't over—it couldn't be over. He needed to rise. It began as a whisper—a subtle unravelling that I initially tried to dismiss. Priya, the woman whose presence once anchored this family with her sharp wit and infectious warmth, started showing signs of something far more sinister than mere fatigue. At first, there were moments of confusion—brief lapses in memory, sentences left unfinished, her thoughts fractured like splintered glass. She grew eerily detached, her eyes wide yet unseeing, fixated on the ceiling as if searching for answers only she could decode. Hours would pass with her lying motionless, muttering incoherently about shadows moving against the walls—shadows none of us could see. And then it escalated. The Priya I knew—the one who lifted any room she walked into, who challenged my stubbornness with her wit, who effortlessly balanced tenderness with tenacity—began to fade. In her place emerged someone I scarcely recognized, someone trapped in a cruel labyrinth of the mind. She started whispering about unseen figures lurking in the corners of the room, eyes darting toward shadows with palpable fear. She accused the nurses of conspiring against her, weaving tales of betrayal that felt terrifyingly real to her. Her voice often broke into panicked shrieks, accusing me of poisoning her food—me, the man who would have moved mountains to see her well. The accusations didn't stop with me. One evening, Siya stumbled from Priya's room, tears streaming down her face. "She said I want her to die," Siya choked out, trembling. As I pulled her into an embrace, trying to soothe her sobs, I realized the depth of the damage Priya's illness was inflicting on all of us. It was like watching her reality fracture in slow motion—pieces of the woman we loved scattering into a mosaic of delusions that no amount of reasoning could piece back together. This isn't her. This isn't my Priya. What is happening? Is this my fault? Am I losing her completely? The questions screamed in my mind, relentless and merciless. I couldn't escape them, no matter how I tried. It was as if the very core of my existence—my ability to protect my family—had been stripped away. Every ounce of corporate confidence I once possessed felt absurdly irrelevant now. I couldn't solve this. I couldn't even comprehend it. The crushing weight of failure dragged me down until I could hardly breathe. I'm failing her. I'm failing all of them. And if her mental state wasn't torture enough, the struggle to find meaningful help made her condition feel insurmountable. With hospitals overwhelmed by the COVID-19 crisis and restrictions limiting in-person consultations, psychiatric care became a distant, elusive hope. Online consultations were all we had—imperfect stabs at a problem that required more than a voice on the other end of a screen. I'd hold the phone to Priya's ear, feeling the bitter sting of helplessness as I described her fragmented thoughts to a distant, disembodied figure. "Doctor, she thinks the walls are moving," I explained during one such call, my voice ragged and tinged with desperation. "She says everyone is conspiring against her. She refuses to eat, convinced everything's poisoned. What do I do?" Dr. Mehta, our psychiatrist, stared back at me from the pixelated screen, her expression weary and restrained. "Mr. Srivastava, I know this is difficult. These symptoms aren't uncommon under conditions like this—we're all navigating uncharted territory. We'll adjust her medication dosage for now and try to manage her stress. Avoid exposing her to news or anything that might agitate her further." I fought the urge to shout, the futility of her advice gnawing at the edges of my frayed patience. "Medication? Stress management?" I snapped, the phone trembling in my grasp. "How can I keep her calm when her mind is a battlefield? How can I ensure her safety when she's bed-bound and disoriented? She needs an actual examination, Doctor—not just words across a screen!" Dr. Mehta remained composed, even as my anger spilled over. His measured tone didn't falter. "I understand, Mr. Srivastava," he said softly. "But in the current situation, in-person consultations simply aren't feasible for non-emergency cases. This is the best we can do for now." It wasn't enough—not by far. Even the medication, prescribed without the benefit of close monitoring, turned into a double-edged sword. The high-power antipsychotics meant to combat Priya's psychosis came laden with side effects: sedation, confusion, and a heightened risk of falls. For Priya, already dealing with mental health triggered by Rohan's long absence and fear and anxiety of covid, a disaster was waiting to happen.

And it did. She began falling in the washroom—a place so small, so ordinary, yet brimming now with danger. I would carefully assist her as she moved, every step a fragile negotiation between her unsteady balance and her disoriented perception. Sometimes she slipped, her body colliding with the cold, unforgiving tiles. The shock of those moments rooted me in place—panic paralyzing my thoughts. Was she bleeding? Was her spine injured further? Would we even get an ambulance if it came to that?

Each fall felt like the culmination of every helpless moment piled into one. The sound reverberated long after the impact—the thud of flesh against tile, the gasps of fear that followed. I'd crouch at her side, trying to lift her, trying to hold her together as her disoriented eyes searched for something real to anchor her. But the truth was, there was no anchor for any of us. The pandemic may have been the backdrop—a storm battering the collective psyche of the world—but inside our home, it had created its own battlefield. Priya's illness wasn't just hers anymore; it was ours—an invisible enemy we were all fighting together. And if I was being honest with myself, there were moments I thought we might lose. Moments when I nearly gave up. Moments when the weight felt unbearable, like I was drowning in a flood that would carry away everything I valued. But even then, I refused to let go entirely. For Priya. For Ananya. For Siya. For every fragile thread that still connected us as a family. Hope may have flickered weakly, but it burned all the same. I had to rise—because giving up was never an option. The crash echoed like a crack of thunder in a world already drenched in chaos. It came from the bathroom—a sound so loud, so final, that for a split second, my mind refused to register what it meant. But instinctively, Siya and I froze at the same moment before lunging forward in unison. The world became a blur as we stumbled toward the source of the sound, dread clawing at my chest, my vision tunnelled, my breathing shallow. When we threw the door open, the scene that greeted us was pure devastation. Priya was splayed across the cold tiled floor, her frail body curled unnaturally, her eyes wide with bewilderment and pain. A fresh bruise bloomed dark and fast on her temple, its edges already a mosaic of purple and blue. A thin, glistening trickle of blood threaded its way from a split in her lip, weaving down toward her chin before disappearing into the folds of her dishevelled nightgown. "Mummy!" Siya cried out, her voice cutting through me like a jagged shard of glass. She flung herself to Priya's side, her small arms trembling as she tried in vain to lift her mother. Her sobs were raw and unrestrained, a desperate, unfiltered plea for the universe to stop its cruelty. My heart pounded, an erratic, frantic rhythm against the walls of my chest as I stood frozen for a moment too long. Another fall. Another injury. Another reminder of just how fragile she had become. My mind raced with spiralling questions, each darker than the last. Is this ever going to end? Is this all there is now—just managing each new catastrophe as it comes? Is this my life, watching helplessly as she deteriorates in front of me? Every fall brought with it the same cycle of terror, guilt, and helplessness, but that didn't make it any easier to stomach. If anything, it felt worse each time because I had already braced myself for the inevitable, yet I still failed to protect her. I had grown to despise the sterile indifference of the healthcare system. The orthopaedic specialists we consulted—whether squeezed into a brief in-person appointment or reduced to pixelated faces on a video call—often seemed clueless about the full scope of Priya's condition. They zeroed in on her back pain issue, as though it existed in a vacuum, casually disregarding the web of interrelated complications: the psychosis, the disorientation exacerbated by her medications, the mounting side effects. It was as if they were dissecting her body into isolated problems, each confined to different parts of an unconnected puzzle. But Priya wasn't a puzzle; she was a person—a fragile, broken, complicated person whose physical and mental ailments fed into one another in ways no one seemed willing or able to consider holistically. I tried to explain it, to plead for them to see what I saw—how her spinal injury, her paranoid delusions, and the medications' effects had transformed even basic mobility into a minefield. But my words seemed to slide off them, like raindrops on smooth glass. The pandemic only magnified the inadequacies of the system. What was once a robust pillar of modern life, a safety net we took for granted, had turned into a fragmented maze of uncertainty. Routine appointments were cancelled. Essential consultations were downgraded to telemedicine, where doctors tried their best to hold focus through video calls but missed the subtle cues that in-person care might reveal. I began to feel like I was captaining a ship without a rudder, navigating through a storm where every turn threatened to capsize us all. And then there was me—the supposed anchor of the family—feeling more rudderless than ever. As I sat that evening, holding Priya's hand while she stared at nothing in particular, the dark corners of my mind began stirring again. They were opportunistic, these thoughts—emerging when the exhaustion and helplessness squeezed my chest too tightly. There's no hope. We're losing her. I'm losing her. And there's nothing I can do. The whispers grew louder, sharper, their cruel logic sinking its hooks into me. I'm useless. All I've done is fail her. Fail them all. I'm not a good husband. I'm not a good father. I'm no longer even a reliable caregiver. Maybe… maybe it would be better if I just disappeared. The thought wasn't entirely new. It had crept in before, a slow, insidious whisper in the dead of night. But now it flashed vividly in my mind's eye like a gash of lightning—its dark promise cold, sharp, and tempting. An escape. A release. If I were gone, there would be no more expectations, no more disappointments, no more failures to shoulder. I closed my eyes tightly, desperate to block out the relentless cacophony of despair.

But escape didn't come—not in the way I wanted. Instead, images of Siya's tear-streaked face, Ananya's taut features, and Priya's vacant eyes played behind my eyelids, swirling pieces of my broken world that refused to fade. Their pain was inescapable—its weight bound to me irrevocably, a chain forged by the love that still tethered us together. I inhaled deeply, the edge of the abyss so close I could almost feel its icy emptiness tugging at me. The darkness offered release, yes, but it also promised oblivion. And as much as I longed for reprieve, I couldn't bear the thought of leaving them behind to weather this storm—our storm—alone. So I opened my eyes, pushed the abyss back one more time, and dug into the last reserves of strength I barely realized I had. Not today. Not yet. Rohan's phone vibrated sharply, jolting him out of the haze that had settled over him. Reality pressed in like an unwelcome guest, demanding his attention as the corporate world beckoned once again—a shimmering mirage of normalcy that felt more disconnected from his life than ever before. The office, now reserved only for senior management, loomed like a ghost town, its empty cubicles silent witnesses to the upheavals of a shattered world. As he stepped inside, the air was heavy with echoes of what once was—a buzzing hive of collaboration now reduced to eerie stillness. What am I even doing here? he wondered, his thoughts tracing their way to the chaos waiting for him at home. Instead of focusing on graphs and spreadsheets, his mind was tethered to Priya—to her haunted eyes, her fragile movements, and the shadow of despair gripping their family. Each meeting blurred into the next, the monotony of corporate deadlines paling in comparison to the urgency of her condition. The office felt like a prison; every moment spent away from home was a painful sacrifice. Finally, the meeting ended, and Rohan bolted out of the conference room. He felt the intensity of his own unease spike until it propelled him toward action. Psychiatrists, he thought desperately. He had to find someone—anyone—who could help Priya. Hours slipped by as he combed through online platforms, his fingers racing over his phone screen, his pulse quickening. His search was relentless, frantic, his hope a precarious flicker in the dark. Finally, after what felt like an eternity, he found one. A reputable psychiatrist willing to do a video consultation—hope, fragile and fleeting, but enough to cling to. Settling on the couch for the appointment, Rohan felt the weight of the oppressive silence that enveloped him. His thoughts churned like storm clouds, each question raised by the doctor a piercing jab against his fragile composure. Would the psychiatrist understand? Would there finally be answers? His heart pounded violently, begging him to calm down, to breathe. But he couldn't—not until something concrete, something definitive, was revealed. And then it came: the doctor's voice, authoritative yet subdued, delivered a revelation that shattered Rohan's world. Priya's diagnosis had been wrong all along. Psychosis—not schizophrenia—was the truth. The medications she had been prescribed were not just unsuitable; they were actively harming her, warping her mind into chaos. It was as if lightning had struck him, the sharp crack of realization slicing through any lingering denial. They tortured her, he thought bitterly, his rage brewing into a storm. They poisoned her mind—slowly, painfully—a cruelty she didn't deserve. As the days passed, the ripple of change began to unfurl in their lives. Priya's medications were adjusted and, like the slow blossoming of spring after a harsh winter, small miracles began to emerge. Fifteen days later, Rohan watched in cautious awe as his wife took hesitant steps out of her cocoon. She wandered into the living room, her movements halting but deliberate, and once again engaged with the world—a tiny spark of the woman she used to be flickering to life. She watched television, her eyes showing interest instead of vacancy, and, for the first time in months, laughter—light and fleeting—escaped her lips. It felt like a resurrection. But hope remained precarious; the shadow of uncertainty hung over them like a storm waiting to break. Priya's progress was fragile, her recovery slow. And amidst this delicate transformation, the crushing pressure of work loomed over Rohan's shoulders, demanding a semblance of normalcy that simply didn't exist. Transitioning to remote work became a refuge for many, but not for Rohan. The office, tethered to him like an unwanted lifeline, demanded his presence, pulling him away from the world where he was most needed. I have to hold everything together, he thought, though the strain of it gnawed at his soul every moment of every day. Every step Priya took, every bathroom visit or attempt at independence, became an unbearable risk. And when—not if—she stumbled again, the sound of it would slash through the paper-thin armour of my composure, leaving me naked to the fear. Siya and I lived in this unending limbo, bound by hyper-vigilance. Every noise, every thud, every creak in the house shot adrenaline through my veins and tightened my chest like a vice. My eyes darted across the room constantly, scanning for hazards, hoping to intercept fate's next cruel blow before it landed. And then came the seismic rupture of September 2, 2020. But that afternoon's fall was simply more brutal—unforgiving in its clarity. She wasn't safe. She was never truly safe. Siya's cries pulled me back to the present, snapping me out of my frozen stupor. I dropped to my knees beside her, my hands shaking as I gently cradled Priya's fragile frame. Her eyes found mine, glassy and unfocused, and for a fleeting moment, an expression of bewildered recognition flickered across her face—but it was gone as quickly as it had come, replaced again by that foreign, vacant stare that had become her default state. "It's okay, Siya," I whispered, though every word felt like a lie. "It's okay. Let's get her up." But it wasn't okay. None of it was okay. The chill settled in his veins, sharp and paralysing. His muscles burned with urgency as he leapt from his chair, every step through the office halls dragging as though he were wading through mud. Not again. Don't let this be another tragedy. That night, during a video consultation, the doctor prompted Priya to try walking. Rohan held his breath as he watched her limp painfully, her right leg betraying her. The sight seared itself into his memory, clawing at his nerves. This doesn't feel okay, he thought sharply, his heart racing against the weight of his fears. September 4 brought more worrying signs as Priya began to complain about intense bloating. Every breath he took was laced with anxiety. Is this a side effect? Or something worse? A video call with the doctor yielded answers but no peace. "It's likely just a side effect," the doctor said dismissively, but Rohan's instincts screamed otherwise. Doubt twisted through him like a hurricane; should he take Priya to a hospital despite the pandemic risks? But the thought of her being put in a COVID hot zone brought its own set of horrors. No. It's too risky. What if it's worse? What if I do the wrong thing? Torn between paralysing fear and cautious hope, Rohan consulted his brother-in-law and mother-in-law, striving for shared wisdom while carrying the weight of indecision. September 5 was supposed to be ordinary—or as ordinary as life could be in their turbulent world. The morning sunlight filtered through the blinds, casting delicate lines across the living room, offering a fleeting illusion of peace. But it shattered abruptly when Rohan found Priya gasping for breath. Her face—blue, ghastly, drained of its warmth—was an image that seared itself into his heart with brutal permanence. "Hell no!" he cried, bolting forward. His hands trembled as he scrambled for the blood pressure monitor. Numbers flashed on the screen like cruel mockery: BP plummeted to 60/40. Heart rate dropped to 52. SpO2 plunged dangerously—78. The world seemed to tilt as desperation overtook him. Every breath he took was weighted with despair, every memory of the woman he loved replaced by this harrowing new reality. When his frantic calls for an ambulance yielded silence, despair escalated into fury. Each unanswered ring felt like a slap, each delay a betrayal. Hours stretched torturously before a private operator agreed to send help, promising a 15-minute arrival that dragged into 75 excruciating minutes. Rohan paced furiously, sweat pouring as he clutched Priya's hand, whispering prayers that felt hollow against the chaos. His mind raced—Why had it come to this? Would they survive this? Would hope hold, or would it crumble under the weight of their anguish? Through the storm pounding at his soul, through the flashes of pain and doubt, Rohan realized one immutable truth: he would not give up. He couldn't afford to. The light Priya brought into their lives had faltered but hadn't gone out—not yet. And he would fight, tooth and nail, through every ounce of pain and chaos to protect it. Hope is all we have left—and I'll save it. I have to.

CHAPTER 11

SILENT SCREAMS, UNSEEN BATTLES

The sterile chaos of the emergency ward swallowed Rohan whole as the stretcher bearing his beloved Priya was pushed through double doors that swung open with an ominous thud. The sound echoed like the tolling of a bell, each clang reverberating in the cavernous space, amplifying his anxiety. The mechanical hum of fluorescent lights and the sterile scent of disinfectant created an environment devoid of warmth, where the walls seemed to close in on him, suffocating him with their cold indifference. "Has a COVID test been done in the last 24 hours?" questioned a junior doctor, her tone as clinical as her demeanour, slicing through Rohan's panicky haze. Her clipped words lacked empathy, coming across as yet another bureaucratic hurdle rather than a genuine inquiry into Priya's condition. Rohan's heart threatened to pound its way out of his chest. Was there time for a COVID test now? The world was spinning too fast for him to catch his bearings, and this question felt absurd against the weight of the crisis he was facing. "No..." he breathed, his voice barely audible—less a definitive answer and more an admission of helplessness. His eyes followed the stretcher as aides hurriedly wheeled Priya toward a designated area. Her figure, nearly lifeless beneath stiff hospital sheets, was now nothing more than an echo of the vibrant, loving woman he knew. He pointed toward the corner reflexively, his hands trembling as the hospital staff moved with the professionalism of someone who had done this far too many times, yet without the urgency he deemed necessary. The waiting area seemed like a cruel purgatory, where time itself mocked those who sat suspended in desperation. Minutes dragged into hours—one, two, three. The room grew colder with each passing moment, despite the harsh glare of buzzing fluorescent lights that drenched every surface in a soulless glow. Around him, others shared the same silent torment, faces strained and etched with their own private burdens. It felt like an abyss of collective anxiety, raw and suffocating. Frustration boiled within Rohan, scalding his throat like molten steel, until he could bear it no more. Reckless and desperate, he surged toward the ward, brushing past a security guard whose attempt to contain his fury was futile at best. He hardly acknowledged the guard's protests. Fear had obliterated any semblance of decorum; his desperation now blurred the lines between logic and lunacy. Nothing mattered except reaching Priya. When Rohan finally entered the ward, a sharp intake of breath clawed at his chest as he glimpsed Priya's frail figure sprawled on the hospital bed. The sterile sheets seemed to engulf her, diminishing her presence into something unrecognisable. Her stillness was like a physical blow, a hollowing reality of how fragile she had become. The bright, sterile light illuminated every strand of her dishevelled hair, every line of her pallid face, and magnified her absence of vitality. "What the hell is taking so long?" Rohan erupted, his voice cracking as his frantic gaze darted around the room, searching for answers—or, at the very least, someone to acknowledge his pain. His wild eyes carried the desperation of a man teetering on the edge, clutching at hope as if it were slipping away grain by grain. "Mr Srivastava, we are prioritising COVID cases," a young resident doctor, Dr Anya, finally responded. Her words were flat, mechanical, worn down by the weight of countless sleepless nights. Her exhaustion hung heavily on her features—the dark crescents under her eyes betraying the toll these days had taken on her. She refused to meet Rohan's frantic gaze, as though shielding herself from the chaos radiating from his panic. "The ICUs are full. The operating theatres are being sanitised. This is systemic, not personal." "Not personal?" The phrase nearly knocked Rohan to his knees.

The clinical detachment of her statement felt like a slap across his face. How could it not be personal? This was Priya—his Priya—his anchor in a world that now felt untethered. Without thinking, he grabbed the doctor's arm, his grip trembling but resolute. "Doctor, my wife is losing sensation! Do you understand? Every hour counts! Every second!" His voice cracked with the desperate urgency of a man clinging to the edge of collapse, his imploring eyes locking onto hers and refusing to relent. Dr Sharma hesitated, seemingly weighed down by the gravity of his pleading words. But before she could respond, a commanding presence entered the room—a man whose greying hair and solemn expression marked him as someone who had weathered many such storms. Dr Ravi Sharma, the senior doctor, addressed Rohan with the calm authority of someone tempered by years in the crucible of medical emergencies. "I understand your emotions, Mr Srivastava," Dr Sharma said, his voice a measured rumble, both reassuring and firm. He gestured for the junior staff lingering at the edges of the room to disperse, as though this interaction required undivided focus. "You might have been a bit late, but you're in the right place now. We will do everything humanly possible for her. Just trust us and give us space." Rohan, still tethered between a suffocating dread and a fragile sliver of hope, latched onto the doctor's words like a drowning man clutching a piece of driftwood. Yet the anxiety gripping his heart refused to entirely abate. "It seems to be a case of spine injury," Dr Sharma continued, his tone tinged with restrained urgency rather than unhelpful optimism. "We can't confirm until the MRI is done. I've alerted Dr Sarkar, our senior neurologist. He's already preparing for emergency surgery if necessary. For now, please wait outside." The last phrase—"please wait"—was a cruel juxtaposition to the severity of Priya's condition. Wait? How could Rohan wait when minutes felt like hours, each one swelling with uncertainty and dragging him closer to the edge? The thunderous silence of the waiting room beckoned him back, its oppressive weight palpable as time coiled around him like a predator ready to strike. Yet he obeyed, knowing that for all his desperation, he could do nothing but cling to fleeting hope. Somewhere deep within Rohan, hope stirred—fragile yet tenacious, like the flicker of a candlelight in the midst of a tempest. Its glow was faint, but it persisted, promising that amidst the chaos, there was still a chance for salvation. For Priya. For their life together. For something unbroken in their world fractured by despair.

It was around 5 PM when Rohan's phone buzzed, a sharp, jarring sound slicing through the oppressive silence that had gripped him all afternoon. The screen flashed with Ananya's name; her voice rang across the line even before he could gather himself enough to answer properly. Siya must have texted her earlier, around 1 PM, letting her know about their hurried departure to the hospital—Ananya was only now catching up after waking from her late-night sleep. "Hi, Dad. How's Mom?" Rohan's throat constricted as if someone had gripped it with iron fingers. His mind swirled, pulling him back to the bleak hospital room and the harrowing uncertainty that hung over them like storm clouds. The sterile environment offered no solace—only dread, magnified with each passing second. He struggled to find words, his voice cracking and fragile as he finally managed to reply. "The doctors… they said… her spine…" The words broke apart into jagged fragments, unwilling to be formed, their weight too heavy to carry. His silence conveyed more than any words could, a cruel testament to the situation they faced. By 9 PM, the hours of waiting had churned his insides into molten anxiety. Yet it was a moment of mixed relief and terror when Dr Anirudh appeared suddenly at the edge of the hall, his silhouette emerging from the shadows of the consulting room. His presence seemed to rearrange the air in the hallway—everything slowed as Rohan followed him into a cramped side room. There, the MRI films lay spread out like a grim mosaic of brokenness. Rohan's eyes darted nervously over the images, but his stomach dropped as Dr Anirudh broke the devastating news. "Your wife has suffered a severe spinal cord injury," he said, his voice steady and clinical, but cold as death itself. "She needs surgery." The words slammed into Rohan like a physical force, the impact leaving him gasping for air. His knees threatened to buckle as the images burned into his consciousness. Spinal cord injury. Emergency surgery. These four words loomed like insurmountable walls, caging him in. Priya—the luminous woman who painted his world with laughter and love—was now teetering on the edge of existence. The prestige of their chosen hospital meant nothing now. The marble floors shimmered under fluorescent lights that gave off no warmth, and the luxurious reception area was rendered a cruel façade in the face of Rohan's escalating desperation. The antiseptic-laden air felt suffocating, heavy with the spectre of a pandemic that seemed to lurk relentlessly outside. Inside these walls, chaos reigned, poorly disguised as order. Nurses darted across hallways, their footsteps echoing hurriedly against the cold floors. Doctors exchanged clipped conversations in rushed tones while navigating crises of their own. Yet through it all, Rohan could barely breathe; he felt trapped in the cacophony, powerless against the maelstrom surrounding him. His head screamed for answers, for action—anything to pull Priya back from the brink. Rohan couldn't hold back as the tension in the room snapped within him. "When are you going to operate?" he demanded, his voice ragged with fury and desperation as he stared at Dr Anirudh. "You can't leave her like this! She's losing sensation—she's going to be paralysed if you wait any longer!" Dr Anirudh regarded him with an eerie calm that felt like mockery in the face of Rohan's spiralling panic. "At the earliest, we could schedule the surgery for tomorrow," he replied, his tone maddeningly detached. "But because it's the weekend, there's a 50% surcharge for Sunday operations. If you can wait until Monday, the process will be less expensive. "What are you saying?" Rohan growled, his voice raw as he cut him off. "Less expensive? My wife is barely hanging on, and you're talking about money? Dr Sharma said Dr Sarkar was alerted for an emergency operation—why hasn't it happened yet?" Dr

Anirudh's expression shifted, hardening into an impenetrable wall of bureaucratic reasoning. "We need to wait on her COVID report, Mr Srivastava," he responded firmly. "It's protocol. We also have to stabilise her vitals first. These precautions are essential to ensure she survives the surgery." Precautions. The word rang out harshly, twisting the pit inside Rohan's stomach into tighter knots. How could they talk of precautions when every second seemed to drag Priya closer to the precipice? Time was no longer a luxury—it was the cruel enemy, slipping away while protocols and systems shackled them. Rohan's pleas remained unanswered, swallowed whole by the immovable weight of regulations imposed by a healthcare system suffocating under endless strain. Grasping for solutions, Rohan frantically dialled every contact he could muster until his fingers landed on the number of Mr Khanna, a senior hospital administrator he had once forged a professional relationship with. Perhaps now that connection could save her. When Mr Khanna's voice finally met his ears, it was calm and apologetic, softened by the kind of measured sympathy that felt rehearsed, hollow. "I'm deeply sorry to hear about Priya," Mr Khanna began, his voice polite but unwavering. "I understand how difficult this must be for you. But I assure you, Mr Srivastava, we cannot bypass protocols—especially during emergencies like these. Stabilisation of vital organs must take precedence. It's not the dramatised version you see in films; every step here is deliberate and necessary." The line went dead before Rohan could argue further, leaving a cavernous void in the wake of Khanna's polished dismissal. The brutal reality sank in deeper: systems built to save lives were now strangling his hopes at every turn. The world felt colder, harder, crueller. Sliding down against the hospital wall, Rohan rested his head in his hands, the weight of the moment pressing heavily against his being. The smooth marble beneath him felt colder than ice. His fight to save Priya remained at the mercy of an overwhelmed hospital and an indifferent set of protocols that showed no sign of faltering. An anguished scream swelled within him, threatening to break through—but it stayed trapped, suffocated by the enormity of what lay before him. Hope teetered on the brink, a fragile ember flickering weakly against the relentless tide of despair that sought to snuff it out entirely. Hours stretched like tantalising strands of anguish, each tick of the clock carving deeper into Rohan's sleepless haze. Priya had been shifted to the ICU, her body preparing—or perhaps bracing—for the surgical procedure that now hung like an impending tempest. The agony of her injury pierced the sterile silence of the hospital ward. Through tears and trembling sobs, Priya eventually succumbed to exhaustion and drifted into an uneasy sleep, her pain lingering in the air like an unbearable presence.

September 6,2020: Rohan sat vigil outside the ICU, tethered by the tenuous promise of being available "should he be required," as the junior doctor advised. The icy, fluorescent-lit corridor blurred the boundary between day and night; it was now 1 AM, and he found himself slumped into one of the cold steel chairs. The middle chair in the row was marked "X" with black paint—a stark reminder of social distancing in the era of invisible contagions that still loomed. The ICU's atmosphere felt like the eye of a storm, deceptively quiet yet brimming with unspoken urgency.

Morning, 8 AM: The sharp voice of a staff nurse sliced through his thoughts: "Mr Rohan Srivastava?" He lurched to his feet, his heart a drumbeat of anxiety. "Yes," he answered quickly, the knot in his stomach tightening as he followed her through a set of swinging doors and into the ICU room where Priya lay. Her frailty was magnified under the harsh light, the hospital bed swallowing her petite frame whole beneath its layers of sheets and wires. Inside, the mood shifted. A ripple of hushed activity signalled the arrival of Dr Mehra, a senior and renowned cardiologist whose reputation preceded him. The air bristled with attentiveness as nurses whispered to one another, darting around with practised efficiency. Dr Mehra's commanding presence filled the room as he walked in, flipping meticulously through the file, pausing to absorb each detail. His demeanour was calm, but his eyes missed nothing. Finally, he spoke, his voice steady but brisk. "Don't worry, Mr Srivastava. We've received her pathological reports, and they're all WNL—within normal range. Her blood sugar is slightly elevated—it's not unusual given the circumstances—but it's manageable and should stabilise. I'll personally oversee her 2-D Echo shortly and advise Dr Sarkar appropriately after that." "Suitably? What does that mean?" Rohan's voice cracked under the strain, frustration creeping in like an unwelcome guest. "Are you saying there's still a chance of delay or postponement if her 2-D Echo shows something unexpected?" Dr Mehra didn't flinch. His words were measured, unyielding. "We follow protocol, Mr Srivastava. Trust the process." The explanation offered no comfort; instead, it exposed the layers of bureaucracy that governed every step of medical intervention, peeling away Rohan's illusions like skin from bone. Rohan muttered to himself as he returned to the steel chair in the hallway, "Now I understand why Mr Khanna said it's not like what you see in films. It's a system where each vital organ needs clearance from its respective expert; only then can the surgeon proceed. And even then, the anaesthetist supervises everything." As his thoughts tumbled into spirals, shards of the previous night's conversations assaulted him. Dr Sinha, the anaesthetist, had explained the risks, the bleak disclaimers, and the labyrinth of legal waivers that absolved the doctors and hospital of responsibility for any adverse outcomes. Rohan had already signed it all, his trembling hands committing to declarations he couldn't dare to question. A deposit of ten lakh rupees had been made, but the weight of money meant little against the enormity of the situation. What stung like an open wound was the stark reality laid bare: the fragile line between compassion and compliance, between human connection and institutional detachment.

Morning, 11 AM: Another voice called out, this time from the OT staff in their crisp blue uniforms. "Mr. Rohan Srivastava?" He stepped forward, his fatigue momentarily eclipsed by the sharp stab of adrenaline. He was escorted through a labyrinth of halls leading to the procedure rooms. Past swinging doors and antiseptic-smelling corridors, he was directed into a consultation space where Dr Sarkar, the neurosurgeon, awaited him. "Good morning, Mr Srivastava," Dr Sarkar greeted curtly before diving straight into business. "We're ready to move forward with the operation. It's going to be a long, complex procedure, possibly spanning six to eight hours. Please make yourself comfortable in the waiting area outside. I'd recommend staying hydrated, and if you believe in God, the prayer room is just down the hallway. Pray if it brings you solace—we'll do our best." Rohan raised the question that clawed at his insides. "Doctor, what are her chances of recovery?" Dr Sarkar paused, his voice solemn but without sugarcoating. "Her spinal nerves are severely damaged. The fracture appears to have occurred three days ago, and prolonged stress on the nerves has complicated matters. I won't give you false hope—I believe her chances are fair, but the golden hours are behind us." Rising from his chair, Dr Sarkar placed his palm on the case file before exiting toward the OT room to prepare for the procedure. Rohan felt a cavern open in his chest, swallowing any resolve he'd clung to. Desperate for strength, he carried himself to the prayer room at the end of the hallway—the doctor's words echoing in his mind. The quiet space smelled faintly of incense, a stark contrast to the sanitised sterility just outside its threshold. Sliding onto the floor, he clasped his hands and began chanting the *Hanuman Chalisa* under his breath, his voice cracked and uneven. Something about the familiar rhythm stabilised him, if only for the briefest moment. When he re-entered the waiting room, he found himself surrounded by other weary relatives. There, amidst the shared suffering, he realised he wasn't alone in his plight. Their whispered words of comfort and exchanged glances spoke volumes—a language crafted from shared grief and quiet resilience. But even as he sat among them, Rohan's mind remained tethered to the operating theatre where Priya's fate hung precariously in balance. Faith momentarily dulled the thorns of his despair, but hope continued its precarious dance on the edge of ruin. The news came like a thunderclap: after hours of agonising uncertainty, Dr Sarkar summoned Rohan to inform him that the operation had been successful. Relief washed over him, an electric wave cutting through the haze of exhaustion that had wrapped itself tightly around him. "She'll remain under the watch of the anaesthetist and ICU staff for a few more hours to monitor her condition," the neurosurgeon explained with a measured tone, his words offering an anchor in the storm. "Once she's stable, we'll shift her." Rohan thanked Dr Sarkar profusely, the gratitude pouring out of him like floodwaters breaking a dam. Still, this victory—the successful surgery—was a fragile lifeline. Priya's recovery was far from assured, and the days ahead stretched out before Rohan like treacherous terrain, marked by uncertainty and relentless vigilance. When Priya was finally shifted back to the ICU, the room became their shared purgatory—a space suspended between hope and despair. Time dissolved into an endless abyss, where each day bled into the next with no beginning or end, marked only by the fluctuations in Priya's condition and the steady rhythm of the monitors that ruled her existence. For Rohan, life outside the hospital had all but ceased to exist. The routines of home—once mundane, now precious—had been abandoned entirely. His once-proud spirit deteriorated, replaced by frayed nerves and sleepless nights in the cramped dormitory opposite the ICU. Siya, left to fend for herself, spiralled into her own brand of chaos. Subsisting on lukewarm Maggi and leftovers, she barely managed to keep it together. The meals Rohan had once prepared with love were now distant memories, replaced by the clumsy, scattered echoes of a life interrupted. His thoughts turned to her often, gnawed by the relentless worry that he was abandoning her to loneliness and despair. But every worry chased itself in a circular storm inside his head, eclipsed by his need to stay as close to Priya as possible. Could he leave her alone in this precarious limbo? What if Priya's condition worsened in his absence? The gnawing questions twisted tighter in his chest with each passing hour.

CHAPTER 12

EVERY LIFE MATTERS

Days turned into weeks, and Rohan began to resemble his own shadow. His once neatly shaven face and meticulously styled black hair had given way to a greying beard and salt-and-pepper disarray. He noticed the worn figure staring back at him in the mirror of the shared, dingy bathroom. The physical toll of sleepless nights compounded with mental exhaustion, but the spectre of COVID lingered in the background. Every time he used that common space, the thought flickered—*What if I fall sick?* And worse, *What happens to Priya?* Even when Priya needed blood—14 units during her first two harrowing years of frequent hospitalisations—it wasn't family that came to donate. It was his loyal staff, dependable not by obligation but by a bond forged through his years of respect and care for them. Rohan subsisted on morning rounds of Batata Wada (potato dumplings) and an evening samosa, a meagre diet that barely sustained him. The only interactions he had outside of his routine were the brief discussions with doctors, each update layered with complex medical jargon that added new wrinkles to his forehead and attending some urgent online office meetings from the waiting room of the ICU ward.

Eleven days into this grim ordeal, a pressing urgency compelled Rohan to leave the hospital temporarily. Siya's voice over their fractured phone conversations had sounded hollow, distant. He was wracked with guilt as he walked through the door of their flat, stepping into a home frozen in a tableau of neglect. Utensils lay stacked on the counter, bearing the stench of forgotten meals, and Siya—his bright, independent daughter—was now a shadow of herself. "I'm okay, Dad," she lied with a shaky voice, her hollow cheeks evidence to the contrary. Rohan's heart ached, his paternal instincts warring with the emotional drain that had left him a shell of his former self. Unable to press her further, he sank into the worn couch, its cushions bearing the weight of his exhaustion. The moment sleep claimed him, it was stolen by the golden hues of dawn creeping through the windows. When he shot upright, panic surged. *How long had I slept?* The thought of leaving Priya alone in the ICU gnawed at him like a wild animal. As he thundered toward the door in haste, his gaze snagged on the remnants of a scarlet streak across the carpet—a smear of blood as haunting as a scream. It was a stark metaphor for his anguish, a reminder of the quiet desolation that had overtaken his world. Yet he had no answers for what it meant, just as there were no guarantees about Priya's fate—a battle fought behind closed doors, gripped in destiny's cruel hand. By the time Priya's condition stabilised and she was shifted to a private ward, fifteen days had blurred into an eternity. The sterile room was far from home, but it offered some solace. The large window framed a magnificent view of the Arabian Sea—a constant, rhythmic motion against a backdrop of uncertainty. The tides ebbed and flowed in languid rhythm, mirroring the turmoil within Rohan's battered soul. He spent hours standing by the window, eyes trained on the sunset as fiery hues painted the waves in amber and azure, a bittersweet reminder of better days. The sea became his silent confidant. Its relentless rise and fall whispered truths he didn't dare voice aloud: *Even amidst chaos, something endures.* Yet hope, he realised, was fickle—fragile as glass. The same sea that offered pearls could just as easily swallow them in its depths, leaving only jagged rocks behind. For Rohan, those jagged rocks were sharp reminders of the precariousness of the life he was fighting desperately to sustain. When Priya slept—as she often did, her laboured breaths stirring faintly in the stillness—Rohan found fleeting refuge in the sunset. It transported him, if only momentarily, to a time untouched by fragility and fear. But tranquillity, as always, was fleeting—a visitor that never lingered. The fiery hues of the horizon melted away, leaving him tethered again to the sterile present, the weight of Priya's fragility anchoring him in the stillness of her recovery. Hope danced like a flame in the wind, flickering but never quite extinguished, its delicate light his only compass in a storm that seemed unending. A week into their supposed sanctuary, Rohan found himself grappling with the fragility of hope. The oppressive air of the hospital began to shift, thickening with a sense of foreboding that made his stomach churn. He sat beside Priya, her pale face illuminated by the cold, clinical light of the ward. Her breathing was shallow, her body trembling as if it were caught in some unseen storm. And then, in the blink of an eye, it happened: her condition plunged into critical territory, an avalanche of chaos disrupting the fragile silence. The shrill tone of the public announcement system cut through the air like a blade. *"Code Blue, Room 15013."* The automated voice echoed down the stark hospital corridors, transforming an ordinary afternoon into a battle for life. The sudden urgency pierced through the humdrum veneer of hospital routine, igniting a coordinated frenzy of movement. Nurses, healthcare assistants, and doctors—regardless of their specialties—all abandoned their tasks, sprinting toward Room 15013 as per the hospital's Standard Operating Procedures. Priya's life was on the line, and the institution's motto—"Every Life Matters"—now stood as both a promise and a test. Among the rush was Priyanka, the daytime nurse assigned to Priya for the past three days. A cheery and talkative professional from Patna, she had become a familiar, reassuring presence in their ordeal. But as she ran at full speed toward Priya's room, her shoes slid across the polished tile floor. Stumbling, she fell hard, twisting her wrist and bruising her knee. Another healthcare assistant, a young man with remarkable composure, immediately took up the stretcher duty she'd intended to fulfil. Within moments, Priya had been transferred onto the stretcher, and instructions were shouted through hastily tapped radios. Elevators were waiting. The ICU team had been alerted. Two minutes was all it took for Priya to be shifted from the ward to the ICU—120 seconds that felt simultaneously immediate and eternal. Dr Reddy, the Critical Care Unit In-Charge, was already at the designated ICU station, his presence like the steady keel of a ship in stormy waters. By the time Priya was wheeled into place, every detail had been orchestrated with military precision. "This is the other face of the hospital," Rohan thought, his mind briefly alighting on the overwhelming dedication playing out before his eyes. "This is why their tagline says, 'Every Life Matters.'" An hour later, once the chaos had subsided, Dr Reddy emerged from the area beyond the glass doors of the ICU. His brows were furrowed, his expression grim. With practised calm, he approached Rohan, each step carrying the weight of news that no one ever truly wants to deliver. "Mr Srivastava," he began, his voice steady yet touched with an undeniable gravity, "your wife has stabilised for now, but I need to be candid with you. Her condition has taken a severe turn. She's extremely critical." Rohan's stomach clenched; the air around him seemed to thin. Each word felt like a hammer blow, striking at his very core. Dr Reddy paused briefly before continuing, "We're currently battling a severe infection that has escalated into septicaemia. This is a life-threatening condition. We are doing everything in our power to fight it, but I must be honest—it is a tough battle." "Septicaemia..." The word echoed in Rohan's mind, heavy and foreign, dripping with menace. His knees felt weak as he struggled to digest the reality being laid before him. Dr Reddy, recognising the anguish his words were causing, pressed a compassionate hand on Rohan's shoulder. "You may want to inform her loved ones. If anyone wishes to see her, now would be a good time," he said, his tone laced with the sincerity of someone who had walked this delicate line between hope and despair many times before. "I'm deeply sorry." Rohan blinked rapidly, his vision clouding with unshed tears as he tried to grasp the enormity of the moment. His lips quivered, but he forced himself to speak, his voice barely audible. "Dr Reddy... she's a fighter. She will pull through. I know it. I trust in God." The doctor gave him a small nod, his eyes a mix of respect and concern, before walking away to continue the fight on Priya's behalf. Meanwhile, Rohan turned to face the waiting room, his legs like lead and his heart like glass, cracking with each passing second. The hours that followed required a resolve Rohan didn't know he possessed. He made the calls, each conversation a painful exercise in managing both his grief and the hope he was trying to conjure against all odds. His elder sister Asha, Priya's mother, and her brother were all notified, their reactions ranging from quiet shock to tearful disbelief. With a trembling voice, he said to each of them, "We need to gather. She's fighting for her life—*but she's still fighting.*" But the hardest conversation was the one he had to have with his daughters. Kneeling before them, their small, innocent faces searching his for answers, he grappled with the weight of balancing truth and hope. "Your mother is very, very sick," he said softly, his voice cracking despite his best efforts to stay strong. "But she's strong, and the doctors are doing everything to help her. And remember... God is with us." Their tears pooled as they nodded, clinging to his words as tightly as they clung to the hem of his shirt. Rohan held them close, his heart breaking as he whispered silent prayers into the void. In the fifteen long days that followed, Priya's battle against the infection became a relentless war, her body oscillating between near collapse and fragments of recovery. Each sunrise felt like an eternity, every glimmer of progress fleeting. Yet against the tidal waves of despair, Priya emerged. Through unmatched grit, skilled medical intervention, and perhaps the divine mercy Rohan had begged for, she clawed her way back toward life. When she was finally removed from the ICU, placed once again in the gentler confines of a private ward, the rays of the setting sun spilled through the window as if to welcome her. The ocean's waves outside glistened with touches of gold and silver, their rhythm no longer merely background noise but a hymn of resilience. Rohan stood at the window, watching the sun dip into the sea. For the first time in weeks, the colours filling the sky didn't ache with desolation. They were a portrait of hope. He exhaled deeply, his breath carrying with it the weight of lessons learned in fire. “She survived,” he whispered to himself, staring at the vast, unending expanse of the horizon. Yet even as relief coursed through him, he knew in his heart that this was about more than survival. It was a transformation. Gratitude coursed through him, not just for her life but for the clarity her ordeal had delivered. “What are you teaching me, God?” he murmured, his thoughts carried out over the waves. “If you’ve given us this second chance, it must be for something greater. Show me the way.” The tides lapped softly against the shore, their harmony a match for the newfound rhythm in his heart. He turned to look at Priya as she slept, her fragile frame softened by the golden light. She was his world, and her fight had become his. Their family had been bent but not broken. Now, with unshakable resolve, Rohan vowed to let this ordeal shape him into a stronger, better man. The storms, he realised, didn’t come only to destroy; sometimes, they came to rebuild.

CHAPTER 13

HOPE BECKONS

After sixty-five gruelling days, Priya was discharged from the hospital—her frail frame a testament to the war her body had fought. As she was wheeled toward the exit, her eyes caught the sunlight streaming through the glass doors for the first time in months. It was as though nature itself welcomed her back to life, wrapping her in its brilliance, whispering, *You made it.* But the journey was far from over; in truth, it had only just begun. The discharge papers came stapled with caveats and protocols that evoked both relief and dread. Instructions to return for review in two weeks. A direct line to the Emergency Unit should her condition take a sudden turn. The sterile threads of hospital life still bound her fragile existence, even as she crossed the threshold into the outside world. Her case was officially referred to Rehabilitation and Palliative Care under Dr Savita Shah, marking a shift from the critical care of Neurology overseen by Dr Sarkar. Clinical victory had evolved into a delicate battle of recovery, with hope balanced perilously against the spectres of relapse. Dr Savita Shah, a stalwart figure in the Rehabilitation Unit, took Priya's case as if it were personal. Tall with eyes that radiated both warmth and unyielding determination, she became the embodiment of care in its purest form. "We're not just healing a body here," she had said during their first session, her voice steady yet empathetic. "We're rebuilding a life—one step, one breath, one heartbeat at a time." Under Dr Shah's guidance, Priya underwent holistic therapy that combined cutting-edge technology with compassionate attention. There was robotic physiotherapy to help retrain her limbs, unlocking movements lost to the trauma of surgery and illness. Hyperbaric Oxygen Therapy (HBO2) became a lifeline, saturating her body with oxygen-rich vitality, accelerating repair in places conventional medicine could not reach. Every session was rigorous, taxing, yet delivered with an unwavering sense of purpose by a doctor who refused mediocrity in the face of Priya's extraordinary fight. But life had turned into a relentless pendulum swing between moments of progress and haunting regressions. The hospital became a recurring chapter in their lives, every quarter bringing a new admission. Some were routine reviews—a clinical tick on the calendar—but others were harrowing emergencies: infections from recurring UTIs, bouts of fever, and medical setbacks that sent them scrambling to the Emergency Unit in the dead of night. Priya's fragile health was like glass—a crack here, a fracture there, always requiring constant vigilance to keep her intact. Through it all, Rohan fought alongside her, his resolve shaped by witnessing Priya's indomitable will. As the months stretched into a year, every hospitalisation became a stark reminder of their precarious reality. The sight of the hospital corridors—once terrifying—morphed into a bittersweet familiarity. The nurses recognised him now, their smiles tinged with both respect and pity for the man who had practically taken up residence between home and hospital for the sake of his wife's survival. Yet, for all the relentless struggles, there remained a profound transformation unfolding—a hidden grace born of hardship. Priya's recovery, though slow, carried glimmers of hope that kept them tethered to the possibilities of tomorrow. Every small victory—a successful physiotherapy session, a day without pain—became a cause for silent celebration. Every setback, though harrowing, became a test of resilience that reminded them of how far they'd come. On the evening she walked unaided for the first time, only a few steps with the help of parallel bars in the therapy room, Rohan found himself uncharacteristically speechless. Watching her tremble but persist—a single foot hesitating before taking its next brave stride—he realized he was witnessing more than just physical recovery. Priya wasn't just fighting to heal her body; she was reclaiming her existence. Reclaiming *them*. Tears pooled in his eyes, unbidden but unstoppable, as he whispered at that moment words meant more for himself and the heavens above than for anyone else: "She's unstoppable." Those sentiments became the quiet anthem of their new reality. Life wasn't the same anymore… maybe it never would be. But beneath the layers of struggle, Priya was no longer just a patient. She was a beacon of resilience, proof that every shattered life could be pieced back together—slowly, agonizingly, beautifully. Rohan understood now that survival was a war that never truly ended; it evolved, demanding new strategies, new strengths, and unrelenting faith. As Priya and Rohan stood at the threshold of their journey—not healed, but healing; not whole yet, but piecing together fragments—they weren't guided by the certainty of victory. They were guided by discovery. New objectives. New definitions of hope. And above all, a new understanding of partnership. Survival—for them—was no longer a task; it was a purpose. She may fall again. There may be more hospital trips, more nights that stretch into infinite despair. But Priya wouldn't back down. And Rohan… Rohan wouldn't let her fight alone. Together, they had learned the true lesson of the storm: survival isn't measured by the absence of hardship; it's measured by the courage to keep walking toward the light—even when the shadows linger close behind.

CHAPTER 14

THE SILENT PILLAR

Priya was always the one to notice the little things. Growing up in the dusty lanes of Orai (a small town in the Bundelkhand region of Uttar Pradesh), where the sun rose lazily over old sandstone buildings and the faint calls of kites circled the sky, she quickly developed a keen eye for unspoken emotions. It was an ability honed in her conservative household, where words often carried consequences and silence was a safer space to exist. She didn't resent her upbringing—it was, after all, a loving one—but she did find herself navigating a labyrinth of subtle expectations, quiet injustices, and unrealised dreams as a girl. As she grew, so did her self-awareness. She often marvelled at the paradox of her life: born to highly educated parents—her father a college professor and her mother a lecturer—yet bound by the traditions of a place that insisted boys were the future while girls were mere caretakers of it. Perhaps that was when she first started to internalise her limiting beliefs. While her parents never openly told her she couldn't achieve what her heart desired, they also never encouraged her to stray too far from the norm. One memory stood out vividly in Priya's mind—a winter evening when she was about 12 years old. She had just returned home from school, bubbling with excitement over an elocution competition she had won. The certificate was clutched tightly in her little hands as she ran to show it to her father. His smile was warm and genuine, yet his words, always laced with pragmatism, never left her. "This is great, Priya," he said, ruffling her hair affectionately. "When you speak so confidently, I can almost see you as a teacher someday, like your mother. It's a respectable path for a woman." A teacher. Respectable, yes. But tied so firmly to the confines of her hometown, her mother's routine, her struggles in juggling between the job and family. In her heart, Priya had wanted to be so much more—an archaeologist, an author, even a classical singer. But over time, as the realities of life unfolded, those dreams lay quietly buried under layers of duty and practicality. Years later, as she sat by the window of her Gurgaon apartment, watching the morning sunlight dance across the balcony plants, Priya reflected on how her life had shifted since her childhood days. She had married Rohan, a charismatic and ambitious man whose corporate schedule often felt like a relentless treadmill. Together, they built a life so full of outward success—big house, talented daughters, elaborate trips to Switzerland—that they appeared almost picture-perfect to the outside world. Yet there were fissures beneath the glossy surface that Priya couldn't ignore. She loved her daughters, Ananya and Siya, with all her heart, but raising them often felt like balancing on a tightrope. As she swept the floor one evening, the faint strains of Siya's guitar reached her ears—a melancholy tune that tugged at her heart. Her youngest daughter had always been like Priya in many ways: soft-spoken, introspective, and prone to retreat inward during times of struggle. But Priya couldn't let her grow up with the same insecurities. Not her Siya. "Why is it easier for fathers to inspire confidence in their children?" Priya whispered to herself as she folded Siya's clothes later that night. "Rohan walks in and says one sentence, and they believe they can conquer the world. But me? I give my entire day to them, and still... am I enough?" These moments of inner conflict were often brushed aside by Priya during the rush of daily life, but they lingered like unspoken conversations. She never told Rohan about her deeper fears—not because she didn't think he cared, but because she worried it might make her seem weak. Instead, she poured her energy into building the kind of stability she herself had longed for growing up. Still, she had her own struggles trying to manage all demands—the demands of Rohan's career and the kids she had sacrificed her own. She still remembered the first of January 2018, New Year's Day, when Rohan came home at 4 a.m. due to the December month closing, which was not an isolated incident but a pattern that had emerged over the last few years every quarter. Unable to hold it any more, she had questioned his being so late, and they had a good verbal duel. The night was wrapping up around him, the city whispering its irresistible lullaby of ambition and chaos, but for the first time in years, Rohan didn't feel its pull. He stood close to the window, his breath fogging the cool glass as he watched the sprawling metropolis stretch infinitely beneath him. Its glittering lights, once emblems of his hunger for success, now seemed like tiny fires extinguished by a deeper, more deliberate yearning. The words he had uttered—*"I will rise, but I will rise for them, I will transform myself as a professional, as a husband, as a father, as a human being"*—lingered in the cavern of his thoughts, echoing with a resolute finality that both terrified and steadied him. Priya moved silently, a quiet presence that both comforted and confronted him. He turned around to see her standing by the marble coffee table, her gaze soft but unreadable, like a precious artifact he had once cherished but forgotten how to hold. For years, she had been the grounding force that tethered him to some semblance of reality, but he had treated her like a constant—an unshakable truth—never realizing that even constants could shift, could shatter under enough strain. "Do you think they'll forgive me?" Rohan's voice cracked, his vulnerability tumbling out in an unfamiliar, fractured tone. This was uncharted territory—exposing the man behind the polished veneer, behind the accolades, the awards, the carefully curated shell of a life lived outwardly but never inwardly. Priya tilted her head slightly, her eyes searching his. For a fleeting moment, he saw a flicker of the woman he had fallen in love with—a vision of uncompromising strength layered with bottomless depth. "Forgiveness isn't what they need, Rohan," she said gently, pulling her arms across her chest, more in solace than defensiveness. "They need to know you're there. Really there. Not a promise, not an apology. Just... you." The simplicity of her words carried a weight that felt like thunder in his chest. They didn't want his success, his sacrifices, his constant justifications. They wanted him. The man Priya had married. The father, his daughters silently worshipped even as his absence stitched invisible wounds across their tender hearts. "Priya," he began, stepping forward cautiously as though approaching a fragile, half-formed truce. "I swear I'll try. I will. I didn't..." He hesitated, afraid to let the next words surface. "I didn't know how far I'd drifted. I thought providing for you, for the girls... ensuring security... that it was enough. That it meant love." Priya let out a soft, almost imperceptible laugh, but it wasn't out of spite. It was the laugh of someone who had heard the same refrain so often that it had become background noise. "We never needed marble floors or priceless paintings, Rohan. What we needed—and still need—is for you to choose us. Every day. Not as an afterthought. Not when it's convenient. But as the heartbeat of your life. That's what love looks like." He felt the truth in her words hit him like an avalanche. It wasn't new—it had always existed, waiting to be acknowledged. But recognition and action had always been distant cousins in his world, divided by years of habitual neglect disguised as noble effort. The image of Siya's quiet struggle flashed across his mind. Her longing gazes, her meek expressions of wanting him there, only to be met with hurried reassurances: "Next time, sweetheart. Daddy has a meeting today." Then, memories of Ananya, their eldest—the way her once bright-eyed admiration for him had dulled into a cautious distance he was only now beginning to recognize as heartache. How she used to tell him everything as a little girl, tugging at his sleeve with uncontainable excitement. And now? She barely spoke during dinners, a wall of polite civility shielding emotions too painful to confront. These cracks—they weren't reflections of fleeting disappointment. They were fissures, scars etched deep into the soul of the family he was supposed to protect. And as much as he feared the truth, Rohan knew one thing with harrowing clarity now: the longer he ignored it, the more permanent those cracks would become. "Will they let me in again?" he asked, voice breaking slightly as he choked on the vulnerability he had long buried beneath layers of perfection. "What if it's too late, Priya?" Her expression softened, something old and tender sparking in her eyes—a flicker of hope, perhaps, or of the love she had never quite stopped carrying for him, even through the years of emotional exile. She crossed the distance between them, her footsteps muffled on the plush carpet, until they were nearly inches apart. Gently, she reached out her hands and rested them lightly on his shoulders. "It's only too late if you stop trying," she said softly, her words barely audible but potent, like a balm to a wound long left unhealed. "Our daughters—they love you, Rohan. They want you in their lives. They just… they don't know how to show it when they think you don't care. Show them you care. Show them that they matter more than anything. Show up. Really, truly show up. That's all they've ever needed." His knees felt weak under the weight of her words, the weight of the truth he had denied himself for so long. "I will," he said, a determined edge creeping into his voice as he straightened under her touch. "I'll show up, Priya. I can't promise I'll have all the answers, but I'll try. I'll start there." "That's all we need, Rohan. A beginning." Something shifted in the room then, a fragile current that carried the promise of renewal. It wasn't a grand resolution. There were no guarantees, no sweeping declarations of redemption. But a fragile hope began to bloom between them—a hope that perhaps they could rebuild the bridge he had let fall to ruins. Not with ease. Not overnight. But piece by painstaking piece. That night, as the stars gradually overtook the weary city, Rohan allowed himself one last glance at the glittering skyline. His reflection stared back at him in the cold glass—no longer an untouchable mogul feigning control, but a man at the cusp of something terrifyingly beautiful. And for the first time in years, the towering city before him felt less like an opulent conquest and more like the fabric of a life worth holding onto. For them. For their laughter. For their love. Tomorrow would be the first of many steps. He didn't know if he'd stumble along the way, but he did know this: he wouldn't walk the path alone. And that? That made all the difference. In the golden summer of 2018, Priya organised a trip to Darjeeling. It was her idea entirely, from booking the charming hillside cottage to packing the picnic baskets she insisted would make their outings unique. She remembered the way she had convinced Rohan, who was forever tethered to his laptop even during vacations. "Just one week," she had said, holding his hand with mock sternness. "Ananya's B.Tech exams are done, Siya won't stop talking about seeing the Himalayas, and I might literally snap if I don't get some fresh air. You can take your calls from the hills." On the second day of the trip, as the family hiked through the mist-covered paths of Cloud's End, Priya's laughter rang out like wind chimes in the crisp air. It was the same laugh that Rohan had fallen in love with all those years ago. At one point, Siya accidentally smeared chocolate on her mother's kurta during a lunch break, which set off a chain of teasing and laughter so contagious that even the usually reserved Ananya joined in. "These are the moments, Rohan," Priya confided to her husband later that night, the children tucked away in their beds. Her face was aglow from the day's adventures, her voice soft but resolute. "Not promotions, not milestones, not plans—you know? Just this. All of us... together." For all her insecurities, Priya had an innate ability to make moments magical, to sew the fabric of life's routines into enchanting memories. She may not have held her Ph.D. as prominently as her peers or framed her achievements in gold-plated certificates on the walls, but she was the heartbeat of her family. The one who remembered to pack hot water bottles during winters, who knew exactly how Ananya liked her aloo parathas, who sang Siya to sleep when anxiety gnawed at her youngest. Priya's life was not just about quietly navigating her own emotions or fulfilling her obligations as a mother and wife; it was also about the lives she touched outside her immediate circle. She was the kind of person who brought warmth into people's lives without drawing attention to herself. Whether it was helping neighbours in need or becoming the unifying figure in family conflicts, Priya had a unique way of bridging gaps and softening the hard edges of life. From the outside, Priya might have seemed like someone too soft-spoken or reserved to embrace the joys of life fully. But that wasn't the case. Behind closed doors, at parties with close friends and her family, she was a woman who danced with abandon, laughed until she couldn't breathe, and enjoyed the beauty of life's fleeting moments. Once at a family wedding, Priya surprised everyone by stepping onto the dance floor during a sangeet ceremony. She swirled around in her silk saree, forgetting herself entirely, and joined a group of cousins performing a choreographed Bollywood number. Even Rohan, usually the stoic type at such gatherings, couldn't help but grin as he watched his wife's infectious joy light up the room. Siya marvelled at her mother's free spirit that evening, later confessing to Priya, "You never told us you could dance like that! You were amazing!" Priya smiled and answered, "Sometimes you have to remind yourself that joy is as important as responsibility, sweetheart. Dancing is just a small way of telling the universe I've not forgotten how to celebrate." She was someone who could balance the gravity of life with moments of levity, bestowing her infectious enthusiasm and energy wherever she went. Priya was someone everyone in the neighbourhood could count on. Whether it was offering advice on school admissions, organising potlucks for festivals, or arranging help for someone in a medical emergency, Priya was a natural problem-solver. She had a knack for finding practical solutions and creating a sense of community wherever she went. Once, when her neighbour, Mrs Bansal fell and fractured her hip, Priya stepped in without second thoughts. She arranged for a nurse to visit daily, cooked extra meals for Mrs Bansal and her husband, and even took over coordinating the paperwork for medical insurance claims. When Mrs Bansal recovered, she tearfully thanked Priya, saying, "I don't know how we would have managed without you. You are an angel!" Priya shrugged off the compliments, replying with her characteristic humility, "That's what neighbours are for. We're all in this together." One of Priya's most poignant life chapters came with her father-in-law, Shankar, who struggled profoundly after losing his wife when Rohan was just a teenager. Shankar had always been a quiet man, but his wife's passing cast him into a shell of sorrow so deep that he barely spoke anymore. The ancestral home in Lucknow, once vibrant with childhood memories, became a place of unbearable emptiness for him. He refused to socialize with relatives or even leave the house. Priya sensed his growing loneliness and knew she had to act. Over months of visiting him, sitting silently by his side, and deep conversations with Rohan, Priya finally made the insistence that would change his life. "Papa, you can't keep staying alone in that big house," Priya gently told him one day when they were sitting by the garden of his home. "We want you to live with us. I'll make sure everything feels just right for you, and the girls will benefit so much from having their Dadu nearby. You deserve to be surrounded by laughter, not emptiness." Initially resistant,

Shankar found himself unable to say no to Priya. Something about the determined compassion in her voice made him relent, and he moved into their Gurgaon home. It wasn't an easy transition for him, but Priya's patience and consistent care made all the difference. She ensured his comfort and gradually brought him out of his shell. She involved him in small family rituals—helping Siya with school projects, reading books with Ananya, and even joining Sunday afternoon tea chats. Slowly but steadily, Shankar began to pull away from his loneliness. Shankar suffered a paralysis attack. Rohan had recently joined a new job in a corporate firm, and the timing couldn't have been worse; he couldn't take leave to attend to Shankar's emergency. It was Priya who stepped up without hesitation. She stayed by his side, managing the hospital routine, ensuring he had the right care, and comforting him during his recovery. Shankar, unable to communicate easily due to his condition, often fixed his weary eyes on Priya, and in those moments, his gratitude was undeniable. "He's my father as well," Priya told a concerned Rohan over a phone call one night. "I know you can't be here right now, but he needs me. And I won't let him handle this alone. You'd do the same if you weren't stuck." Later, when his condition worsened and the inevitable came during his last moments, Priya was holding his hand. Rohan was attending an important Management Development Programme at ISB, and Shankar understood his son's absence, yet he found solace knowing Priya was there for him. In his final seconds of life, he squeezed her hand weakly, and a faint tear rolled down his cheek—his silent way of saying thank you. The pandemic, however, rattled Priya in ways she wasn't prepared for. Each piece of news from the outside world felt like a stone dropped in her chest, compounding her worries for Siya's fragile mental health and Rohan's safety thousands of miles away. Some nights she would pace the living room, wondering if she could have done more with her life, earned money if needed, taken the pressure off her husband. But on better days, Priya reminded herself of who she was: a woman who had learned to make the most of every situation. Someone who could transform scarcity into abundance—not through material wealth, but by creating love-filled homes and nurturing lives. The seeds of anticipation and optimism were still there, buried perhaps, but waiting to bloom yet again. Priya's contradictions—her fears and strengths, her fragility and resilience—made her human, relatable, and the quiet pillar of her family amid the chaos of a pandemic-stricken world. Priya's inner monologues became her solace and torment during the sleepless nights. Sitting alone in darkness, she would whisper into the void like it was her confidante. "*Am I merely a shadow in everyone's life? A giver with nothing left for myself?* I hold them together, but who holds me when I crumble? Am I selfish for wanting..." She stopped, unable to complete the thought. She feared the answer. Her thoughts would oscillate between guilt and anger—both emotions foreign to someone who had always been patient. "*I gave up archaeology, writing, music—all the little pieces of myself—for this. For them. But does anyone see? Do they hear me when my silence screams?*" Rohan, overwhelmed himself, often failed to notice subtle changes in her demeanour—the weariness, the heaviness in her movements, the hollow edge to her soft-spoken voice. Priya despaired silently, fearing she had become invisible not only to the outside world but to him as well—the one person she had counted on to see her, to truly see her. Even her daughters, though loving and attentive, seemed to have inherited Priya's façade of resilience. They noticed but didn't pry; they cared but lacked the language to address her growing distress. Her vulnerability in the ICU was stark—the silent pillar now stripped of her strength, her independence. Yet even in the sterile surroundings of the emergency ward, as machines hummed and beeped a constant reminder of her frailty, Priya found herself battling an inner conflict that refused to cease. Lying still as severe pain and spasm coursed through her body, she thought to herself, "Is this what it takes for them to notice? To see me—not just as their caregiver, their glue, but as a person who bleeds, who breaks? What did I become to deserve this—a martyr or a ghost?" Her bitterness scared her, unfamiliar and volatile. Yet it was accompanied by an equally haunting guilt—a voice of reprimand whispering, "*But they're here now. They love you. Don't let this bitterness taint your survival.*" That night in the ICU, a young man around 35 years had died; she could not sleep. Nurses told her that he was a marathoner, a very health-conscious person and an executive in an MNC. The cardiac specialist had told his family that he had a massive cardiac arrest due to work-related stress. She felt so insecure and was worried more about Rohan than her own pain and spasm seemed nothing. She had seen more than three deaths in her stay in the ICU. Her thoughts wove themselves into knotted loops of despair, fear, and hope. Priya realized, perhaps for the first time, that she was at a crossroads—not just physically but emotionally. Either she would continue to lose herself to everyone else, or she would reclaim her inner world and allow herself to matter too.

When Priya finally stabilised and was shifted to a private ward, her family surrounded her with fragile reassurances. But Priya couldn't verbalize her thoughts. She smiled faintly, nodded gently, but internally, her mind churned with a mixture of feelings and emotions. She felt her strength returning gradually—not physical strength, but a steely resolve. If she were to rise from this, she wouldn't simply return to the silent, invisible figure everyone relied upon. Her silence had served its purpose for years, but now it was time for her to speak, for her heart to reclaim spaces long left vacant.

Moving back home brought new challenges. Being bedridden, Priya's independence was no longer hers to wield. Tasks she once executed effortlessly—cooking, cleaning, coordinating—became impossible. For the first time in her adulthood, Priya had to let others care for her instead. Priya found herself reflecting on this forced dependence as a new chapter of strength. As she listened to Siya play her guitar next to her bedside, she had always meant to repair herself; a quiet sense of pride basked in her heart. Priya, despite her physical confinement, became unyielding in spirit. She insisted on tutoring Siya from the wheelchair, worked on editing Ananya's essays for college applications, and even started dictating chapters for the novel she had once dreamed of writing as a teenager. She titled it The Silent Pillar—a memoir of resilience, loneliness, and hope. Her moments of inner vulnerability were no longer terrifying. They became a reminder of her humanity, not a weakness but an essential rhythm of life she now embraced wholeheartedly. Sitting by the window one afternoon, watching the sunlight bounce off the Boulevard trees, Priya whispered quietly to herself, "I am more than they see. I am not just the woman who gave, sacrificed, and endured. I am Priya—multifaceted, flawed, tender, fierce. I will show them." And as the family rallied around her, shaping their lives into one of shared effort and love, Priya—the woman, the weary mother, the loving wife—was not just their silent pillar but their unshakable cornerstone.

CHAPTER 15

THE SHATTERING ECHOES

The house should have been a refuge, a sanctuary. Instead, it stood transformed, unrecognizable under the heavy weight of Priya's return. Rohan paused at the bedroom doorway, his chest tightening as he took in the scene. Their once cozy retreat, a cocoon of warmth and laughter, now bristled with cold, sterile reminders of fragility—an electric hospital bed taking centre stage, surrounded by the muted hum of oxygen machines and the faint hiss of air from the mattress. The soft curtains let in shards of sunlight, but even the light seemed muted, as if it hesitated to intrude into this fragile new reality. "Welcome home, my love," Rohan murmured, his voice barely audible. He tried to soften his tone, to mask the crack in it, but Priya lifted her eyes toward him, the faintest ghost of a smile flickering across her lips. She was propped against a nest of pillows, her once lively face now drawn and pale. Yet her eyes, though tired, sought him, as if willing herself to ease his burden. The words hung in the room, hollow and uncertain, and Rohan couldn't bring himself to cross the threshold. Somewhere in another corner of the house, an unmistakable stillness pressed in, louder than any noise could ever be. That stillness had crept into Siya's life, too.

Siya had always been the spark in their family, the source of life that seemed to brighten even the dullest of days. For as long as Rohan could remember, she had carried herself with the kind of effortless charm that drew people toward her, like a flower basking in sunlight. Her bubbly laughter echoed through the years in his memory, reminding him of lazy Sunday mornings when she darted around the garden with a camera slung around her neck, endlessly clicking pictures of bugs, flowers, and birds. Her photographs had been more than childlike curiosity; there had been something remarkable there. That raw, budding talent had caught the attention of mentors at *Sanctuary Asia Cub*, a renowned wildlife magazine for young photographers. They had noticed her work after a photo walk in Sanjay Gandhi National Park, Mumbai (SGNP), a trip Rohan had participated in to introduce Siya to nature when she was just 6 years old. One photograph—a brilliantly composed shot of an eagle mid-flight, its wings splayed against a vibrant blue sky—had earned her a feature in the magazine. The editors had praised her skill, calling her a natural with an extraordinary eye for detail. Siya had carried that issue around for weeks, showing it to anyone who cared to listen, as her friends teased her about being "famous already." She thrived in her element, a whirlwind of energy and enthusiasm. At school, she was equally popular—her jokes filling the canteen with laughter, her warmth enveloping everyone she met. She was the girl who could strike up a conversation with anyone, leave them smiling, and somehow juggle horse riding, golf, shooting, and her photo competitions without missing a beat. Siya, their Siya, had been the sun in their orbit. But now, that sun had dimmed. Rohan walked down the hallway to Siya's room that evening, noticing how quiet it had become. He paused outside her door, his heart sinking at the shrill silence beyond it. Pushing it open, he froze at the sight that greeted him. The room that had once been meticulously tidy—walls adorned with her framed photographs, books arranged by size, a mood board pinned with magazine printouts—was now a mess. Her textbooks were scattered across the floor, some with pages curled from being shoved aside. As if the chaos of her room mirrored the storm raging inside her. Siya lay curled up on her bed, her knees drawn tightly to her chest as she stared at the ceiling. Her college sweatshirt hung on her small frame, sagging as though even cloth could sense her shrinking presence. "Siya?" Rohan called softly, stepping in. She didn't stir. "Siya, sweetheart," he tried again, kneeling next to the bed. She slowly turned her face toward him, and he was startled by the absence of her usual vibrancy. Her dark, expressive eyes, eyes that had once captured the beauty of the world through the lens of a camera, now brimmed with tears and something far worse: resignation. "Papa," she choked out, her voice barely above a whisper. The crack in it was a fissure erupting in Rohan's chest. "I can't… I can't do this anymore." "What is it, Siya? What's wrong?" he asked gently, though dread already clawed at his heart. She sat up slowly, her hands trembling as she clutched at her hair. "I can't focus. Every time I try to study, I just see Mummy lying there… like that. And then…" Her breathing quickened, her panicked eyes darting to the floor. "And then my brain… it spirals. I start thinking of her, of me, of how I'll never—that I'll never be able to…" Rohan reached out instinctively, pulling her into his arms. Her body shook against his, her tears soaking into his shirt. "Siya, stop. Stop thinking like that," he said, but the tremor in his own voice betrayed him. She pulled away slightly, looking up at him with an expression so raw it pierced through the numbness he'd been nursing for weeks. "What dreams, Papa?" she whispered brokenly. "What's left for me now? Every time I look at Mummy, I feel… I feel like I'll never be good enough. Not to help her. Not to fix anything. My mind isn't mine anymore. My photos don't matter. My studies don't matter. I got an email that school is reopening next week after lockdown. I don't want to go to my boarding school." Her voice rose, growing frantic. "I'm a failure. I'm ruining everything. I should just withdraw. Stop wasting everyone's time." Her words hit him like a physical blow. Failure? How could she ever think that? She was everything to them—everything—but how could he say it in a way she'd believe? "No," Rohan said firmly, gripping her shoulders as if his grip could anchor her to this moment. "Siya, you… you're the bravest girl I know. Your photographs—do you even know what people said when they saw them?" He smiled, his heart aching. "They weren't just pictures, beta; they were stories. People read those stories in your pictures long after they left the page. That's your gift." She shook her head, tears spilling down her cheeks. "That was before, Papa," she rasped. "Now, I can't even pick up the camera. What's the point? I'm just—" "Stop." His voice cracked. "If you leave school, if you give up on yourself, then yes—then it really will be hopeless. But you, Siya, you're stronger than this. You can get through this, and I'll help you." She didn't reply. But as they sat there in the silence that followed, her head resting on his shoulder, Rohan swore he would fight with everything he had to reignite the spark in his daughter—the girl whose spirit once lit up the darkest corners of their lives. The shadows lingered, yes. But somewhere, barely perceptible in the quiet of the room, was the tiniest glimmer of light. And Rohan resolved to keep stoking it, no matter how faint it became. With Rohan's efforts, Siya felt much better and was escorted by her teacher from Mumbai to her boarding school at Ooty.

CHAPTER 16

THE ACID TEST

The home that had once been a haven of joy and vitality now seemed like the hollowed-out shell of a happier life. It whispered stories of laughter that once spilled into its corners, of dreams nurtured within its walls, and of sunlight that had once painted their mornings gold. Now, that light had dimmed, replaced by shadows that crept in steadily, thickening the air with sorrow and unspoken fears. The living room, once warm and inviting, felt cold and lifeless under the dim yellow glow of a single bulb. Hospital equipment dominated their space—an electric bed standing sentinel, a tall oxygen cylinder anchoring the room to its grim reality, and the constant, low hum of machines like a perpetual reminder of borrowed time. The lingering smell of antiseptic seemed almost sentient, filling every corner and clinging to their world like an uninvited guest. Rohan stood by the granite countertop, his palms pressed against its cool surface, as if its solidity might somehow tether him to reality. The kitchen once bore echoes of warmth: Siya perched on a stool, brushing through her thick hair as she narrated the amusing escapades of her day, and Priya clinking tea cups as she laughed at one of Rohan's terrible jokes. Now, it was a stark contrast—a backdrop of silence as stifling as the storm brewing inside his chest. He stared out at the darkness beyond the windows, the heavy curtains still and lifeless, the world outside muted in comparison to the chaos that churned in his mind. His thoughts zigzagged relentlessly, each one stinging more sharply than the last. He could still hear the piercing wail of the ambulance siren from the night before, a sound that had carved through midnight and embedded itself in his memory. Priya had been rushed to the hospital in the most harrowing hours of the night, her body burning with a fever that threatened to consume her. The doctors, their voices laced with caution, had diagnosed a severe UTI caused by complications with her SPC (suprapubic catheter). She had regained consciousness by morning, but her pale face—her once lively, expressive face—was now a mere shadow of its former self. The sunken eyes that met his gaze seemed to flicker weakly, as if unsure whether to cling to hope or succumb to despair. "She's stable," they had assured him. Stable. What a cruel word—offering neither solace nor certainty, only the hollow assurance of existing on the precipice, waiting for the next disaster to strike. Rohan had returned home to gather some essentials, but the journey back was like walking through molasses. Exhaustion hung on him like the weight of waterlogged clothes, suffocating him and robbing him of clarity. The house felt heavier than ever, not because of the physical strain of caregiving but due to the suffocating emotions coiled within its walls—grief, fear, and, most corrosively, helplessness. The kitchen was drowned in an eerie quiet, save for the distant hum of Priya's oxygen machine down the hall. Rohan hadn't slept in days, his body weary from carrying the weight of their crumbling world. But the silence shattered when his phone vibrated violently on the counter, buzzing like some unholy harbinger. His eyes flicked to the screen. *"Good Shepherd School,"* read the caller ID. Heart pounding, he answered, gripping the phone so tightly his knuckles turned white. The voice on the other end, low and careful, belonged to Dr Albert, the school medical officer. It carried the kind of deliberate gentleness people reserved for delivering blows that could break someone. "Mr Rohan," he began, his words measured but fraught with the gravity of the moment. "Siya fell from the horse during riding practice. She's been rushed to B.S. Hospital, Ooty. It's serious. You need to come immediately." The world seemed to fracture all at once. Rohan grasped the edge of the counter to steady himself, as if gravity itself had betrayed him. Siya—his Siya, the luminous soul who chased butterflies with her camera and peppered their quiet moments with an endless stream of joy—was hurt. His mind panicked, rifling through images of her childhood: her crooked pigtails, the way her voice grew high-pitched when she said the word "ice cream," the sparkle in her eyes when talking about the wild places she longed to visit with her camera. The sharp irony was cruel and unrelenting. First Priya, and now his daughter. Both of them fighting for their lives simultaneously. "How serious is it?" Rohan demanded, his voice trembling, desperate for details he wasn't sure he could bear to hear. The pause on the other end lasted just a moment, but it stretched endlessly in the cavern of his fear. Then came another voice—Ms. Saloni, Siya's class teacher—soft and drenched in tears. "She's critical, sir," she whispered, choking through sobs. "She's on a ventilator." The words ripped through him, biting deeper than he thought humanly possible. An unrelenting pit opened inside his stomach, swallowing his breath and his strength. For one agonizing second, he felt like he was suffocating, consumed by the sheer weight of despair. But then survival instincts kicked in—he dialled Priya. "Siya's unwell," he said firmly, masking the terror in his voice as best as he could. "I have to leave for Ooty immediately. Nisha will be with you, don't worry." He dared not say more, dared not unravel the grim truth. Every movement that followed was sharp and mechanical—packing a bag, booking a flight out of Mumbai to Coimbatore, and grabbing the car keys. He moved as though urgency alone could untangle the cruel knots life had thrown at him. The direct flight had left hours earlier. Forced to settle for a layover in Bengaluru, Rohan sprinted to the airport, his mind a chaotic storm of panic and prayers. By the time he landed in Bengaluru, the exhaustion had caught up to him in ways he didn't expect. His body felt alien, dragged down by invisible anchors tethered to his shoulders. Stepping off the flight, he blinked at the cloudy skies above, but something felt wrong. The world seemed unbalanced. His left eye felt heavy, clouded, like someone had thrown red ink over his vision. He rubbed it vigorously, hoping to clear the haze, but it persisted, a dull ache accompanied by vivid redness. Attempting to mask his growing panic, he stopped a young man with a backpack passing by. "Excuse me," Rohan stammered, fighting to steady his voice. "Do you see anything unusual… about my eye?" The stranger hesitated, taking a wary step back before grimacing. "Your left eye… sir, it's bloody red." Rohan rushed to the restroom, his hands trembling as he pushed open the door. Staring into the mirror, his worst fears confirmed themselves in vivid clarity. His left eye was marooned in blood, as though ruptured from the inside out. A haemorrhage. Panic seized him. His breathing grew shallow, his pulse erratic. He stumbled toward the airport medical unit, clutching at his chest out of some primal instinct to survive, desperate for a lifeline. Inside, the doctor wasted no time. Blood pressure readings followed, the harsh truth spilling from his lips mercilessly. "210/120," the doctor said, his tone incredulous. "It's a miracle you haven't collapsed yet. You need immediate hospitalisation, Mr Rohan. I'm sorry. You are *not fit to fly.*" It felt like the final blow, a cruel and merciless betrayal from his own body. But Rohan wouldn't accept the verdict. His voice cracked, raw with desperation as he pleaded with the doctor. "Listen to me," he begged, his words frantic but resolute. "My wife is in the ICU, recovering from paraplegia. My daughter is on life support in Ooty. *I have to get to her.* You can't stop me." The doctor hesitated. For a moment, his professional resolve, the iron-clad rules of his practice, seemed to waver under the weight of Rohan's desperation. Then—finally, reluctantly—humanity won over policy. After administering an injection to lower his blood pressure and requiring him to rest at the medical unit, the doctor allowed him to leave. When his readings fell to 140/90—still dangerously high but manageable—Rohan was cleared to continue his journey. As he boarded his flight to Coimbatore, his body felt less like something he controlled and more like a weathered, battered machine scraping to survive. But he had to survive. He had no choice. Siya needed him. Priya needed him. Somehow, despite the anguish tearing at his soul, he managed to cling to that one resolute thought. The clouds outside the plane window thickened, promising turbulent skies ahead. But Rohan stared at them unblinking, his hands gripping the armrests as though determination alone could see him through the storm. This wasn't just a journey to Ooty. It was a journey to fight for his family—to salvage what remained of the shattered life they'd all clung to. As the plane climbed higher into the stormy dusk, Rohan clenched his fists. No matter how broken he felt, no matter how much his body screamed at him to rest, he wouldn't stop. Bloodshot eyes and battered heart, he would reach Siya. Because giving up was never an option. The corridors of B.S. Hospital were drenched in a sterile silence, the kind that weighed heavier than the chaos of noises. Rohan's footsteps echoed faintly as he trudged through the dimly lit halls, exhaustion dragging at his every movement. It was close to midnight when he reached Dr Sundaram's office. The senior doctor, a stoic pillar of calm whose reputation had always preceded him, was waiting. Rohan instantly noticed his presence—grave but steady, as though he carried the burden of dozens of broken families on his shoulders. Dr Sundaram rarely entertained meetings past his evening rounds, but tonight, he stayed. Perhaps he had sensed that this father was on the edge of collapse. "She's stable now," Dr Sundaram began, his voice measured, his words deliberate. "But she's fragile. The trauma twisted her diaphragm slightly during the fall, which is why her breathing is compromised. We'll keep her on the ventilator until morning as a precaution and then transfer her to a private ward. She should recover quickly, but only with close monitoring." Relief exploded inside Rohan like a shot of adrenaline, but it was quickly drowned by something heavier—overwhelming fatigue wrapped in fear. For a fleeting moment, his legs threatened to give out beneath him. He nodded mechanically, unable to form coherent responses. Stable wasn't fine, but it wasn't the worst-case scenario either—something he clung to with fingers trembling from despair. When Rohan reached the ICU, the sight before him shattered whatever strength he still possessed. Siya lay in the hospital bed, her small frame dwarfed by machines that hummed and beeped around her as if they were battling death itself. Tubes snaked across her pale skin—one to her nose, another taped to her arm—and her chest rose and fell in perfect rhythm with the ventilator. Rohan froze in the doorway, fear breaking over him like a drowning wave. His mind screamed at him to move closer, but his legs refused to obey. He didn't want to step closer to this terrifying image of fragility, to see the life hanging precariously between breaths. But then, through her laboured breathing, Siya lifted her trembling hand. That frail movement—just inches in the air—was like a distant lighthouse cutting through the storm. It carried a single message: her *spirit* hadn't surrendered. Something inside her was still fighting, clawing its way back from the abyss. Rohan crumbled. Tears streamed down his face like rivers, carving through the exhaustion and pain etched into his skin. With trembling hands, he clasped Siya's fingers in his own, careful not to press too hard. Through the quiet of the machines, he whispered, "I'm here, Siya. I'm here. Rest now, my brave little girl."

The next morning came with difficult choices, the kind that unravel carefully constructed pieces of a life—brick by brick. The school informed Rohan that Siya would need to leave Ooty and return to Mumbai permanently. Her injuries made staying at the boarding school an impossibility despite the fact that they had a well-appointed 60-bed hospital on the school campus with two doctors and four nurses, but it lacked secondary and tertiary care facilities; hence arrangements were made for her to finish her

IBBA Diploma exams remotely. The news struck Rohan like a second blow, yet he couldn't find the energy to grieve it aloud. Siya, on the other hand, clung fiercely to her already fraying threads of connection. Despite the discomfort of her injuries and the weakness gnawing at her limbs, she insisted on saying goodbye to her teachers, her classmates, and the friends she had grown to love. But time and her condition allowed no ceremonious farewells. Ms. Saloni, her class teacher, arrived at the hospital, bags in tow, her hands shaking as she packed Siya's belongings into two backpacks. The weight of those bags seemed to carry layers of unspoken emotions: the laughter shared during classroom pranks, the warmth of impromptu conversations after hours, and the camaraderie of fleeting friendships forged during school plays. It wasn't just luggage—it was a box filled with fragments of a life Siya was being forced to leave behind. "Siya," the teacher choked out softly, brushing stray tears away. "You were the brightest spirit of our class. Don't ever forget that." Siya, her cheeks shallow but her eyes still carrying glints of fight, beckoned for her teacher's phone. With immense effort, she managed to smile—a faint but radiant flicker of her once vibrant self—and posed for a selfie. It was a silent farewell, a token locked away not in words but in pixels; a frozen moment she could clutch when the loss wrapped too tightly around her. Through swollen breaths and faltering strength, Siya whispered, "Tell them I'll miss them. All of them." Ms. Saloni nodded, struggling not to weep. And then, just like that, Siya's chapter in Ooty—her dreams of trekking through lush forests for photography assignments, rifle shooting practice, her afternoons chasing down rabbits during riding practice, and the warm glow of friendships—was closed. It was nearly dawn when they arrived home in Mumbai. Siya dropped her bags at the doorway, exhaustion clouding her every movement, and immediately rushed to Priya's room, looking like a private ward in their house. The frailty of her mother's paraplegic form now mirrored her own, but for a fleeting moment, there was solace in their reunion. Rohan stood behind them, unable to articulate the emotions swirling in his chest. Pain, relief, loss, love—he couldn't untangle where one began and the other ended. As Siya carefully folded herself into the chair beside Priya's bed and they gripped hands trembling from weakness, Rohan sank into the armchair nearby. For the first time in days, he allowed himself a single deep breath. It was quiet now. The chaos had receded—temporarily, perhaps—but in this fragile silence, there was still warmth. His fractured family, broken and battered by forces beyond their control, had somehow come back together. They held onto shadows of what once was, but more importantly, they clung to the threads of love that refused to break. Rohan didn't know what the future would hold. They were healing, yes, but it was a slow and halting process, with moments of light punctuated by relentless battles. Still, as he looked at his two girls, he didn't see despair. He saw *strength*, however fragile, glittering faintly in the cracks. And for now, that was enough. It had to be. After the IBBA diploma, Siya got selected to pursue her BBA in a management school in association with Kedge Business School. She joined as a resident student as Rohan wanted to keep her away from challenges at home. She came home on a long winter break. Siya had always been his buoy in these moments, the beacon of unshakable hope who could drag him from even the darkest depths. But tonight, even Siya was fading. He replayed the scene from earlier in the day over and over again in his mind: her chin trembling, her knees pulled tightly to her chest, her voice trembling as she confessed, "I can't. I can't do this anymore." It was in that moment that Rohan felt the world shift beneath his feet, as if some unseen weight was dragging them down beneath the surface, determined to consume everything they had worked to build together. He had tried to console her, to reassure her, to say the right words. But how could he promise her that things would get better when he wasn't sure himself? How could he convince her to hold on to her dreams when his own were slipping like sand through his fingers? When Siya finally looked at him, her face streaked with tears, some part of him broke irreparably. Together, they had written her withdrawal letter from her management program. The act felt like driving a dagger into his chest—a devastating blow not just to his daughter's aspirations but to the crumbling foundation of the life they had built. Every line of that letter, every carefully chosen word, felt like an admission of defeat, a symbol of his inability to safeguard the dreams of those he loved most. The edges of his mind frayed as he considered all they'd lost. Priya—his anchor, his partner—was now battling her own failing body, confined to a hospital that felt a lifetime away. Siya, his radiant, brilliant, free-spirited daughter, was retreating into herself, her light dimming in ways he didn't know how to fix. The family's finances, once a testament to his ambition and persistence, were now a crumbling ruin, battered by years of hospital bills, therapy costs, and mounting debt. "This is it," Rohan thought bitterly. "This is rock bottom." Siya: The Quiet Flame Siya was the kind of girl who felt deeply but rarely voiced her emotions. While her older sister, Ananya, wore her confidence like armour, Siya moved through the world like a painter carefully navigating a canvas with unpredictable colours. Her introspective nature often made her seem distant, but in reality, Siya was acutely aware of the emotions swirling around her—especially in her family. If Ananya was the blazing sun, full of warmth and assurance, Siya was the moon—soft-spoken, mysterious, and prone to silent reflection. Growing up in the shadow of her capable sister and hardworking parents, Siya often questioned whether there was room for her to be heard. Her love for music had once been her solace, but even that felt muted in the chaos of her family's expectations, unspoken rules, and the mounting emotional strain that hung in the air. But Siya kept her struggles internal, carefully curated behind quiet smiles and the gentle strumming of her guitar strings. When her mother, Priya, was confined to bed during Rohan's absence, Siya found herself thrust into a role she wasn't sure she could fulfil: her mother's caregiver for a good 65 days. For Siya, stepping into the role of caregiver was both a privilege and a burden. She loved her mother deeply, almost fiercely, but that love carried weight. Watching Priya—a woman Siya had always admired for her strength, kindness, and quiet resilience—unable to move freely was more painful than Siya could express. Alone in her room, Siya often whispered her thoughts to the darkness as if it could understand her better than the world could. *"I'm trying, Ma. I am. But what if I'm not enough? I want to be strong for you—you deserve someone strong. But sometimes, I feel like I'm breaking. And I can't … I can't show that to you. You already have enough to deal with. I'll be okay…I always have to be okay. For you."* There were days she felt numb from the expectation of strength, but there were also days her guilt consumed her. On particularly bad nights, when Priya couldn't sleep and Siya sat quietly by her bedside, holding her hand as her mother drifted in and out of restless dreams, a sense of emptiness would creep into Siya's chest. *"Does she know how much I love her? Does she know how hard I try? I'd give up music, time, everything if it would make her pain go away, but all I can do is sit here. Is that enough? God, I should've done more earlier—I should've noticed when things were heavy for her before all this. Would things be different if I had acted sooner?"* Yet even in her moments of self-doubt, Siya found herself holding onto hope, however fragile it was. She would sit by the window after those long nights and watch the first rays of sunlight spill across the quiet streets, whispering softly to herself. *"Maybe this is what love looks like—not always being enough, but trying anyway. I don't know what I'm doing, but I'll keep doing it for Ma. Because she deserves better, even if I'm not sure I'm enough to give it to her."* Siya's Struggles with Mental Health: Contradictions and Vulnerabilities Siya, like her mother, struggled with mental health, though hers had always felt like a shadow she couldn't shake. Anxiety often wormed its way into her thoughts, amplifying every insecurity until it felt deafening. Even before Priya's fall, Siya had wrestled with bouts of quiet sadness—the kind that didn't blaze outwardly but simmered beneath the surface. After her mother's accident, the weight of her own mental battles doubled, as she couldn't afford to crumble when everyone else relied on her to stay steady. There were times when the anxiety became unbearable—when her hands shook so much she couldn't pick up her guitar, when her thoughts spiralled into worst-case scenarios involving her mother's health, her father's absence, her sister's silence. *"Why do*

I feel like this? Why can't I just be normal? Ananya has it figured out—it's like she doesn't feel these highs and lows. I love Ma, but sometimes I just want to cry for myself. That isn't fair, is it? She's the one in pain, not me." Yet Siya was also a contradiction—a girl who felt weak but found herself tending to others; a girl who doubted herself but poured her heart into those she loved. Her inner conflict wasn't about choosing love; it was about navigating the weight of love that demanded too much of her and, at times, asked her to neglect herself. On days when Siya's mind became too overwhelming to bear, she would retreat to the balcony, strumming her guitar softly, tears slipping down her cheeks. Music had once been her escape, but now it echoed with her emotions, raw and unfiltered. It was her therapy, her release, her reminder that she was still here, still trying. *"It's strange. I feel so much, but when I play, I don't need words. I wish Ma could hear this and understand everything I can't explain. I wish I could tell her that she's not alone, that I'm not perfect, but I'll stand with her even when my legs feel shaky. I'll carry her even when my own heart bends under the weight."* While Siya felt torn between her love for Priya and her guilt for not being stronger, she also carried a quiet hope with her—a hope she nurtured by finding beauty in small things. Her mother's faint smile when Siya sang softly from the corner of her room. Her sister's quiet hug on days neither of them could find words. Her father, flawed and distant, trying to show up more often. One rainy evening, as Siya sat beside her mother in the living room, Priya asked her to play something for her. Siya hesitated at first—playing for someone felt raw, vulnerable—but the look in her mother's eyes gave her courage. As her fingers strummed gently, Siya looked at her mother and whispered inside,

"This is for you, Ma. I know you don't expect me to fix everything, and maybe that's the point. Music isn't about solving; it's about healing. I'll heal with you." After her performance, Priya gave her a faint smile and whispered, "You don't know how much light you bring, Siya. Even when you think you're breaking, you make us all complete." Those words stayed with Siya, lingering in her mind like candlelight on dark nights. Siya began to realize that strength could coexist with vulnerability. It wasn't about being perfect or invincible, but about showing up even when it hurt. She started embracing therapy, opening up about her mental health struggles instead of bottling them away. And though her progress felt slow some days, Siya found solace in knowing that healing wasn't linear—it was messy, imperfect, but ultimately possible. Her relationship with Priya deepened during this time, as Siya found her mother was her mirror—a woman who understood vulnerability better than anyone. One evening, as Siya pushed her mother's wheelchair toward the balcony for some fresh air, Priya confessed: "You know, Siya, I used to feel invisible. But not with you. With you, I feel seen." Tears welled in Siya's eyes as she leaned down and hugged her mother tightly. "We're here together, Ma," Siya whispered. Her voice cracked, but her resolve didn't falter. "Even if I'm tired or scared, we'll figure it out. Together." It was a quiet vow born of shared pain and mutual love. It didn't solve everything, but it was enough—a testament to the idea that strength doesn't mean the absence of struggle. It means continuing anyway. For Siya, that realization became her foundation as she journeyed toward healing—herself, her family, and her music. Siya's struggles didn't vanish overnight, but they transformed her. Her love for music became her anchor, helping

her express the emotions words couldn't capture. She scribbled lyrics in earnest, pouring her heart into songs that celebrated hope, heartache, and resilience. Slowly, she began to rebuild herself—not just for Priya's sake, but for her own. Though a quiet dreamer, Siya became her own person—an artist, a caregiver, and a force of compassion. Priya saw this transformation and often marvelled at her youngest daughter's strength. And as their bond grew deeper, Siya realized that even in her darkest moments, she had been a flame—a quiet, persistent light that never stopped fighting for those she loved. For Siya, resilience wasn't just surviving. It was learning to thrive, one note, one word, one day at a time.

CHAPTER 17

THE FRACTURED FAÇADE

The faint amber glow filtering through Rohan's window seemed to mock him, just as the corporate gloss of his office had once done. The air at home felt heavier than ever, suffused with the metallic tang of despair and the sharp edges of dwindling hope. His reflection in the glass was a spectre of the man he had once been—Rohan, the strategist, the corporate gladiator who had clawed his way to the top amidst the machinations of competitors and confidants alike. Now? A defeated figure haunted by questions that pierced him to the core, each one more cruel than the last. The accolades on his wall—plaques shimmering lightly in the dim light—felt void of meaning. Leadership awards, performance trophies, framed endorsements from CEOs—they were no longer symbols of achievement, but hollow relics of a life he had built at the expense of everything else. Trailing his gaze toward the bookshelf, his eyes lingered on a framed photograph of the three of them—himself, Priya, and Siya—taken ten years ago during a rare vacation to Goa. Siya, then a carefree eight-year-old with windswept hair, stood perched on his shoulders, her toothy grin stretching across the frame. Priya, ever radiant, had stood beside them, her hand resting lightly on his arm. That was the last time they had truly laughed together, Rohan realized, free of the encumbrances life and work had since piled on. His whispered question, bitter and biting, broke the suffocating silence. "Was it all worth it, Rohan? The sacrifices, the long hours, the time stolen from Priya and Siya? Look at where it's left you now." The storm within his mind had been brewing for days. His most recent demotion, a reassignment to a non-essential advisory role, left his ambitions hollow and crumbling, caged within a labyrinth of corporate politics that had ultimately betrayed him. The office, once his kingdom, now felt cold and predatory—a mausoleum of egos. It hadn't just been the Annual Strategy Meet he'd missed. Staying back with Siya during her recovery following two harrowing nights in the ICU had cost him dearly at work. The Product Committee Meeting, the Budget Review—he'd stayed away from those too, choosing instead to ferry Priya to therapy appointments or coach Siya through her mounting school anxieties. Three absences in a row, he knew, had painted him as a deserter—a man whose loyalty to his family inconveniently eclipsed that to the company. Weeks earlier, Mahesh Srinivasan, the formidable CEO, had summoned him after his third absence from a top-level meeting. The scene replayed in Rohan's mind like a grating tune he couldn't silence. The CEO's office burned in Rohan's memory like acid on an open wound. The sterile sting of the office greeted Rohan as he stepped into Mahesh's expansive domain. The silence in the room was oppressive, broken only by the faint hum of the air conditioning—a sound too cold, too methodical, like the breath of a predator prowling unseen. The vastness of the space felt calculated to intimidate, the smooth surface of the mahogany desk gleaming under the harsh overhead lights. The CEO's chair—a symbol of unassailable power—loomed like a throne, towering over the room. Mahesh sat at the helm, his monumental mahogany desk commanding the room, as his deep-set eyes pinned Rohan like prey. Frost blanketed the glass walls behind him, matching the chill in his voice as he uttered words that would rearrange Rohan's life forever. In stark contrast, the thin leather seat offered to Rohan seemed designed to sink him into submission. Once upon a time, fellow executives had envied him for enjoying ex-CEO's Favor, for being the man tapped for the toughest projects with the highest stakes. But now, that favour had dissolved—a glass edifice shattered beyond repair. "Rohan," Mahesh began, deliberate as a surgeon sharpening his scalpel, "your attendance record at management meetings has been… concerning. Missing the Quarterly Strategy Meet, the Product Review Meeting, and now the Annual Strategy Meet—it's unimpressive. Your focus, frankly, appears elsewhere." Rohan's jaw tightened, his palms gripping the armrests of his sunken chair with white-knuckled restraint. He had prepared for this moment endlessly, rehearsing rebuttals and appeals in the quiet agony of sleepless nights. Yet now, as he faced Mahesh's impenetrable mask of indifference, his resolve splintered under the weight of exhaustion. Deep lines of fatigue crept across his face, but behind them lived an undeniable fire—a flame stoked by desperation, guilt, and defiance. "Sir," Rohan began carefully, his voice coiled but steady, "I understand how it may look. And I take full responsibility for those absences. But my daughter was critically ill in Ooty, and my wife—" He inhaled sharply, willing himself not to falter. "My wife is still recovering from a spinal injury. I didn't have a choice. My family needed me. More than anything." The faintest tremor betrayed his tone, and he loathed himself for allowing weakness to show. But Mahesh didn't blink. He steepled his fingers, his expression carved in stone, mercilessly unimpressed. "Your challenges are regrettable," Mahesh said, his voice flat as marble, "but the company's priorities cannot be overshadowed by personal matters. Absences—*particularly at critical junctures*—undermine operational excellence. This isn't personal, Rohan. It's a matter of principle." Principle. The word sliced through the air with precision, leaving a sharp aftermath in its wake. Rohan sat straighter, his muscles tightening as he tried to wrangle the simmering anger clawing at his insides. "With all due respect, sir," he countered, his tone trembling but bold, "I *have* been consistent. I attended meetings from the hospital when my wife underwent angiography. While WFH meant 'Work From Home' for the world, it meant 'Work From Hospital' to me. When my daughter battled depression on the eve of her exams, I juggled timelines guiding and mentoring teams who relied on me. I've worked every waking hour to carry my responsibilities in the company as much as I've carried my family. I've fought—every single day—to hold everything together. And I've done it knowing my salary barely covers huge medical bills and overheads despite Group Health Insurance Policy with decent coverage, education fees, and the debts piled on my back." Mahesh's icy expression didn't waver; Rohan's words slid over him as if they had no weight, no meaning. "Consistency," Mahesh repeated lightly, as if testing the word, "means maintaining focus where it matters most. And missing three consecutive leadership meetings? That isn't consistency, Rohan. That's neglect. Missing major committee meetings sends the wrong message to stakeholders. The optics are, frankly, damaging." The word *optics* hung in the air like a sneer, stoking the simmering fire in Rohan's chest. Optics. To Mahesh, his absences weren't the sacrifices of a man torn between two collapsing worlds, but merely blemishes on a corporate report card. Each syllable struck Rohan like a hammer to his ribs, squeezing the air from his lungs until all that remained was bitter fury and the firestorm swelling within. Leaning forward, he locked eyes with Mahesh—the room crackled with unspoken tension as his voice rose. "*Optics?*" he hissed, the venom in his voice spilling free. "My wife is *paralyzed.* My daughter was *fighting for her life.*" "Are you serious? I've sacrificed everything—every ounce of peace, every shred of dignity—for this company. All while you sit there, talking about optics and principles. *Do you even care?* Or am I just another pawn in your game?" he muttered. The room fell silent, the air heavy and suffocating like smoke after a fire. Mahesh leaned back slowly, unmoving, his demeanour absurdly calm in the face of Rohan's unravelling storm. "Effective immediately," he said coolly, "you're being reassigned to an advisory role with no reportee, no secretary, no staff except a shared office boy. I trust you'll adapt." Mahesh's tone was clinical, almost surgical—a precision strike accompanied by hollow formalities designed to administer the final blow. "Advisory role?" The sanitized corporate euphemism for being demoted, stripped of influence, importance, and meaning. The only thing left intact was the shrunken, hollowed-out shell of what his job had once been. For a moment, Rohan just sat there, stunned into silence. All the emotion he had stifled—the pain, the exhaustion, the indignation—clamoured for release. He wanted to fight back, to say something, anything, that would crack through Mahesh's armoured indifference. But his voice failed him. The battle was over, and Mahesh had already moved on. Numbness consumed him, spreading outward from his heart until he felt like a shadow drifting through the city streets. Each step away from the office felt heavier than the last, as if he were leaving behind not just a building but some essential part of himself. His thoughts swirled as he walked—disjointed fragments of pride, regret, and disillusionment colliding like shards of broken glass. He thought of all the late nights he had spent defending those very policies. Of the mentorship sessions with hundreds of juniors. He recalled the words of Amita, the then SVP & Head of Strategic Alliances, who once cautioned him after a committee meeting, "Don't push too hard, Rohan. Play the game until you're the one making the rules." He had ignored her advice, thinking himself above the petty opportunism of corporate politics. But now those same bright-eyed juniors were basking in their quiet satisfaction, the predators feasting on the wounded tiger they had once admired. Was Abhijeet one of them? He couldn't say anymore. In the jungle of the corporate world, loyalty was a fantasy for the naïve, and weakness was an offering to the opportunistic. Rohan's walk had ended where it always did those days—on the worn, faded velvet couch in the living room. The once soft cushions had been pressed into uncomfortable flatness by the weight of years, but tonight, they seemed to mirror his own collapse. He sank into them, his elbows on his knees and face in his hands, the stillness of the house pressing down on him like gravity. "Why me?" he muttered softly, his words barely audible in the dim, empty room. He stared at the faint reflections of city lights trembling on the window, his face faintly visible in the pane. Somewhere in his hollow, bloodshot eyes, a ghost of his former self stared back. "What have I done to deserve this?" The questions spilled out, burning like acid in his chest. He thought of Priya's surgeries and Siya's relentless battle with her depression, their family's savings drained to mere echoes of comfort. He thought of the isolation, the humiliation, the unbearable weight of his demotion. "Is this my punishment?" Rohan whispered, his voice cracking under the strain. "For helping the company? For doing my job? Was this where my downfall was written?" His hands balled into fists, his nails biting into his palms, as anger surged through him again. What simmered inside him needed time to brew—and when it emerged, it would consume everyone standing in his path.

The Shadows Within: That night, Rohan drifted into an uneasy sleep. His thoughts unfolded like a violent theatre production—fractured memories fused with haunting fantasies of revenge. Mahesh's impassive face loomed in his mind's eye, glued to that mahogany fortress, unyielding. But the scene shifted suddenly, grotesquely. Rohan's grip tightened on a cold metallic object—a pistol. His fingers trembled, yet his aim was unwavering. The suppressed click of the safety unlocking echoed in his head like the ticking of a bomb. Everything unfolded in slow motion: Mahesh's smug indifference disintegrating as a bullet tore through him; Jennifer, his loyal secretary, rushing into the room, her cries drowned in the darkness as crimson spilled across the cold floorboards. When Rohan jolted awake, drenched in sweat, the sting of guilt pierced him deep. "What is happening to me? Did I kill him? I should have. He deserves that. But what was the fault of Jennifer? What if she was killed trying to save him, an innocent Jennifer? What will happen to Priya & Siya? Who will take care of them when I am in jail? What is my objective? What do I want out of this messy situation?" he muttered, rubbing his temples in frantic desperation. He had always considered himself kind, rational—a man who solved problems, not created them. Yet here he was, teetering on the edge, his mind consumed by low vibrations of toxic emotions of hate, anger, humiliation, and fear. *They say your thoughts appear as events in your dreams.* But this wasn't just a thought. It was a fracture—his reptilian brain clawing at him, threatening to destroy everything he'd spent decades cultivating. Rohan pressed his face into his hands, trying to rid himself of the primal darkness threatening to consume him. But the sound of gunfire lingered in his ears. And yet, as dawn approached, the firestorm within him began to recede, ever so slightly. It wasn't peace that swept over him—it was something faint, fragile, but alive. Within the ashes of his spirit, a single ember flickered stubbornly, refusing to die. Siya's voice broke his thoughts. "Papa," she said softly, as if she could sense his turmoil. "Kedge Business School just emailed me! An opportunity in France. What do you think? Didi will cheer us on from Boston. We're going to be okay, Papa." Her light was still there. Priya's resilience was still guiding them, faint but unwavering. Rohan inhaled deeply and whispered to himself, a promise forged in steel: "I will fight. For both of you. For everything. This is not the end—it can't be." Hope, fragile but relentless, stirred in his chest—a flicker against the raging void—but sometimes, one ember was enough to reignite a flame. This was not his downfall; this was his call to rise again.

PART
3

CHAPTER 18

THE SEED OF EPIPHANY

Priya's psychosis coupled with her paraplegia clung to her mind like unyielding vines, its tendrils refusing to loosen even slightly despite months of treatment. She remained trapped within its labyrinth, consumed by both paranoia and despair, and it demanded Rohan's relentless presence—every hour of every day—whether they were holed up in the sterile confines of a hospital room or within the fractured sanctuary of their home. For Rohan, life had become a delicate balancing act; his wife's fragile mental state commanding his complete attention on one end while the unrelenting demands of his corporate responsibilities pressed ceaselessly on the other. The toll it exacted seemed immeasurable, a slow bleed of energy and spirit that left him gasping for air. Nowhere was this battle more visceral than in the confines of his quarantine room in Mumbai. The narrow cell-like space seemed to magnify the isolation he felt—not just physically but emotionally and spiritually. The walls, smooth and beige, stood impassive and unfeeling, their sterile monotony mirrored by the rhythm of the air conditioning, a sound that oscillated between comfort and a grating reminder of time ticking away too slowly. Fifteen suffocating days in quarantine weighed heavy on him, compounding the grief he carried. Life, once a relentless climb up the ladder of success, now resembled an unrelenting trial, stripping away every pretence, pride, and illusion, exposing

Rohan's bare existence to the harsh light of truth. He felt as though he was in free fall, plunging deeper into a void, drawn in by despair's seductive, consuming whispers. The years stretched out before Rohan like a dense, impenetrable fog—a haze where his past collided uneasily with an uncertain future. Outside the window of his study room, the sprawling cityscape of Mumbai flickered faintly, a mosaic of muted colours and muffled sounds. His mind was plagued with relentless questioning—about his ambition, his identity, his purpose. Each doubt was a jagged shard of glass carving deeply into the foundation of who he once thought he was. It was in this crushing loneliness that Rohan turned inward, pouring himself onto the blank pages of his journal with a desperation born not of survival but of discovery. The lines of ink felt alive—raw and searing as they carved their truth onto the smooth white canvases. Anger spilled forth like molten lava: anger at Mahesh for robbing him of everything he'd laboured for, anger at himself for prioritizing his career over family when they had needed him most, and anger at the relentless guilt that piled on his chest day by day, suffocating him. But as the words poured out, as the storm roared and raged within, it began to settle—not into peace, but into clarity. His journal was no mere book; it had become his sanctuary, his confessional, the crucible where chaos found its order. Fears he had long buried rose up, fully formed, daring him to look them in the eye. Shadows, which once loomed large and inscrutable, took on new shapes, almost tangible in their vulnerability. These pages bore witness to something profound: a man shedding his old skin, piece by painstaking piece.

Rohan turned inward, channelling the storm within him onto the blank pages of his journal. He poured out his anguish, each word a delicate thread woven from the raw fabric of his soul. The anger roiling within him—toward Mahesh, for his sharp dismissal; toward, for his blind pursuit of external validation—began to unravel on the page. The crushing guilt for the distance he had permitted to grow between himself and his family stared back at him in stark, unapologetic ink. The shadows of loneliness, growing bolder each day, crept across his thoughts like an inevitable tide, but in the act of writing, he named them, confronted them, and piece by piece, lessened their weight. The pages transformed into his sanctuary, a sacred space where truth flowed forth unfiltered. For the first time, his emotions took shape—chaos reduced to order, pain moulded into clarity. As he confessed his hidden fears and contradictions, they crystallized into undeniable revelations. The man on these pages was no longer the same. He had spent a lifetime chasing his career, thriving on strategy, and feeding off the fleeting rush of validation. But in this stillness, a startling paradox emerged: surrender was setting him free. He stood face to face with thoughts he had been repressing. What if this confinement wasn't the end? What if this was the beginning? The thought lingered like a hesitant flame, glowing amidst the ashes of all he had lost. The pseudo demotion, his "non-important side role," which had come carelessly at the hands of Mahesh—seemingly cruel at first—began to shift in significance. What if it wasn't punishment? What if it was a chance? A fragile opportunity for rediscovery, untainted by corporate ego. Rohan didn't seek ways to play the victim. He didn't reach for resentment or spin plausible excuses for his failures. Instead, he chose grace and responsibility.

Life had thrown hardships his way, but he found the courage to own them, unwilling to let despair poison him further. Even Mahesh, whose behaviour had been sharp and lacking empathy, wasn't the villain he once seemed. No, Mahesh hadn't been right, but Rohan realized that blaming him would accomplish nothing. Perhaps Mahesh was nothing more than an instrument of fate—of God's will—in the larger scheme of things. Holding grudges would drown him, while acceptance freed him. This seemingly inconspicuous realization became Rohan's lifeline—a delicate but profound thread linking despair to transformation. He had not been simply a victim of circumstance; he had been chosen by it, forged by it, reshaped by the fire of suffering into something greater. The words attributed to Nelson Mandela in the movie *Invictus*, etched now into his soul: "I am the master of my fate; I am the captain of my soul." And yet, he vowed to imbue this mantra with humility rather than pride. He wasn't a victim anymore. Nor was he a conqueror. He was becoming. Every painful experience became not an obstacle but a stepping stone, a tributary feeding into the river of his transformation. Letting go of his perceived identity—his ambition, his obsession with accolades, his success—felt terrifying at first but ultimately liberating. Slowly, this newfound clarity illuminated paths he had overlooked, leading him to see his suffering as a teacher rather than a tyrant. "It's the choices and decisions we make that determine our destiny," Tony Robbins says.

He was no longer a prisoner but a crucible—a sanctuary for his own burning metamorphosis. This isn't happening to me—it's happening for me became his mantra, each word planting itself deep in the soil of his mind. Rohan, once consumed by external validation, now understood that growth could be messy, imperfect, but deeply meaningful. Life wasn't handing him ruin—it was handing him a second chance. Even in the quietest hours of his quarantine, Rohan was evolving not as an emblem of perfection, but as a flawed man discovering grace within sincerity—transformed slowly by his trials, ready to face the turbulent but redemptive journey ahead. The crucible wasn't behind him yet, but he wasn't afraid to step forward. Change was happening, and this time, Rohan chose to let it lead him instead of resisting its flow. When his colleagues began ignoring and ridiculing him as he was stripped of importance—as is the norm in the corporate world—his current "assignment" became his identity. Rohan reminded himself of the quote by Charles S. Swindoll: "Life is 10% what happens to you and 90% how you react to it." In corporate meetings, he would no longer be invited on stage as he had been removed from the management committee. His former juniors, who once reported to him, were now the guests on stage. He chose to ignore this humiliation and decided not to take it personally, as he had evolved. He sensed a bigger calling on the horizon. Letting go of everything he once clung to—his image, ambition, control—brought him a peace he had never known. It was in this vulnerable yet transformative space that an epiphany hit with full, undeniable force. This wasn't a fleeting flicker of insight or some momentary flash of illumination; he had made his choice—a choice of growing, evolving, metamorphosing. This was a hard-won breakthrough, born of pain, reflection, and the relentless determination to rise. The suffering he had endured was no longer his anchor—it was his awakening. The corporate failures, the familial fractures, the isolation that had threatened to undo him were no longer burdens to bear. They were the alchemy of transformation, reshaping his identity and revealing a higher truth. This trial, cruel and unrelenting as it had been, was not the end of his story. It was the beginning. Rohan had not simply survived his crises—he had been forged by them. What had broken him had also rebuilt him, piece by painstaking piece, into something far more purposeful. He was no longer the man who measured his success through titles, accolades, or the approval of others. He was no longer running the same relentless race. Instead, he had become something deeper, something far more meaningful. The tragedies that had once threatened to consume him—his banishment from the corporate stage, the fragile health of his wife Priya, his fractured sense of self—had woven themselves into an intricate tapestry of renewal. In the ashes of failure, he discovered resilience. In the hollow quiet of solitude, clarity emerged. The very pain he had cursed became the fire that forged his purpose. And that purpose was not just to rebuild his own life; it was larger than him now. It resonated deeply, expanding beyond his own suffering. Rohan understood that his pain had carved a path meant to be shared—meant to guide others. Pain wasn't an obstacle. Pain was the fire that forged him. Rohan extended this newfound clarity to the quiet corners of his home. The Sacred Space: His study, once dominated by the sterile mechanics of corporate strategy—Harvard Business Reviews spilling across the desk, McKinsey agendas pinned to corkboards, frantic notes scrawled in deadlines and margins—now transformed into a haven of wisdom. The room came alive with books that had once gathered dust. The heavy scent of volumes collected over the last thirty years, many of them never read and some only partly read due to impatience and poor time management, brought with it a sense of grounding, each book speaking to him as voices softened through time—philosophical guides, spiritual scriptures, and journals of deep self-reflection. Their words whispered ancient truths back to him, calling him to heal and grow, as if the universe itself were urging his metamorphosis forward. The blended philosophies of the East and the West became his salvation. Rohan devoured lessons from Tony Robbins, Robin Sharma, Deepak Chopra, Joe Vitale, Eckhart Tolle, Viktor Frankl, and many others—not with the urgency of a man seeking salvation, but with the quiet hunger of a soul rediscovering itself. Yet, it was the teachings of Sadhguru and Paramahansa Yogananda that struck his soul with unparalleled precision, ushering him into depths of clarity that no venture capitalist meeting or boardroom strategy ever could. He began practicing Isha Kriya daily, no longer as an experiment but as a lifeline—a sacred ritual banishing the clutter of mindless thoughts and ushering in the still waters of serenity. His once-fragmented days of restless ambition gave way to deliberate hours of calm—embracing life unencumbered by the artificial constructs he had once allowed to define him. It wasn't perfection he sought anymore, but authenticity. The more he leaned into the discomfort, the more he learned about the vast frontiers lying within him. What surprised him, however, was his inner calling and pull toward various healing systems. Reiki, Pranic Healing, Ho'oponopono, the Silva Method, and vibrational sound therapy—all techniques that had once triggered his scepticism—emerged as symbolic conduits for rediscovery. At Priya's bedside, where she lay suspended between fragile health and slow recovery, Rohan practiced visualization exercises. He imagined vibrant threads of energy flowing toward her; he prayed silently—not just for her healing but for his own transformation into the kind of man worthy of their family's needs. In these seemingly small, fragmented moments, seeds of transformation quietly germinated. They whispered of newfound possibilities—a life no longer bound by ambition and control, but guided by purpose and balance. Rohan had been forged, piece by piece, through fire. Not just by his losses, but by his courage to rise in their aftermath. He no longer viewed failure as ruin but as potential—a doorway to meaning. And now, as he sat quietly in his sacred space, gazing at the pages of his journal, the seed planted during quarantine and cultivated during solitude had fully bloomed. Life wasn't happening *to* him. It was happening *for* him. He was ready to embrace the unknown, to let it lead him instead of resisting its flow. The crucible wasn't behind him—but now, it no longer frightened him. It transformed him, revealing a man forged not for accolades, but for purpose. For the first time, Rohan saw his trials not as curses but blessings. Somewhere beyond the horizon lay a bigger calling—a destiny waiting to be shaped. All he had to do was step forward. The Purposeful Radiance: A Mission Unveiled Rohan sat quietly in the dim glow of twilight spilling into his study, the journal resting like an artifact of transformation in his hands. The once blank pages were now alive with his unfiltered truths—each word a fragment of his shattered self-woven into a tapestry of resilience. The air thrummed with quiet revelation as he gazed around the room. Every corner seemed to pulse with meaning, charged by the spirit of purpose that now burned within him like an eternal flame.

What had once been sixty-five days of suffocating confinement, a punishment that had drained the marrow of his soul, had become his chrysalis. London's stark, lonely settings and Mumbai's sterile quarantine had stripped him bare, exposing him to the relentless truth of his humanity. These chambers of despair had shaped his metamorphosis. Heartbreak had bruised him deeply, but that ache had laid the foundation for healing. Suffering had become the soil where service took root. The Rohan emerging now was not just whole—but radiant. As he stared at his written thoughts, a single purpose crystallized within him—the kind of calling that ignites the soul and burns away all debris of lesser ambitions. He would dedicate his life to guiding others lost in the churn of unforgiving corporate ambition, those whose unspoken crises consumed them from within. As Robin Sharma would say in his mentoring sessions, "There are countless people out there—chasing external validation, blinded by unidimensional career success, and grappling alone with the void that follows their victories." "Yes, countless people, countless Rohan Srivastavas need him to be their torchbearer, a beacon in the dark, their lifeline through the storm," he reflected. His mission rang clear, like the striking of a gong in a silent temple. He would help them navigate their shadows, confront their pain, and step into the light of their own transformation. This resolution was no fleeting gesture. It was as solid as the earth beneath him and as profound as the night sky overhead. Rohan now understood why the storms had come—not to drown him, but to teach him how to swim. The cracks carved into him by despair had not marred him; they had let the light through. The tears, the scars, the falls—all had prepared him for this moment. As he closed his journal for the final time and stood to face the horizon ahead, he knew one truth with unshakable certainty: his journey was no longer his own. It was a light meant to illuminate the path for others—the *Purposeful Radiance* that would shine through their darkness.

CHAPTER 19

RIPPLES OF A RADIANT FUTURE

Priya's Triumph and the Family's Renewal

At home, where love and resilience had mended broken places, another story unfolded—a tale of renewal, of hope rekindled from the edges of despair. The energy radiating from Rohan's transformation spilled into his family, suffusing their once-fractured world with the beginnings of harmony. Priya's slow but steady recovery became the heartbeat of their collective triumph. The living room had become a sanctuary, imbued with warmth and intention. The once-cold walls softened with subtle touches—framed nature photography taken by Siya, healing crystals catching beams of sunlight, and the faint aroma of lavender wafting from Priya's essential oil diffuser. The space no longer echoed with the silence of heartbreak but resonated with the quiet hum of renewal. Priya's physical mobility, hampered by the lingering effects of her illness, had significantly improved through determined physiotherapy sessions. Rohan often helped her into her wheelchair, their quiet exchanges radiating a newfound intimacy forged by shared survival. One evening, under a setting sun that bathed their balcony in amber and rose hues, Priya unexpectedly squeezed his hand. Her gaze met his, no longer clouded by the wild storms of psychosis but clear and steady. "Rohan," she said softly, her voice carrying both gratitude and strength, "I remember it all—the darkness, the fear. But more than anything, I remember you. You never let me go. You gave me your light." Rohan swallowed thickly, his chest swelling with pride and relief. "Never, Priya. Through every storm, we faced it together. And look at us now—our love is stronger than the winds that tried to break us." And it was true. Their love had discovered new depths; their wounds had resulted in scars that told the story of survival. The storms may have ravaged them, but they had emerged altered, wiser, and unshakable. Siya's Blossoming

It wasn't just Priya who flourished in the wake of Rohan's transformation—Siya, their youngest daughter, blossomed with a renewed sense of purpose. Once withdrawn and aimless, her struggles had guided her toward a journey of meaning. Depression had forced her to abandon her economics-focused management program—a loss that initially felt devastating. But the detours of life, carefully guided by Rohan's wisdom, became her stepping stones. Siya turned her gaze inward and delved deep into the study of psychology. Mental health advocacy became her passion, with her personal battles offering her a unique perspective and unwavering empathy. Now, Siya stood as a celebrated counsellor, specializing in guiding young adults through the tangled labyrinths of their crises. Her transformation was not hers alone—it illuminated paths for others, mirroring the Purposeful Radiance that Rohan now embraced. Siya often spoke at Rohan's workshops, her voice clear and passionate, her presence magnetic. "It felt like my world ended when depression forced me to abandon my studies," she shared during one seminar. "But Papa showed me that detours aren't endings—they're beginnings. My pain wasn't just something to survive—it became my purpose." Her renewed vibrance infused every aspect of her life, including her rekindled love for nature and photography. It was during an ordinary afternoon, as she flipped through *The Times of India,* that an article caught her attention—a sobering exposé on mass tourism's impact on ecology. The piece planted a seed, and Siya didn't let it remain dormant. She immersed herself in research, pouring over journals, YouTube documentaries, and blogs on sustainable tourism. Then, driven by her burning desire to make a difference, she acted. The Birth of MyEcoTour

Together with Priya, now reinvigorated, Siya co-founded an eco-tourism startup that would redefine travel: MyEcoTour. It was more than a business—it was a movement, a manifesto for conscious wanderers who believed exploration and preservation could coexist. The website launched with a declaration of ethos that stirred hearts: *"Awakening Spirits, Nurturing the Planet. Welcome to MyEcoTour, where we craft transformative travel experiences that ignite your spirit and protect our planet. Our commitment to eco-conscious adventure invites you to explore untouched realms, from ancient forests to starlit waterways. Immerse yourself in vibrant cultures and forge connections that transcend borders, all while treading lightly on the Earth. Join us as we redefine travel—making every journey a step toward a more sustainable and interconnected world."* Their mission was clear: crafting journeys that offset carbon footprints while celebrating humanity's shared responsibility to tread gently. Siya's love for nature intertwined perfectly with Priya's growing wellness philosophy. Their seedling project flourished rapidly, fuelled not by corporate ferocity but by a genuine call to action. A Family Reborn

In the house that had once felt heavy with despair, the light now streamed freely. Priya's healing continued, and Siya's newfound purpose radiated triumph in every smile and word of empowerment she shared. Rohan, the humble architect of this renewal, stood at the centre, his radiance now a flame kindled in every heart around him. This wasn't a story of mere survival—it was one of resurrection. Together, they demonstrated that the deepest trials are not the graves they seem but the soil from which transformation grows. Their journeys entwined, their victories reverberating like echoes across the silent chambers of their shared past. What had once been darkness was now purposeful light—a legacy destined to illuminate countless lives. For Rohan, his family was his greatest testament—not to his own strength but to the power of perseverance, love, and human possibility. As he gazed into their smiling faces that evening, his heart was certain. His fire hadn't just burned—it had ignited those around him, planting seeds of purpose in everyone it touched. This was his legacy. His Purposeful Radiance.

CHAPTER 20

THE RADIANCE OF THE UNBROKEN SPIRIT

The grand ballroom of the Taj Mahal Palace Hotel in Mumbai exuded an opulence that felt almost celestial. Chandeliers hung like cascading constellations, their glass prisms scattering fragmented light across the intricately polished marble floors. Silk-draped tables, adorned with golden centrepieces of roses and lilies, transformed the room into a kaleidoscope of beauty and celebration. The air thrummed with a symphony of clinking glasses and joyous laughter, merging with the faint yet unmistakable hum of a live quartet playing a soulful melody in the background. Priya, seated in her wheelchair, glowed in a deep emerald silk saree, her cheeks flushed more by joy than the artful blush applied by the makeup artist earlier that day. Her hair, streaked with strands of silver that gleamed like faint moonlight, framed a face that radiated serenity yet triumph—a portrait of fortitude hard-earned through a long, arduous battle. She looked toward Ananya, her daughter, standing under a lattice of white orchids and shimmering golden fairy lights, her arm entwined with her new husband, Michael Kennedy. The Irish-American businessman, tall and broad-shouldered, exuded both strength and warmth, his forest-green tie a subtle nod to his heritage. For Rohan and Priya, this wasn't just the union of two lives—it was the culmination of their odyssey, a symbolic emergence from the shadows that had loomed over their family for five long years. This wasn't merely a wedding; it was a testament—a coronation of resilience, hope, and boundless love that could weather any storm. Rohan stood quietly at the edge of the crowd, his tailored Sherwani blending seamlessly into the sea of elegance, but his presence was distinct and magnetic. The man who had once been a mere instrument of corporate identity now carried himself with a warmth that commanded not respect, but reverence. He held a champagne flute, the effervescent bubbles mirroring his mood—a steady, rising joy interspersed with reflective gratitude. The transformation that began during his isolation had crystallized into something almost alchemical, a movement rooted in empathy and purpose. He turned, his eyes locking onto Priya's from across the room. They exchanged a smile—a silent conversation between two souls who had endured immeasurable storms and emerged stronger. His voice, when he spoke, carried a calm resonance. "Look at them," he said to Siya, who had drifted to his side. "Ananya and Michael—they're glowing." Siya, now an accomplished counsellor and co-founder of the eco-tourism startup MyEcoTour, smiled knowingly. "So are you, Papa. Every ship needs a captain. You steered us out of the storm." He chuckled softly, gazing down at his younger daughter. How far she had come—from the withdrawn, uncertain girl battling depression to the radiant young woman inspiring others with her story. Her transformation, like his, proved that darkness did not have to define them; it could forge them into something radiant. The celebration that evening was more than just a family's triumph; it reflected something larger—a growing ripple that had begun with

Rohan's own transformation. The Purposeful Radiance Blueprint had started as a manuscript penned in isolation, but it unfolded into a global movement resonating with millions. Rohan returned to the corporate world, not as the man once shackled to numbers, strategies, and hollow victories. His message was a sharp departure from the ethos of lopsided achievement. Instead of leading leaders against life's current, he taught them to flow with it, a Mindful Transformation approach—a blend of various techniques tailored to Corporate Executives and Entrepreneurs. Empathy replaced ego; soulfulness displaced strategy, and purpose outshone profit. The Radiance Blueprint wasn't just a playbook for executives; it was a philosophy that touched lives across boundaries, industries, and ideologies. At his workshops, which now drew audiences from around the world, Rohan frequently concluded with moments of intimate candour about his journey. His words carried the weight of someone who didn't just teach transformation—he had lived it. "This," he would say while gesturing to the faces before him, "was never just about me. My pain, as isolating as it felt, was never mine alone. Pain has a strange way of illuminating what really matters. I didn't fight the currents—I learned to trust them. And now, my radiance isn't just my own anymore. It belongs to all of you." It wasn't merely rhetoric; it was actionable hope. Attendees left not with abstract inspiration but with the tools, clarity, and courage to rebuild their own lives. What began as a ripple—a single man breaking free from despair—had grown into tidal waves of collective healing. As Rohan observed his family that evening—Ananya waltzing with Michael on the dance floor, Siya sharing a laugh with Priya over a whispered joke, and the endless stream of friends and relatives offering heartfelt congratulations—he felt the profound weight of his journey transform into something lighter. His story had never been merely about survival; it had been about transformation. Every wound, every scar, every moment of darkness had been preparing him to become something greater—not just for himself but for the world. His journey had grown to embody something universal. Like Santiago's quest in *The Alchemist* or Elizabeth Gilbert's search for wholeness in *Eat, Pray, Love,* Rohan's story had become a model for others seeking their own radiant futures. But unlike those fictional or deeply personal journeys, Rohan's path offered something tangible—a blueprint anyone could follow. The Purposeful Radiance Blueprint had extended well beyond the limits of Mumbai. It reached corporate executives suffocated by hollow achievements, artists grappling with self-doubt, and families struggling to piece themselves back together. It flourished through retreats nestled in nature, virtual mentorships that connected continents, and intimate communities where vulnerability was met not with judgment but with understanding. Whether it was a CEO rediscovering the meaning of leadership or a young startup entrepreneur seeking peace amidst chaos, the ripple had evolved into an unrelenting wave of change. Suffering, Rohan had always said, was universal—but so too was the capacity to heal. His journey hadn't been merely about becoming radiant alone; it had been about teaching others how to create their own light, transforming individual scars into shared strength. As the night deepened and the party began to wind down, leaving just the family on the balcony overlooking Mumbai's glittering skyline, the city pulsated below them—a reflection of life itself. Rohan stood at the edge of the balcony, the cool breeze tousling his hair as he clutched the journal he had filled during those gruelling months of isolation. It was worn now, its pages softened from countless readings, its words shaping not just his life but the lives of many others. Priya rolled her wheelchair next to him, her hand resting gently on his arm. She spoke quietly but with conviction. "We didn't just survive, Rohan. We created something beautiful. Out of everything we lost, we found something greater—each other, our family, our purpose." He looked at her, his heart swelling with a love that had deepened through every trial. "You're right," he said, smiling. "We didn't just come back to life. We redefined it." Behind them, Siya and Ananya raised their glasses in a toast, their laughter echoing against the late-night air. Together, the four of them stood under a canopy of stars—a family not just healed but made whole, each one carrying within them a light that would never dim. And so, the ripples of Rohan's radiance flowed outward, merging into the ever-growing current that carried countless others toward their own awakening. His wasn't just the story of one man's triumph; it was the story of all of us—the narrative of how, in the darkest moments, we find the beginnings of light. In his heart, Rohan knew one simple truth that would stay with him forever: The ripple had become a wave. And the wave, unstoppable now, carried with it the promise of a radiant future—The Radiance of the Unbroken Spirit—for everyone.

ABOUT THE AUTHOR

Yogesh Srivastava is a distinguished author celebrated for his poignant exploration in *Resilience of The Unbreakable Spirit*. With over 35 years of experience in high-performance leadership in Corporate World , he serves as a Lead Architect at his new venture -YS Epiphanity, where he has profoundly influenced organizational strategies and talent development of various organizations. Renowned as one of the foremost motivational leaders and transformation coaches, Yogesh's innovative training modules have inspired countless individuals and teams. A proud alumnus of IIM Kozhikode and Jamnalal Bajaj Institute of Management Studies, he embodies a lifelong commitment to learning and personal growth. Yogesh is also a passionate advocate for artificial intelligence, integrating modern technology into his leadership philosophy through his proprietary framework, the "Purposeful Radiance Blueprint," which empowers organizations to "Reimagine, Reignite, and Reboot" their potential. Beyond his professional achievements, he is an avid traveller, wildlife photographer, and collector of numismatics, artifacts, and artwork. These diverse interests enrich his writing, imbuing it with layers of depth and authenticity

Driven by a mission to unlock human potential, Yogesh inspires others to embrace their true selves and navigate life's complexities with resilience and purpose. Explore the transformative world of *Resilience of The Unbreakable Spirit* and let Yogesh's insights illuminate your path toward healing and connection.